FIRST THINGS:

A

Series of Lectures

ON THE

GREAT FACTS AND MORAL LESSONS

FIRST REVEALED TO MANKIND.

BY

GARDINER SPRING, D.D.

PASTOR OF BRICK PRESBYTERIAN CHURCH IN THE CITY OF NEW YORK.

IN TWO VOLUMES.

VOL. I.

NEW YORK:

PUBLISHED BY M. W. DODD,

BRICK CHURCH CHAPEL, CITY HALL SQUARE,

(OPPOSITE THE CITY HALL.)

1851.

STEREOTYPED BY THOMAS B. SMITH,
216 WILLIAM STREET, N. Y.

INTRODUCTION.

THERE are several questions of grave import which naturally present themselves for consideration, in a work bearing the title of these volumes. The facts and principles early revealed to the world, were designed to exert a permanent influence. They form the base of the spiritual edifice in which God himself dwells, and in which his people, as living stones, are built up a spiritual house, an holy temple unto the Lord. They are principles, some of which have given rise to no small diversity of views, and on which the author is not unwilling to leave the testimony of his own thoughts, however humble they may be.

If he has allowed himself to introduce topics and matter of a somewhat varied kind, and portions of it in no elaborate and somewhat discursive form; it is because these topics could not well be overlooked, and a less elaborate view of them would, in his own judgment, be the more useful. If he has omitted some which might naturally have been looked for, it is because they would have exposed him to a still more redundant expression of the same thoughts, and because they have been so frequently and ably presented by other pens.

In dedicating the work to those who compose his own pastorate, he would fain be allowed to include in that number, not only those who now constitute the flock of which the Holy Ghost has made him overseer, but those who no longer attend upon his ministrations, and are dispersed through the metropolis, and still more widely throughout the land. They are delightful memories to his own mind which are thus associated with the past. They bring to his recollection so much that is venerable in the character of those long since gathered into the garner of the great husbandman, and so much that is lovely in youthful piety that lives still, but no longer among men, that he loves to dwell upon them. Nor are they less delightful, because, through much infirmity and more imperfection on his part, he has been so uniformly sustained by the kindness of his people; and more than all, because they so richly savor of the "years of the right-hand of the Most High."

Those who once heard, and now hear the gospel from his lips, will not, he hopes, be displeased, that some of his last thoughts upon First Things are most respectfully dedicated to them, by their affectionate pastor,

THE AUTHOR.

CONTENTS OF VOLUME I.

CHAPTER IX.

CHAPTER X.

CHAPTER XI.

CHAPTER XII.

CHAPTER XIII.

FIRST THINGS.

CHAPTER I.

God Himself before All Things.

It is not the object of the writer to address himself to the popular taste, at the sacrifice of truth. So far from this, the following pages will, he trusts, be found to contain God's truth, presented in the plainest dress.

He has assumed the title, First Things, because his topics are among the first lessons narrated in the Sacred Writings, the first great realities revealed to men.

Of these the adorable and ever-blessed God has the first place. In every view he has the preeminence.

By the great word God, the Scriptures mean that intelligent, eternal First Cause, who created, upholds, and governs all things. We open the sacred pages, and the first words we read are these: "In the beginning, God."

Most of the ancient schools and systems of Pagan philosophy, if not atheistical, were atheistic in their tendency, and in their results showed themselves most successful abettors of atheism. Theoretical atheists are few; yet men still live without God in the world. They speculate coldly on the existence of Him who has existed forever; they reason without emotion of him who is himself the source of all they enjoy and all they admire; they speak with marvellous indifference of him, in whose hand their breath is, and whose are all their ways. They have no affecting impression of his glorious and amiable nature; every thrilling view of God they banish; they feel as if there were no God, and conduct themselves as though He, under whose inspection all their conduct and all their thoughts are naked and open, and who himself has an interest in all they do and are, had no concern with them, nor they with him.

The weighty truth can never be stricken out of existence, that *there is a God;* that he exists independently of every being in the universe, and that he is infinitely above the reach of creatures. The denial of this truth is so palpable an absurdity, that it is no marvel that it has the consent of all nations, and that the belief of it is so universally prevalent. Human consciousness does not more certainly attest the existence of a world within us, nor the human senses more certainly the existence of the world without us, than human reason receives it as an ultimate fact, that these internal and external worlds could not exist without an adequate cause. God's eternal existence is a necessary truth; if other things exist, it is inconceivable, impossible, that he should *not* exist.

Yet, obvious as it is, this is a most exalted idea of God. When he revealed himself to Moses, he made the disclosure in the memorable words, I AM THAT I AM. This is "his name;" this is the impression which he himself has of his own Being. It is without beginning and without end; it has no distinction of parts; what it now is, it always was; what it now is, it always will be. We cannot convey any true idea of what it is; "who by searching can find out God?"* It belongs to creatures to begin to live; to the uncreated One, to live always. And this is the *first* thought by which we would illustrate the truth that God himself is before all things. "Before the mountains were brought forth, or ever thou hadst formed the earth and the world, from everlasting to everlasting thou art God." "Thou art the same, and of

* In the beautiful language of the great Newton, when speaking of God, "Eternus est et infinitus, omnipotens, et omnisciens; id est durat ab eterno in eternum, et adest ab infinito in infinitum. Non est eternitas et infinitas, sed eternus et infinitus; non est duratio et spatium, sed durat et adest. Durat semper, et adest ubique; et existendo semper et ubique durationem et spatium constituit."—*Newton's Principia.*

thy years there is no end." "I am Alpha and Omega, the beginning and the ending, saith the Lord, which is, and which was, and which is to come."

In the next place, God is before all things *in the excellencies of his nature* These can no more be comprehended by creatures than the eternity of his existence. "Touching the Almighty, we cannot find him out." "It is high as heaven, what canst thou do: deeper than hell, what canst thou know: the measure thereof is longer than the earth, and broader than the sea." After the clearest and most extended view of his greatness and majesty,—his spirituality and unchangeableness,—his immensity and infinity,—his omnipotence and omniscience,—his blessedness and his goodness,—his compassion and faithfulness,—his holiness and justice,—his impartiality and sovereignty,—his truth and mercy,—his love and anger; we are constrained to say, "Lo, these are parts of his ways, but how little a portion is heard of him." Our largest and holiest contemplations of his nature leave us insensible of what he is, and almost senseless to his unutterable glory. Our thoughts of him are like shadows; they are the emptiness, the vacancy of thought, as it would fain travel over that shoreless ocean, and as it loses itself in thinking of him who is all and in all, and above all, and over all, God blessed forever. Angels and men have been for centuries employed in contemplating the infinity of his perfections; and though their knowledge of him, and their admiration of his excellence have been continually increasing, and with every new inspection of his works and his word, they have learned something new of him; yet have they never reached the lofty position from which they can survey his fulness, nor have their minds ever been able to take in the full revelations of his nature which he himself has made. O, we are confounded when we think of God. He is "the King eternal, immortal, and invisible;" the "blessed and only potentate, the King of kings and the Lord of lords. "Thine, O Lord, is the greatness, and the power, and the glory, and the victory, and the majesty." Thought, which measures other things, cannot measure the infinite Deity; reason, which penetrates other things, cannot dive into this unsearchable abyss; imagination has no colors by which it can depict him who makes the clouds his chariot, and who dwelleth in light that is inaccessible and full of glory. And faith itself, while it gives his testimony entire and implicit confidence, confessedly believes concerning him what it does not comprehend. Bright excellencies there are in God which eye hath not seen, nor ear heard, nor have entered into the mind of man or seraph. Seraphim do indeed behold him face to face; while they are never more sensible than in their clearest visions of his glory, that there are brighter and still more bright manifestations; and even in view of those that are the more dim and obscure, they cover their faces with their wings. The immensity of God, what is it? the infinity of greatness and goodness, who can comprehend them but his infinite Mind in whom they dwell? Goodness there is in creatures, and greatness, which excite our admiration; but they are borrowed rays from this uncreated sun; no more than floating atoms within his illimitable power and wisdom, his boundless rectitude and love. "All nations before him are as nothing, and they are counted to him as less than nothing and vanity." "Behold, he putteth no trust in his servants, and his angels he charged with folly." Who shall "not fear thee, O Lord, and glorify thy name, for thou only art holy; for all nations shall come and worship before thee."

God is also before all things, *in the claims which he has upon his creatures.* He is of right the lawgiver of the universe; while, in the administration of his government, he doeth according to his will in the armies of heaven, and amid all the inhabitants of the earth. His being and his nature give him this supremacy. In searching for the foundation of moral obligation, we may not push our inquiries beyond the divine existence and the divine nature. It is not without reason that we speak of the eternal and immutable difference between right and wrong; and of the foundations of obligation as existing in the nature of things. But the greatest of all things is God. His law is what it is, because he himself is God. God himself must cease to be what he is, and his intelligent creatures must cease to be what they are, before his claims may hold a secondary place.

What are these claims? Summarily expressed, they are contained in the few words, "*Thou shalt have no other gods before me.*" True religion begins here, with angels and with men, in heaven and on earth. It has peculiarities in the world that is fallen and redeemed, and some shining graces that are unknown to the unfallen; while the elements of these are the same which constitute the character of those who have never sinned, and "have no need of repentance." And what do these claims imply, but that all men should know God, acknowledge him, and from the heart serve and honor him?

Him they must *know*. Ignorance and false views of his character may be, and often are, alike fatal to piety. They not only shroud the mind in darkness, but lead multitudes blindfold to perdition. Nature and providence speak for God; but there are lessons which they do not, cannot read to us. Do we search for views of him that will not mislead our minds; for some strong and express image of the invisible Deity? That great mystery of godliness, "God manifest in the flesh," was *God himself* dwelling among men, imprinting his footsteps on this low earth, and holding intercourse with mortals as a man with his friend. What he was, that God is; Immanuel, "God with us," in all his spotless purity and rectitude, in his attractive loveliness and overawing majesty; "the glory of God in the face of Jesus Christ." In his last and memorable prayer with and for his disciples, he utters the language, "This is life eternal, that they might know thee the only true God, and Jesus Christ whom thou hast sent."

God claims to be *acknowledged* as well as known. He requires an honest and frank avowal of his excellence and prerogative. Where men are brought into collision with idol temples and idol deities; or where, in less degraded lands, fame, pleasure and power set up their altars; where a forgotten God, a slighted Saviour, an unsought Sanctifier proclaim that there are thousands who have other gods before him; where thousands more make a God of self and gold, and worship and serve the creature more than the Creator: it is characteristic of those who serve and honor him, never to be ashamed of him, his truth, or his cause; and while they confess him with their mouths, to inscribe the acknowledgment on the fleshly table of their hearts, "This God is our God forever and ever; he will be our guide even unto death."

His claims thus reach the inner man. It is this internal homage which we owe, and on which he insists. "My son, give me thy heart." Our hearts must be his—so loving, fearing, trusting and rejoicing in him, that we live to praise him, and find our pleasure in doing his will. His being must influence us; all his attributes must influence us; his providence must influence us, as well as his grace and truth. Our time must be his; our labor his; his our property and influence; his our waking, and his our hours of rest; our home his, his our joys, our sorrows; our life his, and his our death. Living and dying, we must be the Lord's. He will have all, if his claims are duly honored.

And the thought may not be lost sight of, that he must have this supremacy in *opposition to all other claims*. There are claims which do not interfere with his; he appoints and honors them, and they are identified with his own. The world has claims, business and friendship have claims, science has claims, and every department of human effort and joy that is honest, true, temperate, pure, and of good report, has claims which he honors. But they must all be subordinate to him; we must turn from every altar to his. No danger may repress, no toil discourage, no external influence subdue this paramount regard to God. No traditions of men may countervail his word; no confessor stand in his place; no sanctuary be set up against his. It is only at his footstool that true devotion kneels.

God also is before all things, *in that his honor and glory should be the first and great object of our pursuit.* When we look into the sacred writings, we find such declarations as these: "The Lord hath made all things for himself."—"I have created him for my glory."—"I wrought for my name's sake that it should not be polluted before the heathen."—"All things were created by him and for him."—"Thou art worthy, O Lord, to receive glory, and honor, and power; for thou hast created all things, and for thy pleasure they do exist, and were created."—"Whether therefore ye eat or drink, do all to the glory of God." We deduce from these and such like declarations, the great truth that God himself is his own great end, and that in all that they do, his creatures should aim to please and honor him. This is his supreme object, and it must be theirs. The supreme and ultimate reason of every created object in the universe is in God himself. What is this material universe, but an expression of his power? the utterance of the Deity as it awoke this universe of matter into being? And when we behold it clothed with verdure, and filled with ten thousand forms of organic life, everywhere displaying its form and beauty; what are these but expressions of his wisdom? And when, in addition to these, we see the myriads of animated and living existences, fitted for life and enjoyment and utility; what are these but expressions of his goodness? And when, to crown the work of his hands, we see a race of thinking, moral, and immortal beings; what do these express but the manifold perfections of their great Author, and what were they made for, if not to show forth his praise? And when we contemplate our race, all the subjects of the divine government; what lesson do they so certainly and emphatically teach us, as the divine authority and control? And when we further contemplate man fallen, man redeemed, man glorified; what do these great and marvellous events so effectually secure as the manifestation of that holiness, justice, mercy, sovereignty, and boundless all-sufficiency of the Godhead, which, without these events, never could have shone forth, and only remained in their original and undiscovered radiance around the throne of the solitary Deity? God would still have been as spiritual, as powerful, as wise, as good, as holy, as just, as gracious and all-sufficient as he is now; but these glorious and burning perfections, which give rise to all the knowledge, holiness, and blessedness of angels and men, and which sustain and are progressively augmenting them all, would have been silent and retired. There would have been no such emphatic utterances of them, no such view of them, as that, "beholding as in a glass the glory of the Lord," creatures themselves might be "changed into the same image, from glory to glory, even as by the Spirit of the Lord." No being in the universe occupies this high eminence but God; he is the Alpha and the Omega; in this he is before all others, and all creatures are but as a drop of a bucket compared with him. Not more certainly was the earth formed for the residence of man, than man was formed for God. Not more certainly were the vapors formed to become condensed in clouds, and the clouds to water the earth, and the rivers to run into the sea, than man was formed for God. Not more certainly was the sun made to shine, and the trees to bear fruit, than man was made for God. It is the great law of man's being, and his chief end to glorify God and enjoy him forever. For this great purpose he was made; and when the fact is demonstrated that he no longer lives to praise, and glorify, and enjoy God, it were better that he did not live. He violates the law of his creation; he does what he can to frustrate the end of his existence; and better were it for him and for the universe where he dwells, that he go back to his original dust. And thither would his Creator remand him, if he were not able to "make the wrath of man praise him," and extort from his folly and wickedness some reluctant tribute.

It is a great thought, that, in this as well as every other respect, God is before all things. We cannot measure it, much less can we utter it. We have a place on this earth more for the purpose of taking a view of this great and glorious Deity, of living to honor him, of so conducting ourselves as to make him appear glorious, excellent, and amiable in the view of our fellow-men, than for any other purpose. We may not aim at a lower end than this: a higher we cannot aim at, nor at one more comprehensive and more controlling. How great the privilege of being permitted to honor One so great, so lovely; One, of whom everything that is venerable in greatness and attractive in goodness in the created universe, is but the faint reflection; One whom holy angels venerate and honor, whom holy men have lived and died to glorify, and in whose faultless character wicked men on earth and devils in hell have been able to find no blemish.

God is also pre-eminently above all others, *as the source of blessedness*. Man is a spiritual and immortal being. He must have joys that are spiritual and immortal; nor does he find them except in God. Those regions of thought and affection where created minds find such rich banquets, were all delineated and mapped out by his hand and heart of love. There is not an emotion in the human mind that makes man wiser, better, or more happy, and that finds such rich and ever-diversified aliment in the contemplation of him and his truth, but is the fruit of his Spirit. It is no abstract theory, no speculation of an abstruse, or sentimental, or transcendental philosophy, that the ever-blessed God is himself as truly the source of blessedness and joy to the soul, as the sun is the source of light and gladness to the otherwise dark and withered creation. There is that in the divine nature, so full-orbed and complete, so glorious in holiness, that the most intense thought, the most ardent affection and desire, the most delighted gratitude, the deepest reverence, the highest admiration, find their ever-increasing and ever-glowing ardor fed at his altars. Such is the Christian's experience, that, when he would be happy, he turns immediately, I had almost said instinctively, to God as his highest good. He has proved the deceitfulness of other confidences, and makes God his refuge; he has tried to find tranquillity elsewhere, but he returns to God as his rest; and even when he has drank deep at other fountains, he can say, "Whom have I in heaven but thee, and there is none on the earth that I desire beside thee!" He loves God and finds his heart gratified; he flees to him, and feels safe; he looks to him in embarrassment, and knows that he will "guide him by his counsel." And when he comes to the last conflict, and there are no sublunary lights to shine upon the dark valley, and no created power to help him as he grapples with the king of terrors; God himself is his "glory and the lifter up of his head." I AM THAT I AM—God's all-sufficiency is his blessedness. It is not the presumption of blind adventurousness that makes him confident; nor the fortitude of insensibility that makes him strong, when unassisted by earth he engages manfully in the great battle with "this last enemy," and "through him that hath loved him," comes off conqueror. It is God alone speaking to the soul in its loneliness, and the thinking spirit uttering its responses, and receiving in return the full promise, "I will never leave thee, never forsake thee." If we would know what it is to be cheered and comforted by the divine presence and love, we may try to think what it is for a creature of thought and sensitiveness to be abandoned of God; separated from the good, separated from the holy, eternally separated from all blessedness and joy. If we search for the two extremes of misery and happiness in the universe, we shall find them, on the one hand, in the soul that is most shut out from God's blessedness; and on the other, in the soul that is permitted to dwell nearest his throne.

Could we know the joys of the pure seraph who has never wandered from his presence, or of the ransomed sinner who occupies a place nearest his feet; we should know that "in his presence is fulness of joy, and at his right hand are pleasures for evermore."

In the eternity of his being, in the excellence of his nature, in the prerogatives of his throne, in the chief and ultimate end of man's being, and as the source of all blessedness, God himself, therefore, is before all things.

Can these high claims be vindicated, and does he deserve his exalted preëminence? We devote a few remaining pages to this inquiry. And we do this, not because we doubt his claims, nor because the inquiry casts any suspicion upon them; but because God himself invites us to inspect them—nay, to *scrutinize* them; well assured that the more they are inspected and scrutinized, the deeper will be our conviction that they deserve to be honored, and that we shall find our own highest holiness, and honor, and happiness in honoring *him.*

The first remark on this part of our discussion is, *That God himself claims this preëminence in his word.* It is the language of his law, that we shall "have no other gods before him;" that we shall "love him with all the heart, and all the understanding." It is the language of his gospel, that if we give him not this preëminence, we shall be anathema. This is man's rule of action; he has no other. This is God's sovereign will, and it may not be disregarded. Yet absolute as it is, we are not justified in regarding it as his mere arbitrary will. He claims this universal preëminence; nor does he act contrary to reason, nor without reason in insisting upon the claim. He would have us acknowledge and honor him of *choice*, and in view of the motives which he sets before our minds. His character as God deserves this supremacy; his authority as God this submission. It is right that creatures should pay him this supreme regard, and always will be right. To insist on such claims would be preposterous and supremely selfish in any other being in the universe; it is not preposterous, nor is it selfishness in God, because he is worthy. Every principle of equity enforces this claim; to abate, or relax it, or allow it to be superseded, were just as absurd as that he should require men to hate that which is lovely, or love that which is hateful. If "there is none like him among the gods," then ought he to have no rival in the affections of men; if he is the only sovereign, then none may challenge his authority; and if he is the First Fair, and the First Good, of no other may it be said, "Their rock is not as our Rock, his enemies themselves being judges." Who may carry about with him the painful consciousness that he is a contemner, or neglecter of God, when he whose "eyes run to and fro throughout the earth to show himself strong on the behalf of them whose heart is perfect toward him," knoweth his down-sitting and his uprising, and understandeth his thoughts afar off. Disguise this heart-idolatry as we will, his eye marks it. "If we have forgotten the name of our God, or stretched out our hands unto a strange God, shall not God search this out?" And what is our disregard of his equitable claim, but a virtual denial of his being, his dominion and glory, or such a dividing and sharing of them with others as moves him to jealousy? He will not hold such a man guiltless. Habits, and principles, and practices, which exalt themselves against God, or give him a subordinate place, ought, like idols of silver and gold, to be "cast to the moles and the bats;" they ought to find their habitation in "the clefts of the rocks, and in the holes of the ragged rocks, for fear of the Lord, and for the glory of his majesty, when he ariseth to shake terribly the earth."

These are claims too, in the next place, which are adapted to man's intellectual and moral nature. He is formed for them; he perceives them, he feels the reasonableness of them, and cannot throw of the obligation of yielding to them. The Bible not more certainly assumes the fact of God's existence, and asserts his excellence and government, than it pre-supposes that man is the fit subject of this government. All its teachings proceed on the principle of accountableness in men, so long as they are not idiots. Men are greatly at fault in their reasonings upon this very plain subject. They would fain persuade themselves that they are not under obligation to give God the first place, because they have already given that place to another; because their carnal mind is at enmity with God and dead in sin; and because this state of moral feeling requires omnipotent grace in order to be subdued. But what sort of theology, and what sort of piety is that, which exempts a man from the obligation to do right, because he does wrong; which relieves him from the duty of having no other God than the living and true, because he sets up idols in his heart, and because he is so wedded to them, that they must be torn from his bosom? His excuse confounds him; he is condemned out of his own mouth. Nothing is more preposterous than such reasoning. If there be any force in it, no man is under obligation to be better than he is; and the worse he is, the less is he under obligation to be better. If there is any force in such reasoning, there is no such thing as sin in the world, because there is no obligation violated, let men be as bad as they will. Never let the truth be forgotten, that human obligation lies back both of human sinfulness and God's imparted grace. "To him that *knoweth* to do good, and doeth it not, to him it is sin." Give men understanding, and conscience, be they ever so perverted by iniquity, and there is no escape from this obligation. They are the fit subjects of God's control; he speaks to them, and what he utters has a determinate meaning. It is understood; conscience feels its authority, and cannot set it aside. It will be a fearful thing for such a man if he goes to the judgment trusting in his refuges of lies. He had better have been numbered with the cattle upon the thousand hills; he had better have been a maniac; or "like the untimely birth of a woman, he had better never have seen the light." The hail will sweep his refuges of lies away, and the waters will overflow his hiding-place. He will have an interview with the insulted Deity at that dread tribunal, and will be speechless.

Nor may we overlook the *affecting relations* which exist between God and man, giving, as they do, additional force to these divine claims. They are not abstract truths which we have been uttering; they are truths addressed to every man's conscience; the conscience of the reader must be the expositor of them.

God is your *Maker*. "Know ye not that the Lord he is God; it is he that hath made us, and not we ourselves." And shall these bodies, so "curiously and wonderfully framed," not become his temple, but be prostituted to the service of other gods? Shall not these hands be employed for him, and these feet "run in the way of his commandments?" Shall these eyes never behold his glory; and these lips, shall they not speak his praise? Shall these thoughts never think of him, and for him; and these sensations never feel for him; and these volitions never respond to the call of their Maker? Shall this heart, which never beats without his wonder-working power, never throb for him, and these warm affections of which he has made us capable, and which give rise to so many social joys, never glow with love, but to show how much others are loved more than him? Shall this immortality, with which he has invested the meanest and the most exalted of our race, be forever alienated from him, and become an eternal exile from his family and favor?

God is your *preserver*. In his hand your breath is, and in him are all your ways. It is he that maketh the outgoings of the morning and the evening to rejoice; that watches you by night, and by day throws around you the shield of his guardianship; that feeds you with the finest of the wheat, makes you suck honey out of the rock, and oil out of the flinty rock, and bears you as on eagles' wings. And does such goodness originate no obligations of grateful acknowledgment and service; or may these mercies be perverted to his dishonor, these deliverances abused, and this forfeited life, so long preserved, never honestly devoted to him by whose visitation it is thus cared for?

God is your *Father*. He has loved you, and instructed you, and chastened you, and borne with you, and guided you with his eye, and carried you in his bosom. He has not left you to be an atheist, nor an infidel, nor a Mohammedan, nor a Pagan. He has reared you in his sanctuary, and given you a place near his altars. Every morning and every evening, you have heard his voice of love, and seen him going forth to direct the arrangements of his providence for your benefit. "If I be a father," says he, "where is mine honor? and if I be a master, where is my fear?" It is no unreasonable, or unfilial duty, and no unreasonable, exacting service that he calls for: it is your own good he is consulting, when he would have you glorify and enjoy him forever.

And what is more than all, God is *your Redeemer*. From the bondage of sin, from all that is terrible in apprehension and agonizing in despair, from corroding guilt and dreadful wrath, from the sting of death and the curse of the law, he sent the Son of his love to rescue you, with a strong hand and a stretched-out arm. When your feet were going down to death, and your steps took hold on hell, he kept you from falling, and snatched you from the pit of destruction. The Destroyer was commissioned to go through your coasts and smite the mother with her children, and lay the first-born low; but the blood of the Paschal Lamb was on your door-posts and on the lintels, and he did not come nigh your dwelling. The enraged foe was in hot pursuit after you; you were foiled and crushed; but this great Deliverer spoiled principalities and powers in order to save you harmless. He spoiled the grave, disappointed hell of its prey, brought hope to the hopeless; and now, with unutterable tenderness, he invites those who are the children of wrath to become the sons of God. And shall the ransomed slave not think of his Deliverer? Shall not the redeemed sinner instinctively say, "O Lord, I am thy servant; *I am thy servant;* thou hast loosed my bonds!"

In every view, therefore, *God is before all things;* and in every view he deserves this preeminence. The obligation thus to regard him is absolute; it is universal and everlasting. We have but to hold up this infinite Deity before the mind of the most benighted Pagan, and he is forever bound to give God this high place. There is no absolution from this bond; and there is no such thing as violating it without peril. It binds the highest and the lowest as truly as it bound Gabriel; as truly as it did the first man before his apostasy; as truly, and just as much as it did the Israelites, when those words were first promulgated, "Thou shalt have no other gods before me." It has never been revoked; nor has its great Author ever said or done anything to lower this high standard of human thought and conduct, but the rather everything to elevate it and give it perpetuity.

Yet, in contemplating this single truth, well may we say, "If thou, Lord, shouldest mark iniquity, O Lord, who shall stand?" There is not one of us but must lay his hand upon his mouth. There is not one of us who is not conscious that many a favorite idol has usurped the throne which belongs to God; and who is not constrained to confess that infinitely inferior claims have been allowed to jostle with the claims of the living Deity. We may well try ourselves by this standard, if it were only to learn how pure and searching it is, and how vile we ourselves are. One reason why multitudes remain so thoughtless in sin, and so unconcerned about their soul's salvation, is that they make light of this great truth. They make light of God, and therefore they make light of his law; and because they make light of these, they make light of sin; and because they make light of sin, they make light of the great salvation. "I was alive," says the apostle, "without the law once; but when the commandment came, sin revived and I died." Sin revives then, and the sinner feels its power; the law utters its penalty, and he sees his danger; his strength withers, and his hopes die. He is condemned; the penalty is death; the day of execution is hastening on; nor is it any marvel that he looks round for some way of escape, and cries out, "What must I do to be saved?" It is no new thing for men to be sensible of their lost condition as sinners; and it is no surprising thing. Resist not these convictions, if the Spirit of God is thus striving with you. Do not stop them, though they make the world look dark, and though they hold your eyes waking.

There is forgiveness with God. There is hope. Yes, there is forgiveness with God that he may be feared. There is hope for the chief of sinners, because "the Son of Man came to seek and save that which is lost." "The wages of sin is death; but the gift of God is eternal life through Jesus Christ." While he lives, and when he dies, this is the Christian's glorying; and this too is his holiness; he lives to Christ and to Christ he dies. This, also, is his greatest joy. For while it is his greatest grief that he has done so little for Jesus Christ, it is his greatest joy that Jesus Christ has done so much for him.

The apostle once said, "I through the law am dead to the law, that I might *live unto God*."

This is the way in which God is enthroned in the heart; and it is this enthroning which constitutes the sum and substance of true religion. It is from this inward obedience, that all outward obedience flows. True morality originates in a supreme regard for God. Morality without, and not within, is a fiction—a dream. Sin began in turning from God; piety begins in turning to him. The point at which men turn to him is giving him the supremacy he claims. Whether the living and true God shall have this supremacy, or whether they give it to another, is the question on which their eternity is suspended. This is the great controversy between man and his Maker. You must yield this controversy, gentle reader; for you cannot help seeing that God is right and you are wrong. God cannot yield it; not because he is arbitrary and will not, but because he is right and may not. Truth is with him; error is with you. His is the rectitude; yours the sin. The throne is his; the footstool yours. You are a creature of yesterday; he is from everlasting. You are abject; he is before all things. Yours is the relenting, the penitence, the submission, the trusting confidence; his the forgiving love, the gracious acceptance, the free salvation.

CHAPTER II.

God's First Work.

THE Book of Genesis is, in every view, a most wonderful book. If it be a fable, Christianity itself is fabulous. Not only does it furnish the earliest narrative of the earliest times, but abounds in facts which lie at the foundation of revealed religion, and render it impregnable to all the assaults of infidelity. The first two chapters speak of times and events which existed before the sun was set in his tabernacle, or man dwelt on the earth. It is not of science and the arts that they treat, nor of the rise and fall of empires, nor of battles lost and won; when its narrative begins, there were no empires, no cities, no din of warfare, no rivalships of art, and no researches of science. The subject of it is the beginning of time; it is GOD'S FIRST WORK,—in its commencement, its progress, its completion; in all the exactness of its design, in all its order and simplicity, beauty and stupendousness.

2*

Yet the writer of it speaks, throughout, with the familiarity and simplicity of one who was an eye-witness of the magnificent scenes he describes; and he does so because, though not an eye-witness, he was taught of God. Nor does he speak with hesitation; he has no doubts to express and no theories to propose, or defend. It is a *statement of facts* which he presents us, on the authority of the revealing Spirit, and therefore everything that he says is consistent and harmonious.

IN THE BEGINNING GOD CREATED THE HEAVENS AND THE EARTH. We read this introductory sentence, and feel a strong desire to know what the book, which is thus introduced to us, contains. What an impregnated announcement is this! how much truth does it affirm! how much error does it refute! how much that is fabulous does it put to shame!

The first great fact here disclosed, is that there was a *beginning* to the heavens and the earth—a period when they did not exist. It is the dream of atheism that they have existed always. We see for ourselves that the *present form* of the world, and the particles of which it is composed, are subject to incessant changes and revolution. "The fashion of this world passeth away;" mutability is stamped upon everything around us; and we cannot fail to demand, can such a world have existed from eternity? That which may be one thing today, another thing to-morrow, and the next day nothing at all, cannot be independent and eternal. Variation in the nature, or mode of the world's existence, is an effect which cannot be produced without a cause. And whence that cause? Not from itself, for it is dead matter and powerless; not from without itself, for this the hypothesis denies. If the matter of which the world is composed be eternal, how came the world to assume its present form? If it existed from eternity with all its parts united and at rest, how was it set in motion? or if it existed from eternity in an infinite number of detached particles, and in motion, in what lucky moment, and by what fortuitous concourse did they come together, and form this beautiful and splendid world? Nor does it owe its existence to an infinite succession of causes. The notion of an infinite progression of dependent causes, without any beginning, or first cause, involves an obvious contradiction. If each distinct cause in the series is dependent, how can the entire series itself be independent? Where nothing in the series is without a beginning, whence is it that there is no beginning to the series? How can an infinite and eternal whole be made up of parts that are not eternal and finite? This hypothesis is adopted in order to get rid of the idea that any one cause in the series is without beginning. If this be so, then there was a beginning to each cause in the succession, so that if this hypothesis be true, "we have a succession of causes infinitely earlier than any cause in the succession," which is an absurdity. Whether this supposed progression commences a thousand years ago, or from eternity, it is equally a contradiction that every link in the chain is supported by one that is antecedent, and that there is no parent link to support the whole.

There is too a total want of testimony in favor of the hypothesis, that the existence of the world runs back to a remoter period than that spoken of by Moses. No human records reach farther back than that period. The traces of higher antiquity said to have been found in the history of Egypt, Phœnicia, Hindostan, and China, have long since been abandoned as fabulous; so far from countervailing, they substantiate the Mosaic history. Had the world existed for any great period beyond the date specified by Moses, it is incredible that numerous evidences of this fact should not exist, and that all veritable history and tradition should terminate within the limits of the scriptural chronology. The scantiness of population, the progress of society, agriculture, and arts and improvements universally, clearly show that this earth began to exist at no very remote period. We are able to ascertain the time when the most useful arts were invented, and the sciences discovered; and can go back to the origin of the earliest nations, and the foundation and progress of the earliest works of man.

We have, moreover, facts which lie at the basis of chronological computations which cannot deceive us.* Jesus Christ was born while Cæsar Augustus was emperor of Rome—a date well known in the history of nations. From the birth of Christ upward to the calling of Abraham, the Scripture chronology, fortified by profane authors almost without number, is exact and determinate. From that period to the exile of the Jews in Babylon were fourteen generations; from the exile in Babylon to David fourteen generations; and from David to Abraham fourteen generations; in all forty-two generations. From Abraham to Noah were four hundred and thirty years; and from Noah to the creation between sixteen and seventeen hundred.† Making all due allowance for the different chronology of the Samaritan copy of the Pentateuch, the Hebrew Scriptures, the Septuagint and Josephus, there are nearly six thousand years from the present date to the creation.

There was a *beginning*, therefore, to the heavens and the earth; the time was when they did not

* See Lightfoot's Hebrew and Talmudical Exercitations upon Matthew. —*Works*, vol. xi. p. 27.

† Comp. Wallace's True Age of the World, Blair's Chronological Tables, Winder's History of Knowledge, and the Encyclopedias.

exist, and when nothing was in existence but the ever-living God. What efforts of the divine power, and what expressions of the divine goodness *may* have been made in the creation of other systems and other worlds besides those of which the Scriptures speak, and which have no revealed relation to "the heavens and the earth," it is at least safe to say *we are utterly ignorant.* To erect any theory at all upon such an hypothesis, is utterly unphilosophical. So far as the Creator himself has informed us, the creation of "the heavens and the earth" was his first work, and constituted the earliest manifestations of his glory, the first ray of the divinity which broke forth.

The *next fact* here taught us is, that the heavens and the earth not only had a beginning, but were *created.* "In the beginning God *created* the heavens and the earth." It is no marvel that the idea of a *creative power* that produced all things out of nothing was above the reach of men who were destitute of a supernatural revelation. Men have no experience, no observation of such a fact as this, and no science that can account for it. We may be allowed to remark, and with emphasis, that the scriptural doctrine of *creation* is so purely a *historical question* that it does not seek any philosophical solution. It is a subject on which science is entitled to no theory, because it is decided by the divine testimony; a subject with which science may not interfere; nor was it ever designed to be investigated by human philosophy.

The great and radical error of modern philosophers lies in supposing that the primeval creation was effected by a process which natural science prescribes. Science may have much to do with the *changes and revolutions* which have taken place in the material world; this is her province; while upon the doctrine of creation itself, she has no claim to be heard. What does science know of *creation?* or what has she to do but "STAND STILL AND CONSIDER the wondrous works of God?" "Dost thou know when God disposed them? dost thou know the wondrous works of him which is perfect in knowledge?" God speaks to these presumptuous world-makers in the language, "Where wast *thou* when I laid the foundations of the earth? declare, if thou hast understanding. Who hath laid the measures thereof if thou knowest? or who hath stretched out the line upon it? Whereupon are the foundations thereof fastened, or who hath laid the corner-stone thereof?" We have no need of the lights of natural science, but to *illustrate*, and to pour their radiance on the works of God. Creation is a MIRACLE, if ever there was a miracle in the world; and what need is there of scientific principles in order to explain a miracle? The Creator does not tread in the footsteps of physical science; true science treads, and treads cautiously in the footsteps of the Creator.

We take our position on the broad and immovable basis of God's word, and ask, what is the scriptural idea of *creation?* Let the answer be given in the first chapter of the book of Genesis. Let it be given in the language of the prophet, "Thou, even thou art Lord alone; thou hast made heaven, the heaven of heavens, with all their hosts, the earth, and all things that are therein, the seas, and all that is therein." Let it be given in the language of the Psalmist, "By the word of the Lord were the heavens made; and all the hosts of them by the breath of his mouth." Let it be given in the language, "Thus saith God the Lord; he that created the heavens and stretched them out; he that spread forth the earth and that which cometh out of it." Let it be given in the language of the apostle, "All things were made by him; and without him was not anything made that was made." It is not to the cabinet of the geologist, nor laboratory of the chemist, that we make our appeal for information on this high subject. It belongs to them to inquire how material things are sustained, and perpetuated, and by what laws they granulate and grow, after they are created; of *creation* they know nothing. The Scriptures mean by creation those acts of omnipotence by which God gives being to that which did not exist before; they mean by it, not only to cause existence, but entire and *completed* existence. "Thus the heavens and the earth were *finished*, and all the host of them." They convey the thought, that creation was the maturèd act of God; it was performed by a word, and under the direct and immediate influence of a divine command. This may not accord with the rationalism of modern science, but is in strict accordance with Christian faith. It is not by science that we arrive at this conclusion. The sacred writers instruct us, that "through FAITH we understand, that the worlds were framed by the *word of God*." The Creator himself knows how the worlds were created; and he has told us. He knows the influence of second causes; for he called them into being at the primeval creation, and gives them their place in his government and control of the natural world. But he claims for himself the prerogative of the mighty Creator.

The third fact here revealed, is that this world was *created in six days*. Here again the Scriptures are at issue with science. Modern geologists tell us that this is not possible; and all we need reply to the bold assertion is, "With men it is impossible, but all things are possible with God." Everything is possible with God that does not involve a contradiction. And where is the contradiction in God's creating this material world in six days? Revealed theology, we are told, must be in "organic connection" with natural science. We are instructed that that theology is not true which is at war with the true science of nature; and that to make revelation and science harmonize with reason, we are driven, from an inspection of the internal organization of our globe, to the conclusion, that "the mere shell of the earth takes us back through an unknown series of ages, in which creation appears to have followed creation at the distance of vast intervals between." There are, it is said, strata, or layers in the earth's foundation, which must have been formed in a certain order; that we scarcely leave the surface of the earth without finding deposits which take us beyond the limits of recorded time; that there are fossil remains, and beds of coal and limestone, which must have been the spoils of other and departed worlds; that countless ages were necessary for this arrangement, and that "the earth itself is a crowded store-house of evidence of its gradual formation." It is enough in reply to such a statement, that it is inconsistent with the Mosaic narrative. Although our main object is to show the inconsistency of these positions with the sacred writings, we may be permitted here to remark, that even upon the hypothesis that the earth exhibits evidence of its formation through the power of natural causes, it does not follow that it was not formed in six days, because the very idea of creation supposes an unwonted energy in those causes. What if it be so, that no small portions of large continents are covered with rocks of many miles in depth, all exhibiting a stratified formation, and arranged in the order of a mineralogical cabinet; where is the evidence that they were not formed by the operation of causes acting with a rapidity and force unknown to modern geology? What if it be so, that these strata contain "pebbles rounded and smoothed as if they had been rolled in water;" can it be shown that God Almighty could not, even by the action of water, have created a round and smooth pebble in six days? And what if it is ascertained, that these strata are fossiliferous and contain the bones of animals; or are carbonic, and contain beds of coal; or are formed of salt and limestone; can it be shown that no organic remains of animals were deposited between the creation and the flood, or that races of animals that are now extinct, were not deposited in mountain and valley by the waters of the deluge? Geologists assume that the operation of natural causes is at all times equal, which they have not demonstrated.

The remark was made on a preceding page, that natural science is concerned with the *changes* that have taken place in the material world; while upon the doctrine of *creation*, she has no claim to be heard. No man supposes that the earth, *as it now is*, is the same earth that was originally created. It was greatly changed by the Deluge; was no doubt gradually changing between the deluge and the creation; it has been subjected to change ever since, sometimes by the laws of a universal providence, sometimes by a providence that is special. Where is the geographer who can now tell us where the rivers are that once bounded the original Paradise? We have abundant proof that what are now large and extensive lakes, were once solid land; and that what is now solid land, was once covered with water. We see for ourselves large tracts of alluvial soil, formed by the accumulation of matter washed down from mountains, and formed by the action of rivers which have changed their beds. Rocks, too, are wearing away by the action of the ocean; while what is now solid land, may in past ages have formed the bed of the ocean itself. Decayed forests are forming new soil beneath. But it does not follow, because the earth has been gradually moulded by the operation of second causes, or changed in many of its aspects by violent concussions and eruptions, that it did not originally possess *the great and distinctive features* of land and water, and in their marked varieties. Geologists tell us that very large portions of the earth were formed gradually and in the progress of indefinite ages; that granite rocks could not have been formed except by the action of subterranean fire; and that the metallic substances which are found in the earth, are all to be traced to the action of natural causes since the creation. But *how do they know this?* This one thing is obvious from the Mosaic narrative, that on the third day of the creation, God said, "Let the dry land appear." Will geologists inform us what were the component elements of the *dry land?* Were there no mountain ranges? no granite hills; no metallic substances; no sand; no gravel; no loam; no clay? Where were Sinai, and Horeb, and Hor, and Gilead, and Paran, and Carmel? Where were the "high hills" that were covered by the flood; and the "everlasting hills" that are spoken of in the book of Genesis; and the "precious things of the everlasting hills;" and the land "whose stones are iron, and out of whose hills thou mayest dig brass?" Whence were the idols of silver and gold in kingdoms far more ancient than the Hebrew state? Whence was it that Tubal Cain, the fourth in descent from Adam, was "an instructor of every artificer in brass and iron?" Did not the "dry land" and the "high hills" which God formed at the creation, contain these metallic substances at that dawn of the world, as truly as they now contain them, and were they not produced by God's creative power? Were there no continents at the original creation; or were they all originally loose and incoherent masses in "the dry land," and formed by "a sediment deposited in the waters," or by "accumulations of transposed matter," and not a few of them by "the melting of other rocks, and cooled down" into their present solidity?

I confess I am no professed geologist, while I have taken some pains to acquaint myself with the best treatises on this interesting department of natural science. And in doing this, I have become satisfied that their theories are far from being satisfactory to the authors themselves. The most candid writers acknowledge that there are difficulties in their system, and phenomena which they cannot account for. It would be no difficult matter to expose the fallacy of their reasoning in its application to the Mosaic narrative of the creation. Take, for example, the following facts. It was asserted not many years since, that a stratum of lava flowed from mount Etna, in the time of the second Punic war, which is about two thousand years ago, which is not sufficiently covered with soil, to produce either corn or vines. The conclusion was hence drawn, that it requires two thousand years to change the surface of lava into fertile soil. Seven distinct lavas, one under the other, have been discovered in digging a pit near Jaci, in the neighborhood of mount Etna, most of them covered with a thick stratum of rich soil.

And the conclusion was that the lowest of these lavas flowed from the mountain fourteen thousand years ago, and that the earth, which, according to the Mosaic narrative, is six thousand years old, is actually more than fourteen thousand. But it has been since ascertained, that the mass which covers *Herculaneum and Pompeii*, consists also of seven distinct lavas, with veins of good soil between them; while it is well known that the lowest of these lavas flowed from Vesuvius in the year 79 of the Christian era, a little more than eighteen hundred years ago; and that, instead of taking two thousand years to be covered with soil, lava is thus covered in a little more than two hundred. Within the memory even of the young among us, it was also the received doctrine of physical science, that there are substances in nature so hard that *it is impossible* to form them except by the slow process of centuries; yet it has since been ascertained by the French chemists, that those very substances, by the force of electricity acting upon water, can be *manufactured* in a week. When the Scriptures teach us, therefore, that the work of creation was completed in six days, we have no questions to ask of geologists.

Geologists not a few are enlightened and Christian men. It may serve our purpose to allude to the construction which *such* writers put upon the Mosaic narrative, in order to make it consistent with geological science. One of these theories is the hypothesis of a material creation prior to that recorded in Scriptures, and of which the Scriptures say nothing. It inculcates the existence of a "pre-adamite earth," which for unnumbered ages was first held in fusion by fire, and afterwards in solution by water; and that during these periods rocks were crystallized, and masses of animal and vegetable matter made their appropriate deposits, in strata conformed to subsequent geological discoveries; and that when the requisite materials were thus laid up in storehouses, *from these* God formed the world we inhabit, as narrated in the book of Genesis. Of this whole theory, we say, and say with confidence, it is the mere *romance* of natural science. It is conjecture simply, unbecoming the name of science. It is mere imagination and theory, in which science not only vaults and soars beyond the limits of known fact, but of remote probability. The most extravagant tales of chivalry do not go beyond it, nor is it transcended by the most fanciful Pagan Cosmogonies. I would as soon believe the account of the generation of the world among the Chaldeans as given by Berosus, or the Phœnician account as given by Sanchoniathon, or the Egyptian as given by Diodorus Siculus, or the Grecian as given by Hesiod, as believe this mere unsupported hypothesis of modern science.

The next of these theories is more sober and plausible. It is, that when the Scriptures assert that the world was created in *six days*, the meaning is *six indefinite periods;* and in support of this construction, it is said that the word *day* is not unfrequently used in this indefinite sense in the Scriptures. Among the modern and more scientific advocates of this hypothesis are Professor Silliman of Yale College and Professor Jameson of Edinburgh. The philological and theological objections to this hypothesis are so many and conclusive, that, so far as my knowledge extends, it is for the most part abandoned. Dr. Buckland, in his Bridgewater Treatise, while he does not deem it necessary to adopt it, ventures to adopt it so far as to believe that the creation was "succeeded by cycles of ages, during which all the physical operations disclosed by geology were going on." To us his ingenious theory appears to be contrary to the plain teachings of Moses. He supposes, for a single example, that the lights of heaven existed long before Moses affirms they were created, and only *came into view* on the day spoken of in the Mosaic narrative; God did not *then create* them. Yet Moses affirms, God then "*made* two great lights," and "*set them* in the firmament." And the Psalmist reiterates the fact when he says, "To him that *made* great lights, the sun to rule by day, and the moon and stars to rule by night;" and he does so in a song that celebrates the work of creation as narrated by Moses.

A still more plausible theory, and that which is now generally adopted by those geologists who disclaim the first, is to give a latitude of interpretation to the first two verses in the book of Genesis, which has not generally been allowed. That paragraph is, "In the *beginning*, God created the heavens and the earth; and the earth was without form and void, and darkness was upon the face of the deep. And the Spirit of God moved upon the face of the waters." The construction put upon this paragraph is, that the time occupied in thus calling into existence the chaotic mass of which the material universe was formed, is not specified, but left entirely open; that it is not included in the six days of the subsequent creation; and that these unarranged materials thus called into being, must have remained untold ages in that forming condition and process; by which time was furnished for the peculiar and stratified organization of the earth as it exhibits itself to the examination of the geologist. The difficulty in adopting this construction is the fact, that, according to the Mosaic narrative, the different *animals* of which the fossil remains are composed, and the vegetable substances which compose the carbonic, and which enter so largely into the interior structure of the earth, *did not exist* in the chaotic period, and were not created until the third, and fifth, and six days of the creation. When, therefore, geologists tell us that the earth must have been in the progress of a gradual and slow formation for millions of years before the days spoken of by Moses, and that there are phenomena in its interior organization that cannot be accounted for but by these millennial processes; we feel authorized and constrained to say to them, "Ye do err, not knowing the Scriptures, nor the power of God." They aim at too much. The knowledge of God's word is too wonderful for them; it is high, they cannot attain unto it. The infinite One can perform what the finite cannot comprehend. When will man, proud, reasoning man, learn to confide in the word of Him who cannot err, and will not deceive? If to the humble and Christian inquirer there are facts in the organic texture of our globe, which *seem* to be inconsistent with the Mosaic history, we may be satisfied that it is but a seeming incoherency. If human science is inconsistent with the sacred record, so much the worse for human science. "Heaven and earth shall pass away, but God's word shall not pass away."

We are not a little alarmed at the tendency of the age to reduce the great facts narrated in the Bible to the standard of natural science. Books of natural science are the text books of our schools;

they supersede the Bible; it is from these, and not from the Bible, that the rising generation are taught how and when God made the world. Yet, what is more fluctuating than such instructions? With all its noble advances, natural science is confessedly progressive, and therefore comparatively crude. Geology is in its infancy. How much does it know of the rapidity with which second causes accomplish their work? how much of the mechanical action of water and fire, and of their chemical effects? how much of galvanism and electricity, directed by omnipotence? how much of the general deluge? What does it know of the internal structure and organization of the earth? Not a thousandth, not a millionth part of our globe has yet been submitted to its inspection. The diameter of the earth is nearly *eight thousand miles.* If we are rightly informed, the deepest mine is a mine in Bohemia, of the depth of three thousand feet; and this, which is little more than half a mile, is scarcely penetrating the earth's crust. A late distinguished European geologist, remarks, "We have attempted to penetrate as far as possible beneath the surface, into the interior of the earth. But if we compare the depth to which we have actually penetrated, with the real diameter of the earth, it will be seen, that we have scarcely broken the surface, and that the scratch of a needle on the varnish of one of our terrestrial globes is proportionally much deeper than the deepest perforations with which we have ever penetrated into the interior of the earth." And may we not ask, if a science which is thus in its infancy, shall be allowed to rob us of our confidence in the verity of the scriptural account of the creation? It has been well remarked, that "the collision is not between the Bible and *nature*, but between the Bible and natural philosophers."

When science is better informed, it will have fewer scruples in endorsing the Mosaic narrative. As the most learned are often said to be more deeply sensible of what is not known, than what it knows, so one of the high attainments of science is, that it is a standing comment, not only upon what it knows, but what it does not know. It is not many years ago that a distinguished astronomer affirmed that the last discovery had been made in the planetary system; and the reason he assigned for the assertion was that the relative motions of the system could be accounted for by the existence of those already discovered, and that the addition of another planet would disturb this harmony. Yet, since that period, other planets have been discovered; and what is remarkable, the last discovery was made by observing the aberration of a planet which human science had thus predicted could never occur. Human science is a changing, restless thing. It is well that it is so; the world is the gainer by all her advances. It is one of her excellencies that she gives rise to more inquiries than she sets at rest. "In not a few of her efforts to explain inexplicable phenomena, she does, in that very explication, add to the mass of inexplicable facts." What science was even twenty years ago is not science now, but is exploded by other and later discoveries.

We demand then, is human science a safe expositor of the word of God, and may it hold a place above the settled principles of biblical exegesis? It is not denied that the physical state of our globe has undergone great *changes* since its creation. What those changes are, is the province of science to search out and disclose, as well as to inquire into their causes, and thus ascertain, as we before intimated, the laws by which the Creator still governs the material creation. But when it would instruct us on the great subject of creation, it is out of its province. God himself is the great teacher here. We are firm believers in the doctrine of CREATION; and we hold that doctrine to be "God's making all things out of nothing, by the word of his power, in the space of six days, and all very good." So God himself instructs us, not only in the revelation to Moses as the selected narrator, but with memorable solemnity, when he said to the nation of Israel 2500 years after the creation itself, "Six *days* shall thou labor and do all thy work; but the *seventh day* is the Sabbath of the Lord thy God; in it thou shall not do any work; for in *six days* the Lord made heaven and earth, the sea and all that in them is." We may not give up the Sabbath from our regard to human science. It will be time enough for science to plead the inconsistency of its discoveries with the literal truth of the Mosaic narrative, when God shall commit to it the work of creation. Creation is *his* work. Human science might as well teach us that God did not in a single day create the oak of the forest, because facts show that it never comes to its maturity except by the growth of years; or that he did not in a single day create the first man, because facts show that the human frame reaches its maturity only by the slow and gradual growth of thirty years; as that the successive formations of aqueous and igneous rock which existed within the earth, required greater time for their formation than the six days spoken of by Moses. It was indeed a wondrous exhibition of his power which thus called all things into being. It was the great miracle. "Power belongeth unto God." From the deep abyss he *bid* this wonderful creation rise, and poised it by its own weight without any other support than his own almighty and invisible hand. "He spake, and it was done; he commanded, and it stood fast."

A *fourth fact* connected with the subject of

which we are speaking, is, that *this great work was prosecuted under the most perfect arrangement.* There is no confusion in the works of God. "In the beginning God created the heavens and the earth. And the earth was without form and void; and darkness was upon the face of the deep, and the Spirit of God moved upon the face of the waters." What the narrator here affirms is, that the first act of creation was the formation of the primordial elements, from which the organized heavens and earth were formed. They constituted a commingled substance, made up of earth and water, light, heat, and electricity, blended in disorder, a rude and shapeless mass, an undigested, dense, and floating chaos. Darkness covered it; and "the Spirit of God moved upon the face of the waters." This life-giving agent brooded there, and made this chaos, this vast valley, this dark ocean of floating death, the first scene of his vivifying power.

It became fitted to be the dwelling-place of man and beast, and to all the purposes of this fair creation, by being reduced to form, order, and beauty. This was effected by the creation of *light*, the most subtle and the most important of all material substances. It was first created after the chaos, because by his own laws of gravity and crystallization, the Creator selected it in his organization of a material world. The sun had been dark without it, or had never been called into existence, and the planetary world had stood still. Without it, the vapors had never ascended from the chaotic mass with which they were inmingled; vegetable and animal life would have found no aliment; living beings would never have found a habitation on the face of the earth; and cold and darkness would have left the original elements of the universe condensed into a solid mass. Heathen writers have expressed their admiration of the sublimity and majesty of the words, "*God* SAID, *let there be light, and there was light!*" Plato is said to have imitated it; and Longinus, the celebrated Athenian philosopher and critic, speaks of it as an instance of the sublime which is unsurpassed. "God said;" what words are these! Who shall speak of the power, the wisdom, the goodness they contain? What wondrous all-sufficiency, what wondrous fulness of the Deity flow out in these few words, "Let there be light!" Before the sun, or the moon, or the stars, this luminous substance was diffused throughout the universe, existing at first in a state of universal expansion, and subsequently distributed into distinct bodies. Truly the light "is sweet, and a pleasant thing it is for the eyes to behold the sun." "And God saw the light that it was good; and *God divided* the light from the darkness. And *God called* the light day, and the darkness he called night."

Ever after, in the progress of time, day and night were thus to succeed each other, each in its proper place, and each fraught with its appropriate blessings; the one bringing tranquillity and repose, the other diffusing wide its beauty, and spreading over the face of the infant creation its assemblage of graces and its coloring of joy.

With this change only, that the light was divided from the darkness, the rude and undigested mass remained the same. There was as yet no separation of the commingled substance; it was an unmeasured, turbid lake, the "vast whirlpool of future things," with all its unseparated elements tossed and agitated in indiscriminate confusion. To separate these mingled substances, and assign them their proper place, *God said*, "Let there be a firmament in the midst of the waters, and let it divide the waters from the waters. And God *made* the firmament, and divided the waters which were under the firmament from the waters which are above the firmament." The agitated and unseparated chaos is described as a mass of *waters*. The earth, when formed, stood between waters: there were waters above, and waters beneath it; and these waters were divided by *a firmament*, or that outstretched arch, or expansion over the earth, in which are placed the atmosphere and the clouds, and which forms the canopy adorned with all the luminaries of heaven. The Scriptures speak of the heavens and the earth as they appear to men; they are optical rather than astronomical or philosophical representations. Such are the representations of Moses, and such is the language of Elihu, when he represents the outspread sky as a "molten looking-glass"—a barrier so formed as to separate the superior from the inferior waters, that it is as impassable as though it were a canopy of brass, fixed and permanent as the statutes and ordinances of the Creator. There it stood, when God gave the decree that the fountains of the great deep should be broken up, and the windows of heaven should be opened, in order to drown the earth by the flood; and there it will stand, in all its varied brilliancy, spread out like a molten mirror, until that last change in its constituent elements, by which this same earth shall be destroyed by fire.

This heavenly, or aerial firmament, thus formed, the waters that were above it were held back and kept in their assigned chambers; but the inferior waters, constituting by far the greater portion of the substance from which the world was formed, overlay the whole of this lower creation. It was the primeval flood. It was the vast deluge. Day and night visited it; it was overhung by a pure atmosphere and a clear sky; but there were no valleys nor plains, nor had it the firmness of dry and solid land. The inspired Psalmist, when praising

God for his goodness, declares, "He gathereth the waters of the sea together as an heap; he layeth up the depth in store-houses." Such is the narrative of Moses. And *God said*, "Let the waters under the heavens be gathered together into one place, and let the dry land appear!" In order to leave the earth a firm and compact globe, there was an upheaving of the submerged land, the everlasting hills lifted themselves up, and the waters were thus drained off. The deep abyss was excavated for them; they were laid up in their appointed channels, and there the sovereign decree was imposed, "Hitherto shalt thou come, and no further; and here shall thy proud waves be stayed!" "And God called the dry land *earth*, and the gathering together of the waters called he *seas*." It was now a terraqueous globe, its surface presenting all the variety of land and water, continent and ocean, sea and island, bay and promontory, hill and plain, mountain and valley, beauty and majesty, while its subterranean apartments unfolded a scene of wonders everywhere exhibiting the depths of the divine wisdom.

Thus prepared, this outspread earth was next clothed with verdure, and devoted to the uses for which it was thus arranged. "And *God said*, Let the earth bring forth grass, the herb yielding seed, and the fruit-tree yielding fruit after his kind, whose seed is in itself upon the earth!" Not a root could germinate, not a tree blossom, nor a spire of grass vegetate throughout the range of the drear earth, without the immediate power of God. When he speaks, this new and almost endlessly diversified creation, with all its grasses and plants, forest and fruit-bearing trees, with all their varieties of structure, form, and foliage, waiting for no tedious process to reach maturity, and delayed by no laws subsequently controlling the world of nature, comes into perfected being with the heaven-imparted power to reproduce itself to the end of time. How emphatic with the signature and stamp of Deity is every plant and leaf and flower! how fragrant with his praise! A day of wonders was this memorable day to this newborn world; hitherto cold and unmantled, now cheered and kissed by the warm breath of heaven, and clothed with budding leaf, and blushing rose, and bending forest, and laughing meadow. "And God saw that it was good."

With the exception of the earth, the whole solar system was created on a subsequent day. By far the largest body in this system is the sun; planets also there are much larger than the earth; yet was the earth the first created world. Though comparatively a little world, our earth is vastly more valuable and important than other planets which are greater. We are thus instructed by the whole scope and design of God's revelation;

nor is it an unnatural, nor illogical conclusion from the order of time in which they were created, that these lights of heaven were formed for the *earth*, and not the earth for *them*. "And *God said*, Let there be lights in the firmament of the heaven, to divide the day from the night; and let them be for signs, and for seasons, and for days, and for years: and let them be for lights in the firmament of heaven, to give light upon the earth; and it was so. And God made two great lights; the greater light to rule the day, and the lesser light to rule the night; he made the stars also." Whatever other and incidental ends they may answer, the Scriptures teach us that they were formed to give light to the earth, to designate the vicissitudes of day and night, to mark their revolutions, and to perform their functions in subservience to the earth. And with what fidelity do they perform this service! with what incredible promptness and velocity! with what wonderful accuracy and precision, no one interrupting the movements of another, but all keeping their prescribed paths and performing their revolutions in their appointed times! And with what persevering obedience to the edict of their great Author have they been thus revolving in majestic order and harmony ever since the morning of their creation, and everywhere so eagerly observed as the unfailing chronometers of the universe!

No sooner was provision made for the animal tribes to subsist upon the thus prepared earth than again "*God said*, Let the waters bring forth abundantly the moving creature that hath life, and fowl that may fly above the earth in the open firmament of heaven!" The creation of the inhabitants of the waters and the firmament appears to have been simultaneous; though the command was first given to the waters, beginning with the lower, and proceeding to the higher orders of being. The waters were commanded to "bring forth *abundantly*:"—a most wise and munificent provision for a large portion of mankind; for while millions of the poor draw their subsistence from these sources, other and richer classes draw from them untold wealth. The riches of the ocean exceeds all calculation. Everything swarms with life in these perpetually replenished departments of the divine bounty; the original blessing still rests with them, "Be fruitful and multiply, and *fill* the waters in the seas, and let fowl multiply in the earth." In the formation of the purely *terrestrial* animals, "God made the *beast of the earth* after his kind, and *cattle* after their kind, and *everything that creepeth upon the earth* after his kind." Everything was formed distinct, "each after his kind;" every class, order, genus and species was distinctly recognized and formed, and so constituted as to produce its kind throughout successive generations.

Man was the last formed of all the animal creation, and was the noblest monument of the Creator's power. We shall say little in this place of this great work of God, because we propose to make it the exclusive topic of the following chapter. When God created this his last and best work, his language is, "*Let us make man.*" And what was the high model after which he was to be made? Wonderful is the recorded answer to this question. "Let us make man in our *own image*, after *our likeness.*" He bore the lineaments of the Deity, reflected his light and love; and though a created and borrowed, a faint and finite, was, nevertheless, a real radiance of his divine glory.

Such was the infancy of our world; such the beginning of the creation of God. "Thus the heavens and the earth were finished, and all the host of them." Survey them, even defaced and spoiled as they are now by the wickedness of man. What power, what wisdom, what greatness, what goodness shine in them all! Surely their great Author has not left himself without witness. What a wonderful Being is God! how vast! how incomprehensible! Great and marvellous are thy works, Lord God Almighty! No marvel that holy men have exclaimed, "Among the gods, there is none like unto Thee, O Lord; neither are there any works like unto thy works!" Atheism, polytheism, idolatry, irreligion and impiety, mournful realities as they are, and impotent to rob the Creator of his glory, would never have found a place on this beautiful earth, but as dark monuments of human apostasy. Reason rebukes them; conscience rebukes them; the works of God rebuke them. The whole creation is the legitimate school of piety, and has a voice that speaks for the mighty Maker. "Their line is gone out throughout all the earth, and their words to the end of the world." They impart instruction everywhere; there is no restriction of time, or place to these universal teachings; they lift up their voice and utter words of knowledge in the hearing of all men. If all that may be learned of God is not gathered from this field of observation, enough may be learned to make men wiser and better, and leave them without excuse. It is no sealed book, but an open volume, legible and beaming throughout with light and truth.

He whose voice was heard in the primeval paradise, and who "walked in the garden in the cool of the day," walks still in the midst of this broad and lofty edifice of nature, whose arch is the unmeasured heaven, whose pillars are the everlasting mountains, and whose lamps have emitted their light from the time when the morning stars first sang together to the present hour. Every motion in unmeasured space indicates the hand, every sound in the immense universe indicates the voice of God. O why is it, that amid these scenes of beauty and sublimity, these smiles of field and forest, this exuberance of land and ocean, this uncounted variety and annual reproduction of all that they can need or ask, thus adding to their enjoyment the freshness of almost perpetual novelty, and pervading every land and clime; men are so slow to bring these lessons home to the mind and heart? True piety here finds copious and consecrated materials for thought. Nature may well become the handmaid to grace, and creation subservient to redemption. The harp of David did not hang upon the willows when creation was his theme. There was no tameness in those notes of praise which sang of "the river of God which is full of water;" nor were they the less sweet because they were elicited by the light of that moon which is "the work of God's fingers;" nor were they discordant when he "covered the heavens with a cloud;" nor, though wild, as they sometimes are, and in keeping with these expressions of majesty, were they less thrilling when the voice of the Thunderer spake, or when he "gave his snow like wool, and scattered his hoar-frost like ashes." An humble and devout mind will gratefully meditate on all the works of God, and muse on the work of his hands.

So true it is that the works of God are seen with new eyes, where the heart is taught by his Spirit. Gratitude has claims in view of the world we occupy. When angels fell, it was a bleak and desert world to which they were destined—a world where no dew descends, and where are no genial skies—a world where the seeds of immortality germinate in weedlike rankness, and fit only for unquenchable flames. Surpassing kindness was it, and sovereign mercy, to assign the fallen race of man to this green earth, where day and night, summer and winter, seed-time and harvest, do not cease, and each successive season bears testimony to the divine mercy and forbearance. It is a privilege to live in such a world, if life be wisely employed; because such a life answers life's great end, and such a world furnishes a fitting education for a brighter and a better. Give place, then, to these grateful thoughts; let them call forth the tribute of praise. Praise him, all, ye nations; laud him, all ye people. To him who by wisdom made the heavens; for his mercy endureth forever! To him that stretched out the earth above the waters; to him that made great lights; for his mercy endureth forever! To him that remembered us in our low estate; for his mercy endureth forever! Praise him in the sanctuary of his power. Praise the Lord, O Jerusalem; praise thy God, O Zion. Let everything that hath breatl praise the Lord.

While the preceding chapter was going through the press, the authoi has fallen in with some observations, to which he may be allowed to refer

"To any one who has watched the progress of theoretical geology for the last few years, where opinion has so often vacillated and changed on the subject, and where so many hasty conclusions have been formed, that scarcely an author has his speculations half through the press, when the last part must accumulate as much on the one side as they hitherto appear to have done on the other."—*The Age of the Earth considered Geologically and Historically, by William Rhind, of Edinburgh.*

"While so large a portion of the globe is geologically unexplored; while all the general views which are to extend our classifications satisfactorily, from one hemisphere to another, from one zone to another, are still unformed; while the organic fossils of the tropics are almost unknown, and their general relations to the existing state of things has not even been conjectured, how can we expect to speculate rightly and securely respecting the history of the whole of our globe? Geologists have only just thrown open the door of a vast labyrinth, which it may employ many generations to traverse, but which they must needs explore before they can penetrate to the oracular chamber of truth."—*Whewell's History of Inductive Sciences.*

Let any one examine the history of geology from the days of Platt, Lester, Leibnitz, Hooke, Woodward, Whiston, and Burnet, to the later theroies by Gesner, Warner, Hutton, Smith, Buckland, Sedgwick, Lyell, and Silliman, and he will see cause to suspend his judgment in all the questions which put any other construction than that which a sound philology puts upon the Mosaic narrative.

"We hold then that the idea of the Adamite strata containing organic remains, in whatever condition these strata are seen, or may be discovered, whether arranged in the order of a first creation, or seen in the position of secondary deposits from this, is at total variance with the narrative of Moses, and was never meant to be implied in his words, or dreamt of by his predecessors or contemporaries. There are also *geological* objections to this theory of a previous world. If it was entirely distinct from the present earth in point of the period of its existence, and if it was completely overthrown at the time of the second creation, how does it happen that existing species are found in contemporary strata with extinct ones?"—*Rhind's Age of the Earth.*

"If the geological creeds of Baron, Cuvier, and Professor Buckland be established as true in science, then must the Book of Genesis be blotted out from the records of inspiration."—*Edinburgh Philosoph. Journ.* vol. xiv.

We are not confident that the mine in Bohemia referred to is the deepest excavation. There are at Schemnitz, on the southern slope of the Carpathian mountains, two silver mines, which are no longer worked on account of their depth; but they do materially differ from 3000 feet.

CHAPTER III.

The First Man.

A glance at the works of God shows that there is progress in them all, and that in them all the Creator has an end in view, which is worthy of himself. Hitherto, the creation which he had so miraculously called into existence, was unintelligent. There was to be a higher and nobler order of beings, transcending the mere material and animal as far as the spiritual and immortal transcends the natural and the mortal, and making new and ever-progressive disclosures of the unsearchable Deity.

Questions there are of deep interest both in theological science and in casuistry, depending upon the views that are entertained of the nature of man. *What am I? To what order of creatures do I belong? What are the peculiarities of my nature and relations? What are my responsibilities? Whence am I, and what is my destiny? I am the progeny of my parents; they of theirs;*

and theirs of an ancestry which extends to a still more remote period of time. Who can tell but men thus exist always and in an eternal series of generations?

To all these inquiries, the word of God gives a definite answer. It teaches us that man, though among the *first things*, began to be; and that there was a time when he did not exist. The atheist himself cannot deny this. If men exist in an eternal series of generations, then infinite generations are already past and gone. If infinite generations are already past and gone, the time was when each in the series was actually present; for if never actually present, it never existed. If each in the series was actually present, then the time was when all except one were future. The hypothesis contradicts itself. It supposes one generation to have been infinite, or the finite beginning of infinity. The absurdity is too palpable to require more than this passing remark. The human race had a beginning. Like the original chaos, and the light and the firmament, man was *created* by the great Author of all things.

There is a marked peculiarity in the Mosaic narrative of the creation of the first man. "*Let us make man in our image, after our likeness; so God created man in his own image, in the image of God made he him.*" God himself was the model, after which he was formed. He was created miraculously. He did not grow up from infancy to youth, and from youth to riper years; but like the plants and trees, like the fishes of the sea, and the fowls of heaven, and the animal creation, and the earth, he was created in full bloom and maturity, the perfection of humanity, and the model of all that is noble in the successive generations of men. When he was first conscious of his own existence, he was conscious of this maturity both of body and of mind. It was not by any agency of his own that he came into being, nor by any consent of his own; nor was he conscious of his dependence on any other being, nor of his obligations to any other but his Almighty Parent. Reason taught him, and his Maker taught him that "he was the son of God," and came into existence by the will and power of Him for whose pleasure he was created.

The sacred writers most certainly do not use flattering words when they speak of *men*. They call things by their right names, and set before us the human character in its true deformity; while at the same time they speak of man as the honored race, and as entitled to regard from the race to which he belongs. When we are told that God created man in his own image, we are made the depositaries of a truth from which we may learn something of God from what we know of man, and something of man from what the Scriptures reveal concerning God.

It was not in his corporeal organization that the first man resembled his Creator; for "God is a Spirit," not to be inspected, not to be analyzed, not even to be fully comprehended. There are visible exhibitions of the Deity; but his essential glory, the pure spirituality of his nature, lies far out of sight. All we know of it is that it is pure, and unmingled, and infinite. His understanding is infinite, his will omnipotent, and his moral dispositions are not only free from all imperfection, but constitute a fountain, an ocean of purity and loveliness that cannot be measured by finite minds. In the different gradations and orders of being, there is first mere inanimate matter; at one remove from this is the exquisite and curious machinery of art; still higher are the beauty, instinct, and consciousness of the animal creation; above this, is the wonderful structure of the human mind; in advance of this, is the angelic creation; while beyond, there is no intermediate existence till we arrive at the infinite God. There is a mighty chasm between the finite and the infinite; we cannot dart our thoughts across it. "Lord, what is *man* that thou art mindful of him, and the son of man that thou visitest him?" There are views of his nature which render him abject; yet are there views of him which we cannot help looking upon with wondrous interest, because he was made but a little lower than the angels, and next to them, holding a position nearest to the Infinite One, and formed in his image.

Man is a complex being, formed of a body and soul. That body of his, dust as it is, and to dust as it will certainly return, is itself a wondrous thing. His face, his form, his lineaments surpass in majesty all the creatures God had made. There is a nobleness written upon his brow, which still marks him as having been the early favorite of his Creator. The *tongue* of man gives him what no other portion of the animal creation possesses; he has the power of articulate speech, and utters a language that can be expressed by symbols and perpetuated by letters. The *hand* of man, adapting itself to every form and shape of matter, and giving him such power of execution; the *eye* of man, that has a meaning from infancy to old age, that speaks almost as intelligibly as his voice, and that has a lustre, a penetration, an authority by which men themselves are in no small degree governed, and which exerts so mysterious a power over the brute creation, are strongly indicative of his preeminent superiority. Strange to say, his physical frame is more enduring of toil than any of the brute creation, and is capable of efforts before which the most gigantic of the lower animals faint and die. He can live in every climate, become accustomed to heat and cold, and be cheerful and happy where few, if any other animals can live and be perpetuated. In the lowest species of animals, there are none of these distinguishing properties; in the ascending scale, we meet with something that bears resemblance to them; while in man we see them in such degrees of perfection, that we are convinced we have reached the highest scale in the series. Who, as he inspects this wondrous mechanism, can refrain from saying with the Psalmist, "I am fearfully and wonderfully made!" Though of lowly origin and allied to earth, the material world does not furnish so striking proofs of the divine wisdom and goodness as are visible in the organization of that animated frame. The least perfect and most summary treatise upon the anatomy and physiology of the human body, is well fitted to fill us with admiration of what we are. From no department of natural science do the elements of natural religion and those first principles of theology which the sacred writers everywhere assume, derive stronger confirmation, or illustrations more curious and ample, than from this complex and beautiful fabric, this earthly house, this tabernacle of clay.

Yet this did not constitute the man; he had a *spiritual*, as well as an animal existence. His body and soul were different and had a different origin. The former was formed of dust, the latter was the immediate inspiration of God himself.

Unhappily, there is a strong tendency in the researches of physical science to stop at *second causes* and terminate their researches in some of the forms of ancient or modern materialism. There are not wanting those who still speculate about the soul of man, as though, with Epicurus and the Stoics, they thought it an attenuated and material substance; a subtile air, or flame, or portion of heavenly light. Not a few among modern Phrenologists maintain that it is the result of some peculiar organization of the brain. They would have us believe there is no definite line of separation between what is material and what is immaterial; that, the bond which unites them is too delicate to be visible, and that the distinction between them is founded on conjecture. They profess to demonstrate that there is an *organ of intelligence*, and that it is unphilosophical to affirm that matter is essentially unintelligent. "If," say they, "matter be capable of gravitation, of elective attraction, of life, of instinct, of sensation, there does not seem to be any absurdity in supposing it is capable of thought." Such an hypothesis might interest us if we were not driven, not less by sound philosophy than by the Scriptures, to recognize the omnipresence of the great First Cause in sustaining and directing the whole material and immaterial creation. When we ask ourselves, what are those mysterious laws of nature by which the movements of organized and inorganic matter are directed; by which light and heat, and magnetism and electricity, develop their wonderful phenomena; by which matter assumes so many shapes, and forms, and textures, and modifications of beauty, life, and enjoyment: we answer in the language of Dr. Paley, "They are the name of an effect whose cause is God." The argument against these materialists lies within a narrow compass. Perceiving, thinking, and willing must be either inherent in matter originally, or they must result from some particular form, or modification, or motion of matter, or from some immaterial substance. Are they then inherent in matter, either in its several parts, or as a whole? If it be intelligent as a whole, it must be intelligent in every atom; for a concourse of the unintelligent cannot produce the intelligent. If intelligent in every atom, whence is it that there are so many unintelligent forms and modifications of it? A clod of earth, a block of marble, does not think. Neither a mountain nor an atom, neither a burning volcano nor a flash of lightning, perceives, thinks, or wills. And if this be so, it is very difficult to conceive how that which is essentially unintelligent as a whole, and also in its several parts, can become intelligent by any peculiar organization. Matter is no nearer thinking for altering its form or position: for being two or three particles, or three hundred; for being gross or refined, condensed or volatile, circular or square, indefinitely large or indefinitely small. Whether in confusion and disorder, or in the most precise and geometrical arrangement; whether in the seed of a vegetable, or in the egg of an animal, in a cord of the nerves, or a gland of the brain, it is still unintelligent. Nor can it approximate to thought by being set in motion. If thought results from matter in motion, then the whole material universe is intelligent; for no part of it is absolutely in a state of rest. The circulation of the blood, no less than the ebbing of the tides, is incompetent to the production of thought. Whatever be the essence of matter or of mind, we know them only by their properties. Matter is an extended, solid, inactive, movable substance; mind is an existence which perceives, thinks, acts, wills. Matter is the object of the senses; mind of consciousness. Matter has none of the properties of mind; mind has none of the properties of matter.

Nor are these conclusions invalidated by the fact, that there are indications of mind in the inferior animals. We do not call this fact in question, while we judge it of some importance to set it in its true light. The inferior animals possess thought and knowledge. The Scriptures teach us, that "the ox *knoweth* his owner, and the ass his master's crib." Yea, "the stork in the heaven *knoweth* her appointed times; and the turtle, and the crane, and the swallow *observe* the time of their coming." But between the intellectual properties of man, and the instinct, or intellectual capacity of animals, there is a wide and strongly marked difference. The knowledge of the inferior animals is confined to a narrow sphere. It is little more than "the law of organized life in a state of action," and extends only to what is necessary for their preservation and comfort. It does not seem capable of progression; it is the gift of the Creator for these definite purposes, and extends not beyond these defined limits. The bird builds her nest, and the bee and the beaver construct their cells now as they constructed them a thousand years ago. So far are they from making any advances in knowledge, that their sagacity is diminished rather than increased, even by human care and culture; while man's capacity is boundless; he is a learner even to old age; and the more he knows, the more is he capable of advancement. The knowledge of brutes is altogether independent of instruction; it is spontaneous; it is without deliberation, and without an object except a provision for its wants. Man has an end in view in his intellectual attainments, and a far-reaching purpose. The inferior animals have little knowledge of the past, and no anticipations of the future; they think only of the present, and only of themselves: man looks backward and forward, searches into the past, surveys the present, and penetrates into futurity. The animal creation cannot reason; they have no powers of imagination and abstraction; they have no perception of cause and effect, no discernment of the marks of wisdom and design, no power of distinguishing between truth and error, fiction and reality, right and wrong. They have not man's conscience, nor his hopes, nor his fears, nor his capacities of enjoyment. They have sensation, perception, and memory, and strong appetites and passions, and strong animal sensitiveness and sensibilities. They have will and choice, but their volitions are determined without the intervention of reason, and are decided by appetite, passion, and habit. God hath "deprived them of wisdom, neither hath he imparted to them understanding."

The soul of man is a wondrous existence; not as its Creator is wondrous, but as his most marvellous work is wondrous. "There is a spirit in man, and the inspiration of the Almighty giveth him understanding." Though mysteriously united to a material substance, it is not amalgamated nor blended with it, nor does it resemble it in any of its properties. It cannot be seen by the eye, nor felt by the touch, nor has it any surface that can be measured, nor can it be separated into parts. The infinite God is a vast and infinite world within himself; and his creature man carries within himself his own finite and little world. Of the more general properties of man's nature, as consisting of a body and a soul, it is not necessary that we say more. But we would utter ourselves more definitely when we speak of his immaterial nature, and endeavor to express some just conceptions of that which constitutes it.

What then is the human soul? In what respects it is *unlike* the Deity, we know; but, if it was created in God's image, there are particulars in which it is *like* him. Is the Deity in his nature intelligent? so is the soul of man. It possesses the *natural faculties* of perception, reason, conscience, and memory; these belong to its intellectual character. There is the same distinction between the natural and moral properties of the human soul, that exists between the natural and moral attributes of the Deity. Is the Deity, in his nature, an acting existence? is he all spirit and action? so is the soul of man. It is an existence whose nature is to act. In its first creation in Paradise, and in its first existence as it comes into being in successive generations, it has, to say the least, intellectual and moral tendencies; and what are these, if not its incipient actings? Wherever that creature exists which may be truly called the soul of man, there is an acting existence. It is that which not merely thinks and reasons, loves and hates, hopes and fears, acts and inspirits; it is itself thought, reason, emotion act. From its nature, there is no inactivity about it; it is activity, because it is spirit. Intellectual philosophers have questioned the truth of this position, and none more than Mr. Locke in his Essay on the Human Understanding. But this is not the only truth disputed by this great philosopher; such a denial is in keeping with the views of his Arminian philosophy, as expressed in his more religious writings. In the language of a living and more evangelical author, "There is a power within us unconscious and incapable of fatigue. Certain exercises of the mind, such as continuous thought and emotion, induce exhaustion and weariness, for in these it employs an organization which requires rest. But the *individual will* is perfectly unsusceptible of fatigue. In its volitions, the mind asserts its proper spirituality. As far as material help is concerned, the will acts from itself. In itself, the mind is an energy, and the source of untiring energy."* These are sound views. It is not the mind that becomes wearied by intellectual effort, but the material organization which it employs; it is not the mind that calls for repose, but the wearied frame in which it dwells, and which sleeps only to be awaked again, and

* Harris on the Constitution and Primitive Condition of the Human Being. Chap. v.

again exhausted by the busy thoughts and untiring will within. The mind like its great parent Spirit, never slumbers and never sleeps. If it were a piece of mechanical clock-work, it might run down and stop, and be wound up again. But the inaction of matter is not one of its properties; and if it once runs down and stops, there is no conceivable cause within itself that can set it in motion, nor could it ever be set in motion except by a new and creating power. It was the glory of the first man, that he was thus "made a living soul." It was his elevation and dignity, that he possessed vast spiritual capacities; that he was endued with a mind capable of unlimited expansion, —a treasure-house of thought, whose intellectual wealth should be ever increasing.

There can be no doubt that God conveyed extensive knowledge to the first man by an immediate and supernatural revelation; nor will it be questioned that these divine communications were the means of invigorating his intellectual capacities. And though the intellectual powers of his descendants are darkened and impoverished by sin, it is impossible for us to describe the fields of thought over which the mind of man, even now, is capable of expatiating. The gold has become dim, but it is still gold. It is mind and not matter; it is intelligence and not idiocy; it is the activity and powei of thought and will, and not the inertness, and age, and decay of a mere material organization. Its moral assimilation to the Deity it has lost; while it retains this intellectual resemblance. The former was "the glory that excelleth," the latter is the glory that remains. Were the mass of men idiots, how should we venerate the few that were intelligent; or were there but one in a million known and distinguished for intellect, how should we venerate him, and approach him as a being of superior rank! Our first father deserves our homage, were it only for his high capacity of thought. This fair jewel is the inheritance of the race. And though it shone brighter on his unscathed and unfurrowed brow than it has since shone, it still belongs to man, and sparkles even in its degradation. If the most fine gold be changed, there is even in this casket of clay a gem which twinkles in borrowed rays from the "Father of lights."

The soul of man was also created *moral* and *accountable.* A moral and accountable being is one who possesses a character that has moral qualities, and capable of being judged by a moral law. Much as men are disposed to honor intellect, we all feel that no man ought to be measured by his intellect alone; they are his moral attributes which constitute his glory. The first man was created in the full possession of his intellectual and moral faculties; and was therefore created under moral obligation. He was capable of distinguishing, not only between reality and fiction, truth and error, but between what is right and what is wrong. Once let the obligations of religion and morality be set before such a mind, and it feels the weight of them as certainly and as necessarily as his senses are affected by the objects of sense. This is a truth intuitively discerned: we can give no other account of it except that the Author of our being has so constituted us. The first man knew his relations to his Maker, and the biddings of his conscience told him that his Maker's will was law. He could not divest himself of the feeling that he was bound to do what God required, and to abstain from doing what God forbade. It was the obligation of rectitude, and he felt it. He could not throw it off, nor renounce nor resign this responsibility. There was a voice within him that enforced it, and a voice which nothing could silence. It was inwrought in his nature; it was concreated with his created soul, and formed a constituent element of his being. And it is common to all men; man everywhere recognizes the distinction between right and wrong. Even Hume confesses, that "the principles upon which men reason in morals are always the same. Let a man's insensibility be ever so great," says this infidel writer, "he must often be touched with the images of right and wrong; and let his prejudices be ever so obstinate, he must observe that others are susceptible of like impressions."* Understanding and conscience constitute men moral and accountable wherever they are found. It was not a mere irresponsible sagacity with which the first man was invested; the brutes had these, but they were not accountable. The light did its Maker's bidding; and so did the sea and the dry land, and so did every herb of the field; but none of these were moral and accountable. The physical and the animal creation were subject to law, but it was not a moral law. God gave man a law commanding what is right and forbidding what is wrong; this law was the rule of his duty and of his accountableness.

There were greater things in the created universe; but there was no created existence so important as man, on account of his moral and responsible nature. The sun and the stars of heaven could accomplish that to which his arm was incompetent; but be their action ever so useful or injurious, it could not be either approved or condemned. Man possessed a nature capable of doing good or evil; and in this, a nature capable of setting in motion a train of causes whose influence should be felt to the utmost verge of the divine empire. His character and conduct were allied to the most magnificent and glorious interests in the universe. He was free to do right or

* Hume's Essays: Inquiry Concerning the Principles of Morals. Sect. i.

wrong; to honor or dishonor the God that made him; to obey or disobey; to increase the aggregate of virtue and happiness in the universe, or to open the sluices of wickedness, and swell the tide of vice and wretchedness. He was capable of holiness and happiness, and he was capable of sin and misery, and of making continual progress in both. The foundations of this responsibility are laid deep; too deep ever to be disturbed without annihilating the soul of man itself.

Not only was this first man created moral and accountable, but he was created *holy*. As he came from the hands of his Creator, he was bright and pure. The earth was fair and beautiful; the heavens were decked with lights which single and alone, or in clustered galaxy, declared the glory of God. And when he created *man* to inhabit this beautiful earth, he formed him fitted for his select abode and high destiny. He was formed in the image of his Maker, not because he was a partaker of the divine intelligence only, and not simply in that, like his Maker, he was a spiritual and moral existence; but because he was a partaker of the divine holiness. The statement that he was made in the image of God, implies that all his intellectual and moral powers were in a state of perfection; and that, in the excellency of his disposition and character, he was every way a finished and perfected existence, and fit to be the adornment of the new-created world. Metaphysical theologians of the Arminian school profess to see insurmountable difficulties in the doctrine of *created* holiness. They affirm that holiness is the act of the creature, and because the creatures act, must be caused by the creature. But even upon the hypothesis that holiness *is* the act of the creature, and nothing but his act, it does not follow that it is not caused by the Creator. The soul of man itself is a created thing, and like all other created things, is constantly dependent on the will of God for its continuance in being. The soul of Adam was not sufficient of itself to think anything of itself; it lived, and moved, and had its being in God. It was an acting existence, but it was a dependent existence, and dependent for its activity. All its springs were in God. If God had not created him holy, or made him holy after his creation, he never would have been holy. Nor does the idea of created holiness at all interfere with the idea that it is the creature's act. We challenge philosophy to show that the acts of a holy creature cannot be caused by the Creator, or that they are the less voluntary because they are the effects of divine power. The Scriptures teach us that the gracious affections in the heart of the Christian are an effect of God's power; nor are they on this account, any the less the acts of the Christian's mind. His love to God is his own act; he himself performs it, but it is "shed abroad in his heart by the Holy Ghost." The first man needed more than to be created with intellectual and moral faculties, just as the material universe needed more than to be created, and then left "to go alone;" it was necessary that the right exercise of these faculties should be produced by divine power. And this is everywhere the teaching of the Bible. "So God *created* man in his own image; in the *image of God* created he him." If there be any doubt as to the nature of this resemblance, let the doubt be solved by the Apostle when he says, "And that ye put on the new man which after God is created in righteousness and true holiness." The new creation makes men holy, and is in the image of God; the first creation, which was in God's image, made the first man holy. The author of the Book of Ecclesiastes declares, "Lo this only have I found, that God *made* man upright, but they have sought out many inventions." God did not create sin; wickedness is not from him. He made man upright; this is his greatest preëminence. It was created holiness that he possessed,—a borrowed holiness; but it was not the less holiness because created. Nor was it the less lovely. It was "the beauty of holiness"—beautiful as the blossoms of the young paradise, stainless as angelic purity, a mild reflection, and miniature resemblance of the Uncreated One. With the single exception of the

Second Adam, there never has been, in this beautiful world, so delightful an object of contemplation as the perfect character of the first man.

The first man was also created *immortal.* This soul of his was deathless. When the dust which contained it, "returned to the earth as it was, the spirit returned to God who gave it." Its very nature favors this thought; its instinctive dread of annihilation favors it; it is indicated still more clearly by its vast capacities, and more clearly still by the equal justice and vast designs of the divine government; but it finds its confirmation only in God's revealed will. What he has created, he can annihilate; nor have we any certain evidence that he will not annihilate the mind of man, except his own declared purpose. From the first moment of his creation, the first man bore the seal of heaven to his immortality. Nothing else bore this impress. The sun and the moon did not; they were made to be extinguished and set in darkness. The earth did not; it was made to wax old, and stagger like a drunken man, and be burnt up. Time did not; for time itself shall pass away and be no longer. But *man*, the first as well as the last, was formed the inheritor of eternity. Once created, by the decree of his eternal Author, he shall never be blotted out of being. That same first man into whose nostrils God breathed the breath of life now lives. Six thousand years have passed away, and his existence is but just begun. Long since did he slough off this body of earth, and come forth pure and happy, robed in light, and crowned with more than his pristine honor and glory. Nor shall he ever lose the high attribute of his immortality.

Thus created and thus endued, he was constituted the *deputed lord of this lower creation.* He came from his Maker's hands to take his place at the head of the kingdoms of nature and the whole animal world. Everything around him recognized his authority and influence. They were his property, and he had a right to use them as his own. The law of their being was that they were all to be subservient to man.

God gave man this dominion when he gave him his first blessing; and the gift is one which furnishes a beautiful illustration of the Creator's bounty. Because there was nothing within the wide compass of the world he had made, which presented so noble a specimen of his finished workmanship as man, he thus honored him. The spacious earth, the trackless ocean, were his. Every other part of the creation was but the preface and the prelude to the more distinguished honor he thus put upon man. He was indeed but a single link in the chain of created things; but he was the last and most important link, and was placed at the head of the creation itself. "The heaven and the heaven of heavens," says the Psalmist, "are the Lord's, but the earth hath he given to the children of men." Everything was made subject to his usefulness, his enjoyment, and his sway. Nor were these rights which he ever would have claimed but for God, nor have dared to exercise without the divine permission. Nor would the material and animal creation have been thus subservient, but for its Maker's high command. But God gave man this high precedence, and made him the world's monarch and proprietor. Though in size, and strength, and swiftness, he was inferior to a multitude of the animal creation, they were to be his subjects. He was crowned this earth's emperor, and it is a part of his mission to exercise this authority. It is a commission, too, which he has executed. Animal tribes have made war upon him; but there are none so fell and savage that he has not the skill and power to tame or subdue. The "fear of man and the dread of man" is, to the present hour, upon every class of animal existence. Man's voice is their law, and man's presence their restraint; they do his bidding, he does not theirs. With a supremacy to be maintained until the dissolution of all things, man is preëminent in his authority over them all, and not more certainly does the foot of man encroach upon the wilderness where they roam, and the voice of man is heard amid their forest recesses, than they gradually retire to the more remote deserts.

This delegated authority is expressed in very comprehensive terms. "Subdue the earth and have dominion," is broad enough to cover every enterprise which employs human ingenuity and labor. The sun now shines for man, and the rains descend, and day and night, summer and winter, seed-time and harvest, do not cease. The earth on which he treads is barren, or fruitful, as he cultivates it; it ministers to his necessities, his comforts, his luxury, his wealth, as he wills it. Every department of the material creation, from the bowels of the earth to its verdure, fruits, and flowers, and even its circumambient atmosphere, are placed under tribute to man. Man's great mission is, in humble dependence upon his Maker, in the fear and love of God, and in grateful acknowledgment of his goodness, to go forth and *subdue* it. And as the result of this munificence, the mind, the eye, the hand of man, have been directed to wondrous achievements. Had we lived in the earlier and more rude states of society, we might well have doubted if it were possible for him to effect what we now know he has effected, and what we see him performing every day. He has felled the forests, and made the wilderness blossom as the rose; and through him the solitary place has been made glad. He has founded empires, erected pyramids and towers, and beautified the earth with cottage and palace. He has reclaimed the wandering savage of his own species, called into existence and governed political communities, given to social life the security of its laws, and adorned it with the arts and refinement of civilization, science, and religion. He has scanned the heavens, penetrated the earth, and navigated its seas. He has converted deserts into cities, made islands in the ocean, and turned in the sea upon the solid land. He has shown that the animal and vegetable kingdoms are made to balance and sustain each other, according to general laws; he has recorded the general facts or results which proceed from the skilful adjustment in the natural world made by the great Creator. By his advancement in science and the arts, he has contended successfully with the elements of nature, and decomposed or combined them, neutralized them or given them vigor. By his acquaintance with the laws of mechanism and motion, he has asserted his power over the material world, and directed its agencies almost at his pleasure. The analytical powers of his mind have been successfully employed in pursuits that have furnished noble specimens of thought and intellect. He has busied himself with whatever can be numbered and measured, and with a clearness, caution, and accuracy that have surpassed even his own hopes. The painted canvass, the sculptured marble, receive life and beauty from his hands; while he so concentrates and directs the scattered rays of the light of heaven, that, at his bidding, they perform more accurate and delicate tracings. There is no enterprise, and no sphere of knowledge, in which he has been employed, which has not acknowledged his authority. Prose has recorded his deeds, and they have been sung in poetry. Libraries are the monuments of his toil and perseverance; alcove upon alcove, in the deep recesses of time, have treasured up the records of his dominion. This dominion is man's immunity as God's creature; he has a divine right to it, because he is a man. He is a prince in earth's empire, and not a subject. He has but one superior; he himself is sovereign in the dominion thus delegated to him by the great Lord of all.

There is one more thought which here deserves consideration, and that is, that this first man was the *parent of the race.* This thought must furnish the subject of our next chapter. In the mean time, we may not dismiss our general topic, without a single reflection.

We are *men.* Yet is there something within us that forces the conviction upon our minds, that our honor is tarnished. The comeliness of our humanity is obscured; its high adornment is departed. O, why is it, that we cannot look toward heaven without the blush of shame upon our cheek! Some foul enemy has been busy with our race. "Man that is in honor abode not." *Sin* has effected this mournful degradation in this highest and noblest work of God. "The crown is fallen from our head; woe unto us, for we have sinned!" Yet are we not outcasts, and banished like Cain. Everlasting thanks to God, this reproach of humanity may be wiped away. Man's nature is even more than ever dignified by its alliance with the second Adam, who, when it lost all its redeeming qualities, embodied it with his own, and for disgrace gave it honor. It was the promise to the first man, that there should be One, "of woman born," who would rescue from degradation and shame. He has rescued. Multitudes have by him been made kings and priests to God, and live and reign with him forever. Self-respect ought to make every man a Christian. He must forget that he is a *man*, and lose all consciousness of his real worth, if he aim not thus at humanity's prize and high calling. An unchristian man! no, let me not be an unchristian man. An unchristian life, an unchristian death, an unchristian eternity, O my soul, come not thou into their secret, to their assembly, mine honor be not thou united! The time is coming when such a man will be indeed dishonored. No voice of love will greet him in his exile, and his punishment will be greater than he can bear. The star of hope will never rise over his dark way in that far-off land of sin and shame.

Seek then to elevate the intellectual above the animal, the moral above the physical, the spiritual and eternal above the material and temporal. The redemption that has been achieved for man, more than all things else, indicates his destiny. His aspirations and hopes indicate it; it remains for him to watch and pray that he commit not the suicidal act of destroying his own soul.

CHAPTER IV.

The Unity of the Human Race.

We proceed, as we intimated in the last chapter, to call the attention of the reader to the question of the *unity of the human race.* Whether the first man spoken of by Moses, was literally the *first* man, and the *parent* of the entire race of human beings, is an inquiry to which different answers have for the most part been given, as different authors have been believers, or disbelievers, in a supernatural revelation. Where the subject is investigated simply by the phenomena of nature and the lights of science, there indeed are those who have come to the conclusion, that all mankind are not the descendants of one common pair. Men imbued with Christian truth do not complain of these philosophical inquiries; for they are more and more satisfied that on this subject, as well as every other, the works and the word of God, when both are known and understood, are perfectly harmonious. The greatest naturalists in all ages, however diversified may have been their views in regard to Christianity, regarded all the races of men as composed of one species.* We are not a little surprised, therefore, when we find men who express their unhesitating confidence in the Scriptures, advocating the doctrine of a plurality of races, as has been recently done by two authors of eminence in our own country.† One of the writers here referred to affirms, that "the Mosaic history affords a fair, and very strong presumption, that man was divided into several species by the Creator." He expresses the belief that Adam and Eve were not the first and only created beings in the world; that the race spoken of by Moses, of which Adam was the first, is simply the race to which the Scriptures have reference, and which were to be employed by God in the design of redeeming mercy. The other affirms that the Bible professes to give "the history of the *white* race, with special reference to the history of the Jews;" and, strange as it may appear to those who read the Scriptures, he asserts that "nowhere the colored races, as such, are even

* Among these were Linnæus, Leibnitz, Buffon, Schrobler, Erxleben, Humboldt, Blumenbach, Cuvier, Owen, and others, who were the lights of the world, and studied all the departments of nature.

† See "The Natural History of Man," a work of more than seven hundred octavo pages, by William Frederic Van Amringe, of the state of New York; and a work "On the Diversity and Origin of the Human Races," by Prof. Agassiz, of Cambridge College.

alluded to;" while he "challenges those who maintain that mankind originated from a single pair, to quote a single passage in the whole Scriptures, pointing at those physical differences, which may be adduced as evidence that the sacred writers regarded them as descended from a common stock."

In the following discussion, therefore, we are concerned mainly with the scriptural argument in favor of the unity of the race. All arguments against this position are, as it appears to us, arguments against the Scriptures; the verity of Moses and of Paul depend alike on the common origin of the species. In defence of this view, we remark—

In the first place, *there is no intimation in the Scriptures that there was a race of men prior to the creation of Adam and Eve.* It has been alleged as a reason of the belief that there was such a race, that it is most improbable that the wife of Cain could have been the daughter of Adam and Eve; because, it does not appear that they had daughters at the time Cain was driven into exile, nor indeed until after the birth of Seth, who was born after Canaan's son Enoch. And in keeping with this hypothesis, it is supposed that the unhallowed marriages subsequently spoken of between the "sons of God" and the "daughters of men," and through which the earth became degenerate, were alliances between the descendants of

Adam, and the descendants of a race which existed prior to the creation, spoken of by Moses. This is no new hypothesis; it was known, at least as early as the days of Voltaire, and has often been repeated. No fact is more obvious than that in the genealogy of the Scriptures, there is an *incomplete* record of *female* descendants. The sons of Adam and Eve must have married their sisters; yet the names of his daughters are not once mentioned in the sacred writings. The first female on the record is the wife of Cain, and the next two are the wives of Lamech. It does not appear from the book of Genesis that even so late as the time of Cain's exile, Adam and Eve had any female children; yet in a subsequent paragraph, which covers his entire life, we are told that Adam lived nine hundred and thirty years, and "begat sons and *daughters*." The sacred records trace the events of patriarchal history, and the age of the world from Adam to Noah, through a period of 2000 years; they give us the intermediate names of Seth, Enos, Cainan, Mahalaleel, Jared, Enoch, Methusaleh, and Lamech; but the most we know of the female descendants of any of them is the bald record that "they begat sons and *daughters*." That the wife of Cain could not have been the daughter of Adam and Eve is entirely destitute of proof. The supposition assumes that the narrative contains an account of *all* the children of our first parents; while this was by no means necessary to the objects of the writer, or the accuracy of the narrative. There is no intimation in the narrative itself that our first parents had no daughters before Cain's exile, or none between his exile and his marriage. He was banished during the life of his parents, and not until about one hundred and thirty years after their creation; so that there was abundant time for them to have a numerous and dispersed progeny before the marriage of Cain. Though the Scriptures do not inform us when that marriage took place, they give no intimation that it did not take place previous to his banishment; but on the other hand speak of "his wife" as one well known to the family of Adam, and as one who, as such, had been familiarly recognized.

In opposition to the hypothesis on which we are animadverting, it may be remarked, that the narrative in the book of Genesis cannot fairly receive any other fair construction than that Adam was the first created of the race. It is compendious, but perfectly explicit. It is a narrative of the *creation* in its beautiful and divine order; first the commingled materials which formed the heavens and the earth—then light—then the firmament—then the sea and the dry land—then the vegetable world—then the sun, moon, and stars—then fishes and fowl—then cattle, and creeping things, and beast of the earth—and last of all *man*, the first created man, as the crown of the creation and the parent of the race. Do we want anything more than this to satisfy us that the first male and female ever created were Adam and Eve? If so, we have it in the fact that they were invested with universal dominion, and that to them the command was given, "Be fruitful, and multiply, and replenish the *earth*"—not inhabited and replenished by a prior race, but to be inhabited and replenished by the new created-pair. Besides; if there were a prior race, where are they? Who are they? And what has become of this anomalous race of human beings, so separated from the race of Adam, that they hail from a different ancestry, and amid all the interlacing of the nations are not mentioned in the word of God, and have preserved no tradition of their origin? In addition to this, the *Scriptures expressly assert that Adam was the first man.* "The *first* man Adam was made a living soul; the last Adam a quickening spirit:" —"The *first* man is of the earth, earthy; the second man is the Lord from heaven."

In proof of the common origin of the race, it may be again remarked that the *Scriptures attribute to them all the same common properties.* In the question we are considering, due weight is to be given to the fact, that in their view of the nations, the Scriptures take a wide survey. There is not a distinct, or a mingled people on the face of the earth, known to the records of ethnology, certainly not then in its infant state, whose history they do not trace, or of whom they do not give some intimation. They have respect to the entire race of man, and overlook no part of it. To a great extent, the Bible is definite in its notices of the nations, and where it is not thus definite, it speaks of them as "all the ends of the earth," and as "dwelling afar off upon the sea." People of every age of time, of every longitude and zone, under every form of government, and in all their diversities of descent, color, language and habits, are comprised in the descriptions, or allusions of Moses and the prophets, Christ and the apostles. The same dissimilarities in the various races of men existed at the time the Scriptures were written which have existed since, and which exist at the present day. It is not a little marvellous that a man distinguished for learning should hazard the bold assertion, that "the colored races are nowhere alluded to by the sacred writers." Most abundantly do they allude to them. They speak of *Ethiopia*, and they refer to its different families. Moses and the prophets were not unacquainted with the imbrowned inhabitants of Egypt, Nubia and Abyssinia; nor with the darker inhabitants of the interior and equatorial regions. They were Ethiopian princes who, at various times, occupied the throne of the Pharaohs; an Ethiopian princess is mentioned by St. Luke in the Acts of the Apostles; the inhabitants of Ethiopia were better known to the Hebrews than they are even to ourselves. Did Professor Agassiz never read of a Cushite chieftain whose name was Nimrod? Did he never hear of a Cushite woman who was the daughter of Jethro? or of a Cushite invader of Judah in the days of Asa? or of "recovering the remnant left from Cush?" or of the Ethiopian slave belonging to the household of king Zedekiah? or of "Ethiopia stretching out her hands unto God?" or of the glorious things spoken of Zion, in the day when it shall be said, "Behold Philistia and Tyre, with *Ethiopia:* this man was born there?" Or does he suppose the sacred writers knew nothing of the peculiarities of this people, when they demand, "Can the Ethiopian change his skin, or the leopard his spots?" The Cush and the Ethiopia of the Scriptures are the same; Cush is always rendered by the Septuagint translators Ethiopia. The historical fact is, that the word Ethiopian denoted the negro race. So the Greeks used it; to "wash the Ethiopian white," was with them a proverbial expression applied to a hopeless attempt. They were the darkest race of people known to the Greeks, and in earlier times to the Hebrews. Yet the Scriptures everywhere speak of this race of men, who, in configuration, color, and constitutional peculiarity, are the very antipodes of the white races, as possessing a common humanity with them. No fact is more obvious, than that whatever there be in one portion of the world that constitutes its inhabitants human, *that* the Scriptures decide belongs to the inhabitants of every other portion.

We know from an investigation of the laws of nature, and from the anatomy and physiology of the human frame, that all the varieties of the race, many as they are, and not a few of them from their immingling with other varieties almost imperceptible in degree, possess the same *physical* properties. In the structure of his body, and in that physical organization which distinguishes him from every other species of animals, man is the same being in Labrador and South Wales, on the Caucasian mountains, and on the burning sands of Africa. Change his condition; transplant him from his natural soil and climate; take him in the wilds of the forest, or under the culture of civilized and polished life; and he has everywhere the characteristics which designate the same species. These characteristics are obvious, striking, and permanent, even to the number of teeth and bones, the number and arrangement of the muscles, and the digestive, circulatory, secretory, and respiratory organs. There is no difference in these particulars which has as yet been detected among the different races; there is the same uniformity in the white and black, the Mongolian, the Malay, and the American. They are all omniverous, and capable of living on all kinds of food, and of inhabiting all climates; while all have the same period of gestation, the same slow growth, are subject to the same diseases, possess the same average longevity, and in all their varieties, and in every shade of amalgamation, produce a fertile offspring.

It is now a well-ascertained fact, that animals of different species are incapable of producing and perpetuating themselves. Our learned countryman, Dr. Bachman, has shown, with a force of testimony that cannot be resisted, that in no instance has a fertile progeny arisen from the amalgamation of distinct species. Prichard, in his work on the Natural History of Man, mentions that Dr. Wagner, of Germany, has proved by the dissection of animals of mixed blood, that nature has interposed in the anatomical structure of hybrids, an absolute barrier to their reproduction. Yet the proof is abundant from the Scriptures, that the different varieties of the race mingle without limit, and reproduce indefinitely. They do not fail to criminate the illicit intercourse of the sexes who form different varieties of the race, as the prohibited intercourse with beings who are human, and belonging to the same species.

The more important properties, and those which the Scriptures dwell upon as characteristics of the race, are man's intellectual and moral nature, and his indestructible immortality. Indeed, this whole subject is important, chiefly for its moral ends, and in relation to man's responsibility as a being who is *human* in all the varieties of his descent. It is a spiritual nature which he possesses. He is a percipient, thinking, willing existence. He has reason and conscience. He possesses a mind which is capable of progress and expansion; he is so far a religious being, that he possesses a sense of right and wrong, is capable of holiness and happiness, and of wickedness and misery. He was formed for immortality, and is constituted the deputed lord of this lower creation. These are high prerogatives, but they belong to man wherever he is found; the Scriptures everywhere attribute them to all the races, of every variety on the face of the globe.

In the next place, the Scriptures represent *all the varieties of the race as having a common interest in the truths which they reveal.* No matter from what proximate parentage he is descended, or what his peculiarities of form and color, they look upon man as the subject of God's moral government, and as having an interest in his revealed truth. The great truths of the Bible are man's apostasy and God's redemption; while, as the consequence, or rather as part and parcel of these revelations, they disclose to us man's accountability, and his final and irrevocable award to the retributious of eternity. They speak of him as a transgressor, but as the prisoner of hope; enjoying a reprieve from condemnation, living under the mediatorial reign of mercy, and to whom the offer of salvation is made on revealed conditions. In all these particulars, so descriptive of what is exclusively human, the Bible addresses itself equally, and with equal appropriateness, to all the varieties of the race. It requires that the same instruction should be given to them all; the same obligation enforced; the same offers of mercy proclaimed; and the same divine solicitude for their salvation made known. It requires that the same class of motives, drawn from truth and duty, from all that is authoritative in the divine government, and all that is persuasive in the tenderness of infinite love, be urged upon all men as inducements to accept its great salvation. It tells them that this day of grace and hope terminates at death; that none may look for a subsequent opportunity of repentance; that then the righteous hath hope, and the wicked is driven away in his wickedness; and that after death is the final and irrevocable sentence to heaven, or hell. Just look at these leading truths. Is it of human sinfulness that the Scriptures speak; they speak of *man* wherever he is found, of every form of humanity in all its varieties, of Jew and Gentile, slave and freeman: "All have sinned and come short of the glory of God." Is it of the salvation by Christ; their language is, "For if *by one man's offence* death reigned by one; much more they which receive abundance of grace and of the gift of righteousness, shall reign in life *by One, Jesus Christ.*" If there be a truth they state with clearness, it is the ruined condition of the race from the apostasy of the first man; and with the same clearness its blessed counterpart, the salvation by Christ. They require that "the gospel be preached to *every creature*," and affirm that "according to the commandment of the everlasting God, it is made known *to all nations* for the obedience of faith." Is it of repentance they speak; their language is, "God now commandeth all men everywhere to repent." Or do they lift the veil of future things, and tell of the resurrection both of the just and the unjust; their language is, "All that are in their graves shall hear his voice and come forth;" "The sea gave up the dead which were in it, and death and hell delivered up the dead which were in them;" "As in *Adam all* die, so in Christ, shall all be made alive." And when they speak of the judgment, they say, "I saw the dead, *small and great*, stand before God;" we shall "*all* stand before the judgment-seat of Christ;" "*Every one of us* shall give an account of himself before God;" "Christ shall judge the *quick* and the *dead* at his appearing and his kingdom."

There are phrases here which certainly include all the varieties of the race, and which regard the race itself as one. What is there of humanity that is not comprehended in the word, *Christ?* Who shall shut out Christ from the great brotherhood of man, when he stands as the God-man Mediator, as embodying humanity, and as the brother of the race—stands in the very centre of the stream of time, bound alike to the first and the last man? And who that is *human* has not these characteristics—that he is a fallen sinner—that his only hope is in the gospel of the grace of God—and that the federal personages by which he is bound to these great realities, are on the one hand the first, and on the other the second Adam? Perish the infidel thought that there is any portion of the human race, who are so isolated from the common parentage as to be cut off from all access to the common Saviour! Surely wherever man is found, the relation he bears to the Saviour of men identifies him with Adam's posterity. If there was a prior race, or if there be any other race, the Scriptures nowhere give the least intimation of it. If there be such a race, it is one not affected by Adam's apostasy; nor have they any interest in the Redeemer of his descendants; nor do they come within the sphere of the commission given to those who preach his gospel; nor may it be preached to them; nor are they entitled to any of its promises or hopes; nor have any lot nor part in this matter. Do the Scriptures anywhere recognize such a race? We can understand why it was that such a man as Voltaire should advocate the doctrine of a variety of races, because his object was to invalidate the truth of the Sacred Writings; but it is not easy for us to understand why professed believers in the Sacred Scriptures should be the advocates of this doctrine, and urge in favor of it the established laws of science. We marvel not a little at the inconsistency which puts the question upon such an issue. It becomes such writers, as men of science, if not as Christians, to *show*, with some precision, what those distinctive differences in the race are, which necessarily give men a different origin; from what, and how many, different sources they have originated; and how, in the dispensation of the gospel, we are to discriminate them from the descendants of Adam. When they have done this, we, in our turn, will undertake to show that those very lines of demarcation are distinctly recognized in the Scriptures, not as characteristics of a different origin, but as belonging to those who are the descendants of the same pair, and as component parts of the one great family to all of whom the Scriptures address the truths and hopes of the common salvation.

This leads me to another and a distinct topic, which is, that *in their references to the various nations, and tribes of men, and in all their diversities, the Scriptures do in fact trace their genealogy to one common parentage.* The common objection to the doctrine we are advocating is, that men are so widely diffused over the earth, that it is irrational to suppose them to have originated from a common centre. Man is found everywhere; and in varieties so numerous, so great, and so permanent, that it is more consistent with analogy to suppose him to have originated from different sources, than to have sprung from the same source. If we were to answer this objection on philosophical principles merely, we would undertake to show with Dr. Pickering, "on zoological grounds, that the human family is foreign to the American continent." It has been shown, as we judge, from the migratory habits of man, and from the facilities and motives to his migration, that it is no absurd, nor unnatural hypothesis, that he migrated from that portion of the earth which the Scriptures assign as the place of his creation. The theory of Professor Agassiz is that men are traceable to *different creations*, as they inhabit different zoological regions, or zones. Yet it might be shown, that large districts of country, comprising different zones, are inhabited by tribes and nations which all ethnological writers trace to the same common stock. This theory has been well tested by a recent reviewer in our own country.* Within the American continent, says this searching writer, "are *four* provinces, reaching through a greater extent of climate than any other body of land upon the globe can supply—from the north star to the southern cross—occupied through all its length by one aboriginal race. This American race, whose distribution over four zoological provinces is not questioned, affords the most convincing proof of the utter futility of this attempt to connect each race of men whose limits are naturally circumscribed with a particular organized province. It is not like the *Aztec* race, of no real foundation in nature; nor like the *Mongol*, of undecided extent; nor like the *Malay*, mingled throughout its extent with other races; nor like the negro, blended in every direction with other and related tribes. It is of almost *pure blood*, and is limited in every direction by the ocean, which cuts it off from all association."† This fact alone is a perfect confutation of the Professor's theory, and a perfect refutation of his whole argument.

But our concern is more with the argument as it is presented in the Scriptures. The genealogical tables contained in the Scriptures present a remarkable feature in the Sacred Writings. I

* The New Englander for Oct. 1850.

† In proof the common origin of the American Aborigines. See Stone's Life of Red Jacket.

call them genealogical; and while some of them are strictly so, others are rather *statements*, and ethnological sketches, by which the inhabitants of the earth are traced down from earlier to later periods. The author of the Book of Genesis furnishes a succinct history of the inhabitants of the earth from the creation to the Deluge, and from the Deluge to his own times; a period of twenty-five hundred years, and during which men had greatly multiplied, and formed different clans, and large and powerful nations. This enumeration contains a great *variety* of the human race; so great, that science might be justified in advocating the doctrine of a plurality of races from this diversity as it then existed, for as good reasons as justify the doctrine at the present day. There were the same diversities of color and form; yet it will not be questioned, that Moses traces them to a common origin; with all their diversity, there was the same lineal descent from Adam and from Noah. It would be an instructive work on ethnology which should follow in the track of Moses, and trace up the different nations of the earth to the point where he left them, and show that all the great branches of the race sprang from Noah's three sons. We may be pardoned for suggesting that this *threefold* classification is the more natural one. Cuvier, in substance, retains it, and divides the race into three varieties, Caucasian, Mongolian, and

Ethiopian. Blumenbach, and his classification has been more generally received, makes five varieties, the Caucasian, the Mongolian, the American, the Negro, and the Malay. This classification appears to us objectionable on many accounts; nor is it at once comprehended by the ordinary reader. Nor is that classification of one of our learned countrymen less objectionable, by which he designates the varieties as the Shemitic species, the Japhetic, the Ishmaelitic and the Canaanitic species. These two latter classifications separate what God has historically joined together. Philologists have traced the languages of the earth to the languages originally spoken by the descendants of Shem, Ham and Japheth; would not the work of the ethnologist be facilitated by thus classifying the great varieties of the race?

Would it be impracticable to define with very considerable precision the branches of the *Shemitic* family, or the descendants of Shem? Moses traces his descendants down to Abraham; and from Abraham are traced all the varieties of the *Jews proper*, all the ramifications of *Moabite and Ammonite origin*, and the still greater varieties descended from *Hagar through Ishmael*, forming as his descendants did one of the most extensive empires in the world; extending themselves over Syria, Palestine, Egypt, and civilized Africa—penetrating Europe and invading Tartary—overrun-ning Spain and the larger islands of the Mediterranean—reaching from the Ganges to the Atlantic, and from the Pyrenees to the deserts of Africa—combining the scattered Saracen tribes, everywhere marked by peculiarities and customs of their own, a people "dwelling in the presence of their brethren," and proclaiming their descent from the archer in the wilderness of Paran. The ancient inhabitants of Mesopotamia, Syria, and Ophir were all the descendants of Shem. If we carefully compare the ethnological portions of the Book of Genesis with the ethnological portions of the First Book of Chronicles, we may collect no small amount of knowledge in regard to this portion of the human race.

Though not without its difficulties, there is still less embarrassment in tracing the descendants of *Ham.* They had a different destiny from the descendants of Shem. For the unnatural, unfilial, and foul sin of their father, they were the accursed race, and doomed to be "the servant of servants," to the descendants of Shem and Japheth. Nothing is more obvious than that this race must, in some way, be kept so distinct from the other races, that this curse could be visibly executed. Without some line of demarcation, either physical or geographical, or both, the frequent intermarriages between these races would have gradually blotted out their predicted isolation, and rendered the descendants of Ham, in the progress of time, undistinguished from the descendants of Shem and Japheth. We know from all history and observation, that there is a race of men who possess strong specific differences of color and features; that these differences have prevailed from the earliest times, and that, let them be removed to whatever portion of the earth, and live under whatever regimen they may, these specific differences exist still. Ham had four sons, and they were early assigned to a well-defined portion of the earth. *Cush* was the oldest, and as we have already seen, was but another name for Ethiopia. *Mizraim* was the second son; he peopled Egypt; Egypt is called the *land of Mizraim*. *Canaan*, the youngest, early occupied Palestine; but this fair land was reserved for the posterity of Shem, and the idolatrous Canaanites were conquered by Joshua, and driven into Egypt, where they founded Carthage. *Ham* is supposed to have settled in Egypt, together with his son Mizraim. Egypt is called the land of Ham, not only by ancient historians, but in the Old Testament. The Greeks called it Egypt; but its proper name in the Hebrew Scriptures is Mizraim. The Libyans, inhabiting a country in Africa, west of Egypt, were the descendants of Lehabim, one of Mizraim's sons. Phut, another of the sons of Ham, occupied Africa also, and by the Septuagint translators, is identified with the Libyans.

They are associated with Cush and Lud and Egypt; and the evidence preponderates in favor of their occupying the Barbary coast. From Cush descended those who are more appropriately called the Ethiopian race. A colony of them early removed from the land of Shinar, and settled in that part of Africa which lies south of Egypt, in the western part of the continent, and bounded on the north by the Great Desert. Africa was peopled by the sons of Ham. All the other races, which have from time to time inhabited it, were not indigenous races. Africa is not, we are sorry to say, their permanent residence; for they are found everywhere; in India, in China, in Japan, among the Jews, the Greeks, and the Romans, in the islands of the Indian and West Indian oceans, and in North and South America. But, though thus scattered, they are known as the race of Ham. Yet, strange to say, it is with this peculiar variety of the human race, so easily traced to one of the sons of Noah, that naturalists find the greatest difficulty in allowing to belong to the common family of man.

The descendants of *Japheth* comprise the Caucasian, or white races, scattered over the earth, dwelling in the tents of Shem, inhabiting a large portion of the finer parts of the habitable globe, and comprising the most civilized and powerful nations. They peopled the northern parts of Asia and all Europe, including the ancient Persians, Scythians, Celts, Greeks, Romans and Gauls, the various Gothic and Teutonic and Tartar races, and those insular portions of the earth in Lesser Asia and Europe which are described in the Scriptures as the "isles of the Gentiles." Japheth had seven sons. From *Gomer* descended the ancient Galatians, the Trojans of the Hellespont, the Phrygians, the inhabitants of the Axanian islands, or the coasts of the Euxine, the Gomerians, or early Germans of the Danube, and from Germany spread themselves into Gaul. The ancient Britons, too, as well as our own Saxon ancestors, were the descendants of Japheth, through his first-born son Gomer. The descendants of his second son, *Magog*, I have not the means of tracing more extensively than to learn they were the Scythians, the Tartars and the Goths, who overran the Roman empire. *Madai*, his third son, was the ancestor of the Medes and the Samaritans. From *Javan*, the fourth son, descended the inhabitants of Cilicia, Tarshish, Chittim, the ancient Dorians, and the islands lying between Europe and Asia, or what the prophet Ezekiel calls "the *isles of Elisha*"—the Elisæ Pontus, or the Hellespont, and the colonies of Tarshish. *Tubal and Meshech*, the fifth and sixth sons, names so often united in the sacred writings, spread themselves over Cappadocia and Armenia, ancient Albania, and, according to the prophet Ezekiel, carried on an extensive slave-trade with Tyre. Wells, in his Historical Geography of the Old Testament, says that the Spaniards have a tradition that they are descendants from Tubal; for they were the Asiatic Iberi. The Muscovites were a colony descended from Meshech. Of *Tyras*, the youngest son of Japheth, it is generally agreed that he was the progenitor of the ancient Thracians, and first settled in the country of Thrace, and spread over the north side of the Euxine sea.*

The thought is not always present to those advocates of the doctrine of plurality of races who profess to submit to the teachings of the Scriptures, that these writings refer to a *very great number* of distinct nations and tribes of men, to all of which they not only ascribe a common origin, but, notwithstanding all their varieties, and all these gradations of difference, historically trace them to a common parentage in one of the sons of Noah. If these historic facts lay unembarrassed by local differences in the mind of the sacred historian, why should these differences be perplexing to *us?*

The ethnological sketching of the sacred writers, subsequent to the days of Moses, while it is far from being full, is also far from being impov-

* See Well's Hist. Geog. of the Old Test., vol. i.—The Commentaries—Calmel's Dictionary—and some valuable hints from Lempriere's Class. Dict. by Anthon—Bedford's Chronology.

erished and bald. There are so many scraps of history and ethnology, scattered throughout the classics and classic historians, as well as throughout some of the larger commentaries on the Scriptures, the more valuable biblical and biographical dictionaries and charts of history,* that it demands no great credulity, even independently of the sacred writings, to adopt the conclusion, that the various races of men may, in fact, be traced to a common origin. The great outlines of this descent are in some good degree obvious; nor are they obliterated by the unnumbered crossings of blood which assign some portions of the earth to two, or even more proximate races. Nor do we entertain a doubt, that with the rapid progress of scientific knowledge, the more thorough research into the natural history of our race, and a more extended acquaintance with the descent, and immingled population of the nations, facts will abundantly illustrate and confirm the Mosaic narrative in regard to the origin of mankind.

The only consideration that detracts from the force of this general outline is, that it is necessarily

* See a most valuable depository of facts entitled *Atlas und Tabellen*, &c., by Frederich Kruse, Leipzig: also the *Annales Antiquitatis*, or Oxford Chronological Tables of Ancient History, synchronistically and ethnologically arranged. Also *Atlas Historique et Chronologique*, A. Jarry De Mancy: in the Astor Library.

Not a few valuable hints on this topic may be also gathered from Hallam's Literature of Europe.

so imperfect. The different nations are so immingled, that is difficult to trace them with precision to their national origin. But does not this fact itself confirm the general argument? Does it not show that the farther back we trace the origin of the nations, the more we find these streams commingled, and issuing from the same fountain? Even the Jews themselves are not a perfectly unmingled race. It would be a remarkable fact, if not an unaccountable one, that so few of the nations of the earth have been able to retain with certainty the knowledge of their distinct origin, if they originated from as many new creations, as their zoological zones. Upon the hypothesis that they are all descended from one common origin, this is perfectly natural, and just what might be looked for. The different branches became gradually more and more ramified from their very growth. Necessity, policy, their own arrangement and choice, dispersed them over the earth so widely, that while the main trunk and the principal branches are visible, it requires a minuteness of inspection, a microscopic view, of which the human mind is not capable, to affirm with certainty, amid the ten thousand graftings, to which of the main branches the more remote and dense twigs and foliage belong. This general fact is ascertained, that all tradition, monuments, hieroglyphical writing, and history, point to a common origin of the race.

Science is bound by all her own laws, if she insists on a plurality of sources, to *prove* what those sources are. This she has not done; this she cannot do. She is pressed with this difficulty, and does not attempt what she knows is impossible. Yet, as the lawyers would say, the *onus probandi* lies upon her. According to all the laws of fair reasoning, her bold affirmative that the different races proceeded from different sources, we call upon her to support, by defining at least some of those sources. To speak with the confidence with which Agassiz has spoken, and then retire from the field in his own covert way, is presumption and not science. The Mosaic history never was palmed upon the world; there is every reason to place the fullest confidence in its representations.

I remark also, that the Scriptures *expressly affirm, that the entire race of men, with all their varieties, have one and the same origin.* They do not leave us to deduce this doctrine from their great design and object merely, nor from their ethnological records; they explicitly instruct us that Adam and Eve were the parents of the race. In Genesis it is written, "Let us make *man* in our own image, after our own likeness; and let *them* have dominion." The plural verb here shows that the word man, or Adam, is employed collectively, as equivalent to *mankind.* Afterwards it is written, "And God created the *man* in his own image;

in the image of God created he him; male and female created he *them*."

The application of male and female to the *Adam*, and the plural pronoun, at the end of the verse, show that the name is used generically, or to denote the first of *mankind*. Nor may it be denied that the word Adam is often used in the Old Testament as an appellative noun for the species, and in this collective sense denotes mankind—the human race. Was not this then the germ, the original stock? In chap. iii. v. 20, we have the following declaration, "And Adam called his wife's name Eve"—life—"because she was the mother *of all living*." Was she not the mother of the whole human race? The scriptural account of the flood proves incontestably the same fact. By that catastrophe we are told that "all flesh died that moved upon the earth"—"every man—every living substance, both man and cattle"—and that "Noah only remained and they that were with him in the ark." Where were those who, as Professor Agassiz supposes, were descended from other pairs? And then again, by what evasion can the subsequent declaration be set aside, that of the three sons of Noah "was the *whole earth* overspread?" In the book of Deuteronomy it is affirmed, that "when God divided to the nations their inheritance, when he separated the sons of Adam, he set the bounds of the people according to the number of the children of Israel." Are not the *divided nations* here called the *sons of Adam?* The prophet Malachi, also, writing four thousand years after the creation, demands, "And did he not make *one?* And wherefore *one*; that he might seek a godly seed?" In the 17th ch. of the Acts of the Apostles, Paul addresses the learned men of Athens in the following language: God that made the world, "hath made of *one blood* all *nations of men*, for to dwell on the face of the earth, and determined the bounds of their habitation." Does not this declaration assert that God formed the whole race of men of one family; and that, however widely scattered, and by whatever external varieties they may be distinguished, these diversities, and this different locality, are consistent with their common parentage?* Can language be more plain or more decisive, than such statements as these? In view of such declarations, what becomes of the hypothesis of that class of Christian writers, who would fain have us believe that the Scriptures have reference only to the Caucasian race; and that other races of men exist who were of a different origin from the posterity of Adam? If the earth is "replenished" and peopled from one common pair; if "all the living," and the "di-

* The summary manner in which Professor Agassiz disposes of this passage is as summarily disposed of by an able and characteristic Review in the Biblical Repertory for Oct. 1850.

vided nations," and "all nations of men" have this common parentage, this natural descent, this blood relationship; where is the tribe, or family, or man, be he Greek or Jew, Ethiopian or Caucasian, monarch or slave, that hails not from the same primogenitors?

There is one more consideration in favor of the unity of the race, which rests, also, originally on the testimony of the Scriptures. The last enumeration gives us 3664 known languages now in the world. Yet the Bible teaches us that the *languages* of the earth had a common origin. At the time of the division of the nations after the flood, "the whole earth was of one language, and one speech." At the building of the tower of Babel, God confounded their language, and thereby more effectually scattered them abroad. It is generally agreed, that the Hebrew language was the primitive language of men; and that it was retained among the descendants of Heber long before the calling of Abraham. The immediate descendants of Abraham probably spoke the Chaldaic tongue, as he was from Chaldea; or if that nation spoke the Hebrew language, there is no doubt of the fact that they no longer preserved it in its purity after they were carried captive to Babylon; for there it became mixed with the language of the Chaldeans. The Chaldee, or Chaldaic, is said to comprise the Aramean, Syriac, Arabic, Ethiopic,

Samaritan, and Coptic; while these are said to be linked by unquestionable affinities with all the languages spoken by the great Indo-European and Shemitic races. The Japhetic race, scattered throughout Asia Minor, the northern parts of Asia, and all Europe, including the Celtic and Teutonic families, had a different language, while their radical words are proved to have been essentially the same, and the difference between this family of languages and that of the Shemitic family, consists in its inflections and combinations. The Greek language is formed on the same radical words as the Celtic and Teutonic languages; while the affinities between the Latin and the Teutonic show that they are of the same origin. It is admitted, too, that the Sanscrit, or ancient language of India, the parent of all the dialects in the great Peninsula, is radically from the same stock as the Greek and Latin. The modern Italian, Spanish, French, and Portuguese are all from the Latin, retaining some words of Celtic, and Carthaginian, and Gothic origin. The German, Belgian, Anglo-Saxon, Danish, and Swedish languages are all of Gothic parentage. The languages of the Chinese, of Polynesia, and original America, belong to the same group with the languages of northern Asia, and of parts of northern Europe. "In proportion as a careful inquiry has penetrated into the past, the streams of speech have been traced upward to their points of divergence from their parent channels; while these channels have been found to converge and unite in a common source." Nor is this any inconsiderable witness to the common origin of the nations which speak them. If we have good evidence of the common origin of all languages, we have good evidence in confirmation of the Mosaic account of the unity of the race.

It appears to us that there is no small temerity in the hypothesis, that there are other races of men, of a different origin from the posterity of Adam, and some weakness in the considerations by which it is supported. Its authors are too clearly under the influence of their romantic love of theory, rather than inflexible love of truth. For humanity's sake, we hope better things of human science. We are alarmed at such things, lest they prove the incipient step to a more arrogant infidelity.

We have not, in this discussion, except incidentally, designed to present the philosophical argument in favor of the common origin of mankind. Few questions have been more ably or more abundantly discussed upon the mere principles of natural science. In adverting to these discussions, one fact is quite obvious, that if we once wander from the unity of the race, we know not where to stop. Our distinguished countryman, Dr. Pickering, himself an eminent naturalist, and employed by the government in the scientific corps of the Exploring Expedition, which sailed around the world, has written ably on this general subject, and sums up his views in the following sentence: "There is, I conceive, no middle ground between the admission of eleven distinct species in the human family, and the reduction to one;" while a still later writer affirms, that "if there be five different sources, he sees not why there must not be five hundred." The all-wise Disposer of the human race has assigned to natural causes their appropriate agency, in the varieties of our race, but he has limited their power; and when the naturalist expects to find a solution for all the varieties in the sole agency of natural causes, he finds himself at fault. There are anomalies which natural science does not account for; our true resort is to the word of God. Our convictions are continually strengthening, that the laws of natural science, on this, as well as every subject, the more they are known, confer abundant honor on the sacred Scriptures.

And on this firm basis of God's word do we rest the question. There is no safety, no true science, but in the scriptural account of the origin of the human family. The subject is one of *history*, and not of natural science. God is the author of the race, and he has plainly indicated its origin. He has given man a physical constitution fitted to all climates, and fitted to produce those varieties which are adapted to their condition, their wants, and their responsibilities. Man goes everywhere, and everywhere carries with him his distinctive humanity, and therefore his obligations to God and his fellow-men.

It is a mischievous, an infidel thought, that we may look upon any portion of the human family as a distinct race from ourselves, and not entitled to our love and sympathy. There are no diversities which do not carry with them the evidence of their common humanity, and enforce its claims. Shem, Ham, and Japheth are still impersonated in the different nations of men; but they are brethren; there should be no strife between them. The weak may not envy the strong; nor the strong oppress the weak. The polished and the rude, the black and the white, the master and the slave, the rich and the poor, meet together; the Lord is the Maker of them all. The things in which they differ are neither so many nor so important as those in which they agree. All are creatures of the same God; descended from the same ancestry; fallen by their iniquity; subjected to the same wants and trials; if saved, saved by the same grace. All are born to die, destined to the same final account, and heirs of a deathless immortality. Tried by such standards, we see the true and proper value of the race; while thus tried, all the varieties that are incidental to their existence in the present world, vanishes away. It behooves us to take heed, lest with the spirit of the first murderer we say, "Am I my brother's keeper?" "No man," saith the Apostle, "ever hateth his own flesh." It was a powerful appeal once uttered by Wilberforce in behalf of an abused and crushed people, "Am I not a man and a brother?" Born under whatever skies, and however degraded their condition, *men*, and because they are *men*, are all linked together by these fraternal bonds. "Love worketh no ill to his neighbor." Unkindness and revenge, oppression and injury, desolation and bloodshed, do not rest in the bosom of love. There is no poison of asps under her lips; she has no venomous breath, and no deadly sting. She mingles no bitter ingredients in the cup of man, and no poison with his joys. She plants no thorns in his path, and never blights the verdure of his hopes. Nay, she knows no cold indifference and chilling neglect; it is no barren heart that beats within her warm bosom; it is light and cheerfulness beaming on the dark places of the earth, and making the wilderness blossom as the rose. She does not say to the voice of the needy, or to the sighing of the prisoner, he is an Indian—he is a poor negro—he belongs to another race. Never may men thus lose sight of the obligations of humanity, associated as they are by a common origin, common responsibilities, common trials, and a common eternity. There is another and a better world, where the saved of all nations will meet, and the elevated will be no more elevated than their meaner brethren on the earth, and the degraded will be degraded no more. It was a rapturous vision beheld by the exiled apostle, when he said, "And after this I beheld, and lo a great multitude which no man could number, of all *nations*, and *kindreds*, and *people*, and *tongues*, stood before the throne and before the Lamb, clothed with white robes and palms in their hands; and cried with a loud voice saying, Salvation to our God which sitteth upon the throne and unto the Lamb!"

CHAPTER V.

The First Woman.

FROM nothing did the first man learn so mu of God, as from the creation of a "second human being with faculties and senses like his own." Although we have not a detailed narrative of the creation of *woman*, until after the seventh day, there is reason to believe that she was created on the same day with man. Both sexes of all organized bodies, of plants and animals, were created together. In his account of the creation of man on the sixth day, the sacred historian remarks, "So God created man in his own image, in the image of God created he him; *male and female* created he them." In the next paragraph he proceeds to say, "And on the seventh day God *ended* his work which he had made; and he rested on the seventh day from *all* his work which he had made." From these premises, it is the more natural conclusion, that the woman was included in the creation that was accomplished on the sixth day. She was not an appendage to the perfected creation; it was not perfect without her.

Of the manner of her creation we have a more full account in a subsequent paragraph. It is in the following words: "And the Lord God caused a deep sleep to fall upon Adam, and he slept: and he took one of his ribs, and closed up the flesh instead thereof; and the *rib which the Lord God had taken from man* made he *a woman.*" Man himself was not created out of nothing, as was the original chaos; he was formed out of the dust of the earth; it was a secondary creation from a prior existing substance. The creation of the woman was also a secondary creation; she was formed from a substance previously existing; not out of the dust of the earth, but from a portion of the newly-created man himself. "She was called woman, because she was taken out of man." The intimacy was perfect; there was oneness between them. She was identified with the man; she formed a part of the man; she was his second self. She was not to be either his master or his slave; but his associate, his equal, imbued with the same spirit, possessing interests in common with him, aiming at common objects, and pursuing the same joyous course of obedience and immortality. The man originally had no priority except in the single fact, that "Adam was first formed, then Eve;" nor was this equality disturbed, until she became the first transgressor, and the sentence uttered, "thy husband shall rule over thee."

Woman comprises one half the human race; the birth of males and females is about equal. It has been supposed that, taking the aggregate population of the globe, males are more numerous than females; and that this surplusage is called for by the waste of human life by war, and by those calamities to which the retired habits of females are less exposed than the ordinary habits of the male population. Yet is it to be observed, that the average of human life is not so long among females as among males; and that in Asiatic and Mohammedan countries, and in all countries where polygamy prevails, there are more females than males. There is no good reason to believe that the original arrangement of a wise providence in the equality of numbers in the different sexes, has been seriously disturbed.

What are the peculiarities of woman? What is the sphere which she is destined to occupy? And what are the qualifications which best fit her to occupy that sphere? Let us devote a few moments to each of these topics.

In speaking of *the peculiarities of woman*, we are not so blind as to suppose that she is faultless. She belongs to a fallen race—herself the first transgressor. *By nature*, she differs not from those "every imagination of the thoughts of whose heart is only evil continually." Her sinfulness, like man's, until she is renewed by grace, is strong and constant. Her "heart is fully set in her to do evil," and in her unrenewed state she does nothing to please God. She is "dead in trespasses and sins," a "child of wrath even as others." Her "neck is as an iron sinew, and her brow brass." There is "no fear of God before her eyes;" she "hates him without a cause." She "casts his law behind her back;" she "sets at naught all his counsel, and would none of his reproof." "Of the Rock that begat her she is unmindful, and has forgotten the God that formed her."

Yet we have strong impressions that she presents the fairer side of fallen humanity. She has excellencies which do not belong to the other sex; they are peculiarities that are obvious, and that excite our admiration of the divine wisdom and goodness. Man has the advantage over her in physical power, and in some intellectual endowments; while there are intellectual endowments in which the superiority belongs to her. Her powers of patient research and reasoning, and her powers of invention, are not equal to those of men; while her perceptions are quicker than the perceptions of men; her judgment and common sense are more worthy of confidence; her memory is more retentive, her imagination more vivid, her taste more delicate and refined, and her curiosity more wakeful.

Her great and distinctive peculiarity will be found in the fact, that *she lives in her affections.* To this fact, if we mistake not, may be attributed her peculiar excellencies and faults. Man lives in the world; he lives amid the contentions of self-interest and the strife of passion; his life is bound up in wealth, pleasure, and fame; nor is he ever happier than when employed in such pursuits most intensely and most successfully. Woman has more heart than man; she was made to love and be beloved.

> "Her crown is in her heart, not on her head;
> Not decked with diamonds and Indian stones,
> Nor to be seen.
> A crown it is that seldom kings enjoy."

She may love wealth; but it is not so much for wealth's sake, as for the sake of those she loves. She may love pleasure; but it is more to gratify the objects of her affection than for her own enjoyment. She may be ambitious, and love fame, but it is not for herself. She is gifted far above man in native sweetness and gentleness, and in the winning graces and charities of the heart. "I have observed," says the celebrated traveller Ledyard, "That women, in all countries, are civil, obliging, tender and humane. I never addressed myself to them in the language of decency and friendship, without receiving a decent and friendly answer. With man it has often been otherwise. In wandering over the barren plains of inhospitable Denmark, through honest Sweden and frozen Lapland, rude and churlish Finland, unprincipled Russia, and the wide-spread regions of the wandering Tartar, if hungry, dry, cold, wet, or sick, the women have ever been friendly to me, and uniformly so. And to add to this virtue, these actions have been performed in so free and kind a manner, that if I was thirsty, I drank the sweetest draughts, and if hungry, ate the coarsest morsel with a double relish." God has given woman this lovely and loving nature. She lives and would live in the hearts of others. The objects of her affection live in her thoughts; they live in her memory, live in her hopes and in her fears, in her toil and in her repose. She is more frank and has fewer imprisoned thoughts than man, because her affections govern her. She has more eagerness and intensity of character, because her affections are intense. When her affections are crossed, she may have a degree of bitterness that is not ordinarily possessed by men, because her affections are despotic, and her heart would fain play the tyrant. If her pride is more exacting, and her vanity more easily flattered; if her emotions are less impenetrable, and less under the control of skill and habit, it is because there are strong affections within her which disdain concealment, and will not brook control. She may love cautiously; but where she loves, she loves ardently and long. She is the creature of affection. Even long before her heart is touched by definite attachments, there are within her bosom strong and deep affections, and the unignited materials of attachment that is warm and ardent. With those exceptions in which injury and wrong have driven her to desperation, she does not sink beneath this high-born excellence. You may bruise and crush her; but it is by bruising and crushing her unsoiled affections. Even then she is perhaps more lovely than ever; just as the sweetest herbs and flowers, when bruised, give forth their sweetest fragrance. This is her great peculiarity; in this lies her power. Ignorance, or mistake of this amiable trait of her character, has been the source of no small portion of the domestic evils and sorrows which have desolated the world. Not to know and not to value this great excellence of her nature is to misinterpret and defame her—is to know nothing of woman. Nor does that man deserve anything better than to be denied the thousand little attentions and delicacies which flow from the strength of her love whose mind is disciplined to mock its tenderness.

Woman is also more *self-sacrificing* than man. There are selfish women; but it is not so natural for woman to be selfish; there are more kindly, and generous, and noble feelings in her bosom. She loves more than man, and therefore will give up more. There is nothing she will not sacrifice for those she loves. The life of woman is a life of self-denying sacrifice; the history of woman is the history of one who so identifies the interests of others with her own, that she seeks her own in advancing theirs. Ease, comfort, pride, wealth, pleasure, society, and long-cherished habits, all she was, and all she is, she renounces for those she loves. Could days of anxiety and sleepless nights, could deeds of self-renunciation and mortified pride testify, how accumulated would be the testimony to woman's self-sacrificing spirit! To feel thus, and to conduct thus, is her *pleasure*. She could not have the joy of a clear conscience, she would not be happy, she would not be *woman*, without giving up her own good for the good of others.

It is not less true that woman is *more patient in suffering* than man. The burden of suffering was laid upon her at her first apostasy; and God has prepared her to endure it quietly. Her spirit is more subdued than the spirit of man. Be the suffering bodily or mental, be it poverty, or reproach, or injury, she meets it; nobly indeed does she meet it. I have seen examples of heroic suffering in woman, that made me envy her lofty bearing. Woman will suffer wrongfully, as man will not suffer. I know of but one exception to the truth of this remark: *disappointment* cuts deeper in woman than in man. It lingers longer; shut up as she is, and excluded from external excitement, it is brooded over and dwelt upon. She may not *anticipate* danger with the same unblanched countenance and unmoved nerve and muscle as man anticipates it; she may tremble in view of it, and shrink from it more instinctively. Where flight is possible, she will flee from it; and make almost frantic efforts to escape from it. She will dart from it like the swallow from the vulture's beak; but when it is inevitable, and comes crowding upon her, and when the blow falls, it is not woman's heart that is the first to complain.

Woman is likewise *more sensible of her dependence than man.* God has made her dependent, and she feels it. Man is her natural guardian; it is not only her nature to feel her dependence upon him, but her strength and joy. Place her in danger, and she instinctively looks to man; and even if her husband is far away, her thoughts at once centre in him. She cries out for him, though she knows he is distant; nay, though sleeping in his grave, in sudden danger she may peradventure instantly call for her *husband.* Next to God, he is her confidence. Man summons his own firmness, and girds himself for the conflict, while woman retires and retreats to her natural refuge. You see this spirit from her very girlhood. The girl flies to the boy for protection, the sister to her brother. She early imbibes this depending, confiding spirit, and it goes with her to old age, and to her last rest. She rejoices in it; it is her happiness to feel that she has some one to look up to, and cling to. There are exceptions to this great law of her sex, like Semiramis of Assyria, Catherine of Russia, and Elizabeth of England. When Xerxes invaded Greece, Artemisia, a distinguished female of Halicarnassus, displayed so much valor and skill at the battle of Salamis, as to call from the proud Persian the well-known remark, that "the men had acted like women, and the women like men." There are masculine and Amazonian women, as there are men who are effeminate. They are women who unsex themselves. This is not woman's amiable and affectionate nature; nor was it the character of the first woman. Nothing is more natural to woman than to feel this dependence; it is not mortifying to her, as it is to man; she is not ashamed of it, but rather is it her pride.

> "God is thy law, thou mine; to know no more
> Is woman's happiest knowledge and her praise."

There is a peculiarity also *in woman's love of power;* it is not like the love of power in man. She is proud and ambitious; but it is not so much the love of domination, as the love of influence, that distinguishes her. Man would carry his point, no matter how; woman would carry it by her persuasive and insinuating attractiveness. She does not ask it, she does not seek it to be reluctantly gained and grudgingly bestowed; on such terms she would rather be without it. She seeks power, but it is the power of love; she is not apt to triumph over conquests, of whatever kind they be, where she carries not the heart. This is the power she delights in, and these the conquests she boasts of. She is a very tyrant then, and well knows how to sway her gilded sceptre.

> "Mightier far
> Than strength of nerve or sinew, or the sway
> Of magic, potent over sun and star,
> Is *love*,
> Though his favorite seat be feeble woman's breast."

Woman also is *more fond of embellishment than man, and embellishment of every kind.* It is well that she is so; else would the world we occupy be a degraded world. It is not without reason that classic mythology represents the *Graces* as three young sisters, who were the symbols of all that is beautiful and attractive in the physical as well as the social world. What marvel that a creature thus formed, and for such ends, should be fond of embellishment? that she should be more susceptible to beauty than man, more embellished in her thoughts and writings, more embellished in her person, and possess greater delicacy of taste in all her domestic arrangements ? She was formed for this ; she has a keener sense of fitness and propriety ; she is the presiding genius in this department ; the grace, and polish, and elegance of society are attributable to her ; she strews the desert with flowers, and is herself the flower of the desert. This too is woman's nature ; she seeks embellishment not so much for her *sons* as for her *daughters*. Her and their personal charms are her treasure ; and if she polish and adorn them, she does no more, I doubt not, than did our first mother even before she fell. I will not say that this is woman's weakness ; it may be, it is, where it is excessive, and degenerates to the love of show. Nor may I say that this does not belong to woman more than to man ; the love of admiration may be her ruling passion ; and it is proof of her womanly ingenuousness that she herself is not insensible to the infirmity, nor slow to confess that her true honor is found in higher adornment.

Of the two sexes, woman, it must also be confessed, is *more cheerful than man*. That would be a gloomy continent that were inhabited only by a colony of men ; there would be nothing there to tame man's lion-heart. Man is naturally more silent and pensive than woman, though God has so greatly multiplied her sorrows. She has a more elastic and buoyant spirit, and one that bounds over the inequalities of life with a more sylph-like step. Man breaks before the storm; woman bends before it, and regains her courage. Man's mirth is occasional, and boisterous; woman's is more uniform and safe. Her face is lighted up, and her voice is gladsome. Her spirit is familiar with the land of song, and her luxuriant smile skirts it with its richest verdure. A virtuous and cheerful woman, especially if she have the graces and hopes of Christianity, is among the bright things, if not the brightest thing in this low world. Woman's imperfections are not ordinarily dark and sombre shades of character. It is not the leaden cloud of gloom that enshrouds us in the society of woman; we can scarcely help feeling that there are thoughts and emotions passing within her bosom, which, if we sympathize with them, must banish gloom. The suavity of her disposition, the softness of her manners, and the cheerfulness of her spirit, is just what man requires. This world were cheerless and melancholy, a withered, autumnal, wintry world, were it never cheered by woman's smile. A thousand times have I thought on this beautiful characteristic of woman with thankfulness.

Men are not unfrequently so frigid and crusty, that nothing thaws them but the presence of woman. No matter how overwhelmed with care and depressed a man is, and no matter what the circumstances of woman are; *her* effort is to lighten the burden. Never is he so depressed, but her gladsome eye and voice cheer him. Man *sympathizes* with her in her depression, but he does not so naturally lift her out of it. Woman not only bears up under sorrow, but enables others to bear up. We do not say too much for her, when we say that she is a well-spring of cheerfulness. There are, no doubt, exceptions to this remark, and they demand our sympathy. There are those whose contentions "are like a continual dropping in a rainy day." There is the dissatisfied woman, whom nothing can please. And there is the angry woman, whose eye flashes with outrageous passion, and who is like a wasp in a garden of flowers. Woman, like man, never feels her own impotence so much as when she is driven to moody sullenness, or has no other resort than uproar and tumult. Would to God that those who constitute these exceptions were elevated above this moody and sentimental gloom! An austere, gloomy, sullen, woe-begone woman—from all such may the good Lord deliver us!

Not a little to our shame, we must also add, that woman has *more self-respect than man.* Such is the wise organization of society, and such the decree of God, that more depends upon her character, and she can survive fewer faults. From a few incautious steps and self-inflicted blows, it is very difficult for her to recover. Her circumspection is her safety. And to her honor be it said, she is distinguished for her self-respect. Woman is often artful; I have sometimes thought that she was more artful than man, because when her heart is strongly enlisted, it is difficult for her not to encourage a little "pious fraud." Those there are who affect to overbear and depress by their superiority. If you associate with them without the fear of mortification, you still keep them at a distance, and treat them rather with studied caution than unembarrassed courtesy. There is a *blue-light* splendor in some females, which a sensible man enjoys for a moment, but despises at his leisure. There are those, too, who affect to be what they are not, and who are weak enough to desire to be extolled for qualities which they know they do not possess. But though sometimes artful, affected, and of high pretensions, she is *not often vicious. When she is vicious, she is vile—viler even than man—more dishonest and faithless, more impudent in wickedness and more irreclaimable, because her heart is poisoned*, and her affections have not even hope to feed upon. The same classic mythology that represents the *Graces* as symbolized by female excellence and loveliness, when it would represent the extreme of wickedness, true to nature, impersonates the

Furies,—"Furæ Diræ,"—in female forms. As there are characteristic faults in men, in sufficient abundance, so they are not wanting in woman. Milton, when urged by his daughters to describe the character of their mother, and the object of his first love, replied, that she was

"Like the fresh sweet-brier, and early May,
Like the fresh, cool, pure air of opening day,
Like the gay lark, sprung from the glittering dew,
An angel, yet—a *very woman too*."

We pass to another topic on which we proposed to submit a few remarks. It is not unnatural that woman, with these peculiarities, should be formed for a sphere of her own; *what is that sphere?* "Nature herself," one would think, gives a full and sufficient answer to this question. A moment's reflection must show us, that there are characteristics in her physical constitution which render her unfit for those spheres that are occupied by the other sex, and which, if she attempts to occupy, necessarily throw her into inextricable embarrassment. It is not her mission, because it is not her nature, to plunge wildly into the perilous enterprises and active warfare of human life. She was not formed to fell the forest, nor to traverse the ocean, nor to excavate the bowels of the earth. Nor are they the noisy scenes of barter and exchange for which she possesses any natural accomplishments; nor are they places of power, and trust, and emolument which she is fitted for. Nor was she ever commissioned to occupy the Pulpit, or become a debater in the Forum, or maintain her country's cause in the Senate, or to sit on the bench of Justice, or wield the sword on the field of battle. True it is that there have been instances in which woman has thrust herself into spheres thus uncongenial to her soft and gentle nature. Catharine de Medicis assumed the throne of France; but she was despised for her cruelties and perfidy, and the infamous features of her masculine mind were evinced by massacres so fearful as to have made the land that witnessed them drink blood because it was worthy. Mary of England well deserved the appellation of the bloody Mary, and died of disappointed ambition. Yet have there been better female sovereigns than these. Zenobia, of Palmyra memory, and the famed daughter of the Arab chieftain—Isabella of Spain—Maria Theresa, of Austria—and Joanna of Sicily were, worthy of the throne, and distinguished for vigor of intellect and comprehensive policy. But after all, this is not woman's place. The exceptions which history furnishes to this natural law, do but confirm the law itself. Such women are anomalies; they wage war upon nature, and nature enters her protest against the usurpation. Woman is man's *helper;* she is his friend, his counsellor. When he girds his robust frame for the toil of human life, and nerves his heart and arm for its varied conflicts, she is his solace, his comforter. Her place is *at home*, amid those social duties which give tranquillity and joy to domestic life; of which she herself is the queen; whence she sends forth a universally conservative influence, and where she weaves the thousand silken cords which are stronger than bands of iron, and by which the otherwise disjointed and jarring and effervescing elements of society are amalgamated and bound together.

It is amid the endearments and duties of conjugal life, that she so emphatically *lives in her affections*, her best and strongest, her purest and noblest affections. This is her throne; this her little world. It is here that she makes the cup of life sweeter by instilling into it exhilarating ingredients that are never thought of, except by her own sovereign alchemy. It is here that she diffuses that pleasant and balmy atmosphere, which is so imperceptible that we scarcely notice it, yet so necessary, that without it we droop and wither. It were not easy to describe the extent of her gentle influence, even where it falls short of being religiously exerted. Woman's heart is so formed, that it is bound up in the heart of her husband; and even though she be not a lover of God, if she be affectionate, beloved, and respected, her highest wish, and her most delightful employment are to render her husband respected, useful, and happy. Sympathy with her husband is one of the marked features in her character. She enters into all his feelings, all his occupations, all his interests, all his sorrows, all his joys, all his defeats, all his honors, and all his usefulness. There is a community of feeling and interest between them; a sympathy in weal and in woe, which in prosperity makes everything light and gladsome, and in adversity alleviates its trials, and chases away its depression and gloom. Wearisome care loses its perplexity, toil its hardship, affliction its bitterness, reproach its mortification, and the subtleties and deception of the world their sickening repulsiveness, amid her artless simplicity, undissembled tenderness, buoyant hope and cheerful love. Bad men are made good, and good men better through the influence of woman. Few men possess so hardy and gross a temperament as not to be withdrawn from the seductions of vice and licentiousness by the discretion and firmness of an affectionate wife. Where woman is what she ought to be, home has endearments and charms that cannot be easily exchanged for the snares of a corrupt and corrupting world. I would never abandon a wild and harebrained youth while there is any hope that his heart may be enchained by a virtuous woman; nor would I ever calculate with confidence on the course which the most promising young man will pursue, without counting on the domestic influences which may animate or depress him, extend or contract his usefulness, without knowing something of the goddess he worships.

It is in this relation, that woman occupies the most responsible of all positions, ordinarily known to her sex. In the physical, intellectual, and moral endowments of her children, and more especially in the whole business of forming their character, the mother is the more important parent. Napoleon once said to Madame Campan, "The old systems of education are good for nothing; what do young women stand in need of to be well brought up in France?" The reply of this intelligent and accomplished lady was, "OF MOTHERS." And it speaks volumes. Give a mother ordinary intelligence, and ordinary accomplishments, and she is the centre of attraction alike to her husband, to her sons and daughters. Her ear and her heart are always accessible, because she is rarely absent from her children, and cherishes in them the habits of unrestrained familiarity. She forms their opinions, their habits, their manners, their character, almost as she pleases. I know of no earthly restraint, and no moral power, that can be compared with the wishes of a mother. That tongue of hers in which is the law of kindness; that heart which is all gentleness and love; that wakeful discretion and unwearied patience; that self-sacrificing spirit, and those tears which sometimes drop as the rain; give her a control which the sterner and more severe government of a father is rarely able to secure. Many a youth of rash and impetuous temperament would venture to disregard the strong bonds of paternal authority, whose heart would fail him in rudely bursting the cord that binds him to a mother's bosom.

> "A mother's love!
> If there be one thing pure,
> Where all beside is sullied;
> That can endure
> When all else pass away;
> If there be aught
> Surpassing human deed, or word, or thought—
> It is a *mother's love!*"

And what daughter is there, in whose bosom there is a spark of womanly virtue and nobleness, who would ever trample on a mother's love? The world does not know its indebtedness to mothers. Even when left to struggle with their responsible and arduous duties, unaided and alone, they have accomplished that for mankind which demands the most grateful acknowledgment. Who does not dwell with tenderness on the sacred name of *mother!* When we read the biographical notices of such a man as Byron, much as we abhor his character, we pity him; because the ostrich cruelty of a proud and insensate mother made that diamond mind an outcast. Mothers hold in their hands the destinies of millions. Who can estimate the value of a devoted mother? Of how little avail are the authority, power, and laws of the world, compared with the silent and unobtrusive influence of woman? "Her price is above rubies." They are honors that never wither, when, at a mother's grave, her children rise up and call her blessed!

There are also domestic relations of a less important kind which woman sustains. We have no misgivings at the wisdom of divine providence when we survey a family where there is a large preponderance of *daughters*. They are the charm of the domestic circle. The sacred penman beautifully compares them to "corner-stones" in a splendid edifice, that "are polished after the similitude of a palace." As daughters, we love to look upon them; as sisters, it is their province to give preëminence to the domestic circle above every society, and to make their own happy dwelling more serene and happy. Nor let the forbidding thought ever enter the proud heart of woman, that, though her maidenly honors come thick upon her, her womanly character and influence are of little, or no account. God judges otherwise, or, in his wise providence, he would have disposed it otherwise. Some of the loveliest, and some of the noblest and most estimable traits of the female character, as well as some of its most enviable and active virtues, adorn those who themselves would have adorned the most elevated of the social relations; but to whom the all-wise Disposer has refused the responsibilities, the joys and the sorrows of wedded life. Though denied this inheritance, there are reserved for them spheres of usefulness and honor, which none but woman's mind and heart can occupy. No matter what sphere she fills, if she fills it well she shines. The savor of her feminine virtues and the blessing of her example are no twilight dawning upon this dark and frozen world. She interests, she endears. Wherever she goes, she is man's guardian and friend. Her love is wakeful, even when she watches alone. It sounds the note of alarm at man's exposure; unsought, it shields him. She is never obscure; nor can she ever exclude herself from her share in the concerns of this great world. In her modest reserve, she may feel that she is a cypher; while her capacious heart may embrace greater good than thousands more ostentatious and exacting. Be it where it may, unless it is degenerate to unwomanly abjectness, the influence of woman has a predominant sway. Public taste and manners, public virtues and vices, are under her control. Her sway is scarcely less absolute in the empire of morals than in the empire of fashion. Her unseen hand is everywhere forming the character of men, and giving a complexion to the society and age in which she holds a place. She has not the less influence, because she is the more retired. And if she does not so often appear in the pompous emblazonment of heraldry, it is because she would occupy too wide a place, and her power would be too implicitly acknowledged.

This view of the sphere she occupies, suggests our last topic of remark, which is the *suitable requisites for the fulfilment of her appropriate duties.* The inquiry is a practical one—How shall she best employ herself in this her appropriate sphere, and what are the qualifications she requires in order to act out the peculiarities of her character, and to the best advantage fulfil her high destiny? There are befitting attainments for her, not only as God's creature, and constituting so large a part of the human family; there are attainments befitting her as *woman*, and without which her natural excellencies must be suppressed, her lustre obscured, and her name remain unembalmed.

Let it not be thought that we are degrading our subject, while we say, that among these attainments, we hold in high estimation *the homely virtues of industry and economy.* No beauty, no wealth, no embellishment can supply the want of these. It is woman's calling to excel in a practical acquaintance with the arts and duties of domestic life. So far from being beneath her station, they adorn and exalt the most distinguished of her sex. When, in the days of the Tarquins, the Roman army lay encamped around the walls of the capital of the Rutuli, the princes of the Tarquin blood, in their gay boasting, each of the beauty and virtue of his wife, consented to yield the palm to the one who was found at midnight, with her handmaids around her, working at the loom. Were I the biographer of female excellence, my judgment, my heart, my imagination would induce me to select for my theme some illustrious Christian woman who is preëminent for her domestic virtues. No woman is well educated, who is not qualified to "look well to the ways of her household." To "eat the bread of idleness" is more befitting the slave of an Eastern despot, than the elevated station assigned to woman in Christian lands. I pity the man who is wedded to a woman who, so far from sharing with her husband the burdens of human life, satisfies herself that she has nothing to do but spend and be supported; and who, when rebuked for her inactivity, can do nothing but weep. Nor do I wonder that many such a man, under a load which he finds it impossible to bear, sinks to a premature grave. We have no apology for the idle, pleasure-loving spendthrift, and hard-hearted husband. There would be fewer *widowers*, if husbands were more kind, and affectionate, and industrious. And we have no apology for the pleasure-loving and spendthrift wife; there would be fewer *widows*, if wives were more industrious and economical. There is no such thing as throwing off the original curse of care and labor either from man or woman. The obligation and the necessity of toil in her own proper sphere, rests as truly upon all the daughters of Eve, as upon all the sons of Adam. Wealth may furnish a partial exemption from labor; it is no exemption from care. Solomon, in describing a virtuous woman, says that "her candle goeth not out by night." The most splendid women the world has seen, have been those who were most familiar with care and toil. It would be difficult to find more distinguished women than the Countess of Huntingdon, the Lady Rachel Russel, whose husband was beheaded by Charles II., and Mrs. Lucy Hutchinson, who flourished during the civil wars in England, and died in prison after the Restoration. But they were women not less distinguished for forethought and toil, than for the high stations they occupied. And the more retired scenes of private life furnish thousands not less distinguished than they, and not less worthy to be immortalized on the page of history. The woman who would not be a sufferer, must, in the ordinary course of providence, be alive, awake, and in earnest in the superintendence and management of her domestic affairs. If her hand is not everywhere, her eye must be everywhere, and her authority everywhere in her own household. A cheerful submission to this great law forms one of the prominent virtues of her character, and where this is wanting she is a stranger to woman's true worth and excellence.

Allied to this is a *well-cultivated mind.* Her intellectual endowments qualify her for high degrees of mental embellishment; nor are there any departments even of solid learning and science which, with suitable training, auxiliaries, and incitement, she might not adorn. The fact that she lives in her affections, rather than in the ambition which stimulates to high attainments in the profound sciences, indicates the limits beyond which, in ordinary cases, her intellectual researches may not be extended; while the station she occupies, the influence she exerts, and the power she possesses over the minds of the young, indicate not less clearly that, where her domestic qualifications are not interfered with, she is the more esteemed and honored by all her advances in knowledge. Aside from the men who are employed in the learned professions, the great mass of females in this land of enterprise and hope, are better educated than the males. In the ordinary intercourse of the middle classes, as well as in more polished circles, the number of females who are well grounded in all the branches of a good English education, and who are capable of thinking, and of expressing their thoughts with propriety, force, and elegance, is far greater than that of the other sex. Not many years since, an intelligent lady from a foreign land remarked, that nothing more surprised her than to find so much attention paid in the United States to female education. I will not say, that in reference to the other sex, this is as it ought to be; while it is highly creditable to woman. She is the better informed class of the community; nor is society the loser by her preeminence. Her keen perceptions, her intuitive judgment, her ready wit, her vivid fancy, and her retentive memory, cultivated, enriched, and adorned, render her her husband's pride, the glory of her children, and the charm of the social circle. We regret to express the opinion that, in a solid and well-measured education, the women of the present age are not so far in advance of their predecessors as their opportunities of advancement. They are exposed to magnify the mere elegancies of education above its more useful and practical tendencies; they live in the song and the dance; or they revel in romance, and melt away in dreamy sentimentalism, when they ought to be more intent on storing their minds with facts and principles; in becoming acquainted with standard authors, and in learning how to turn their attainments to good account. Woman's object is to please; and sooner or later she will learn that she cannot do this with becoming grace and dignity, and cannot do it permanently, where her society is not *instructive*. Men there are who are too proud to be instructed by a woman; but so far is this from being their general character, that the insinuation of female loveliness and modesty is never more welcome than when most instructive. By such teaching, the unthinking of the stronger sex imperceptibly slide into new truths, and make them their own. We need not fear cultivated intellect in woman. Where the God of nature has given her the force, and opportunity the furniture, of a well-disciplined and richly-cultivated mind, she is not the less lovely, nor beloved.

But the most important attainment of woman is *personal piety*. Though in adverting to the peculiarities of woman, we have remarked that she presents the fairer side of human apostasy, we are not to forget that she is one for whom there is no redemption but through Him who "came to call, not the righteous, but sinners to repentance." She was the first to fall, and man's successful tempter. It were no marvel, that the blighting effects of sin should pass over her, and leave her scathed with the tokens of God's displeasure. With all her defencelessness and sorrows, there is nothing which woman so much needs as personal piety. Frail woman must have the Eternal God for her refuge.

The keen storms of adversity will pass over her, and she will sink beneath its billows, if she have not this refuge, and her defenceless head be not covered with the shadow of his wing.

When we speak of *piety*, we mean something more than a name. By piety, we mean the religion of principle, in distinction from the religion of impulse; a spiritual religion, in distinction from a religion of forms; a religion of which the Spirit of God, and not the wisdom or the will of man, is the author; a self-denying and not a self-indulgent religion; a religion that has a heavenward, and not an earthly tendency; a practical religion, in opposition to the abstractions of theory; and a religion that is so full of Christ, that the crucified One is at the basis of its duties and hopes, its centre, its living head, and its glory. "Favor is deceitful, and beauty is vain; but the woman that feareth the Lord, she shall be praised." Other things there are which constitute her adornment; this is the brightest jewel in her crown. Separate her inferior and incidental adornments from a heart-felt and practical Christianity; associate them with immorality, imbue them with infidelity or atheism; and they are worse than snares—they are a curse to herself and the world. There is nothing of more dangerous tendency and influence than an impious or infidel woman. There are few men in the world so degenerate, and so utterly lost to all sense of right and shame, as to congratulate themselves on an infidel wife, or an infidel mother.

It is without doubt a truth, that there are more pious women in the world than pious men, and that their piety is of a higher order. Nor is this difficult to account for, from the peculiarities of the female character and condition. The fact that she lives in her affections; that she is formed to be confiding; that she is separated from the grosser snares of the world; that she is not unaccustomed to submission; and that God " hath chosen her in the furnace of affliction," are all in keeping with the abounding grace of God to her sex. When piety is engrafted upon woman's loveliness, I know of nothing so lovely. It is a mantle that covers all her faults and foibles, more than they are veiled even by her beauty. The sweetest emblem of piety, selected by the sacred writers, is *woman.* She is "the daughter of Zion;" a high-born progeny, attired from heaven's wardrobe, "coming up from the wilderness leaning upon her Beloved." Piety makes her everything she can be this side heaven. It elevates and beautifies her when the charms of personal beauty are fled; it supplies her with resources of joy, when the adulations of earth have become faint, its affection cold, and its trials severe; it sanctifies the infirmities of age, and gives her bright anticipations when the bloom and flower of earthly hope languish and decay. It hallows all her domestic virtues, makes her toil pleasant and her self-denial welcome, and carries along with it its own reward. It makes her the better wife, stimulating her husband in his spiritual career, and rejoicing with him as he goes; or if he has not entered upon that career, restrains him from the paths of sin and death, allures him to heavenly wisdom, and by discretion, love, tenderness, sympathy and prayer, it brings him within the fold of God. And does it not make her the better mother? Of all the untold millions that are now in heaven, how many, think you, are there, whose conversion is to be attributed to the counsels, the solicitude, the prayers, the tears, the ever-stimulated, *ever-hoping* faith of her that bare them? As a daughter, a sister, or even a faithful and pious servant, how much has piety done for woman, and what dews of Hermon has it distilled upon her path! In her own unostentatious and retired department, how has she scattered seeds of mercy, which have sprung up, and been cherished, and transplanted to scatter their fragrance under purer and brighter skies!

Piety is essentially the same thing both in man and woman; yet in woman it has her own beautiful and womanly characteristics. Woman's love and woman's tenderness adorn it. It has her meek-eyed humility and her robe of cheerfulness. It blends her timidity and her confidence. It has her cautious delicacy and all the refinement of her manners. It has her nobleness and her instinctive abhorrence of all that is mean and grovelling. It has her unsleeping watchfulness, her patient toil, her self-denying devotement, and her angel ministrations. And while it has her shrinking fears, it has also her unchanging faithfulness and unshrinking valor. Woman, if she cannot contend for Christ, can die for him. The pages of history do not record finer exemplifications of Christian fortitude and valor, than are furnished by the noble doing, brave daring, and patient suffering of woman. Apathy does not belong to her; stoical indifference forms no part of her nature; a calculating policy finds no place in her warm bosom. It is not she who consults with flesh and blood, when God calls her to advance with an undaunted heart and a firm, undeviating step to the torture, or the death. Flattery cannot move her then; nor is she dismayed by cruel mockings; nor is she confounded before the envenomed tongue of man; nor does desertion leave her deserted. Man's vigilance sleeps when his Saviour lies prostrate. Man's love hesitates, and falters when his Saviour is crowned with thorns. Man denies him, and man betrays. Woman's heart is faithful.

"Not she, with treach'rous kiss, her Saviour stung,
Not she denied him with unholy tongue,
She, when apostles shrunk, could danger brave,
Last at his cross and earliest at his grave."

We honor woman, and hold that she is to be honored. We would give her "the fruit of her hands, and let her own works praise her in the gates." "Giving honor to the wife," and because she is the weaker and more dependent, is an obligation delightfully in keeping with the dignified spirit, and sweet charities of the Sacred Volume. She has trials enough to bear, arising from the delicacy and dependence of her condition, not to be called on to encounter disesteem or reproach. She has no security but in the magnanimity of the stronger sex; and that man deserves to be held in very low estimation, who himself cherishes low and mean thoughts of woman. I not only look upon such a man as an ill-bred man, but I cannot help suspecting that he had a bad mother, or that he has a bad wife, or that in his associations with the female sex, he has been unfortunate, if not vicious. The history of nations and of men instructs us that their personal and national advancement stand abreast with their treatment of woman. Man is never free, where woman is a slave; and where she is degraded, in vain may you search for a cultivated and polished community. Degrade woman, and you degrade her offspring, and in every view make man more degraded. Nature herself inflicts the penalty; the retribution is sure to be felt in unfailing accuracy and full measure. The records of the past, and a careful inspection of the present, show nothing more clearly, than that just in the proportion to woman's advancement is man the more exalted, virtuous, and happy. One of the first rays of light that broke upon the night of the dark ages, was the gallant and heroic deportment of the stronger toward the weaker sex, which was fostered by the laws of chivalry; while from that day to this, not only have the social and moral culture of the nations of Europe been progressive with the culture of the female mind and heart, but the peculiarity of their national character has received its impress from the peculiarity of that culture, and from the degree in which woman has been allowed to retain her own womanly character and station. The Creator honored her by making her his last and fairest work. Her Saviour honored her; man might not share the honor, even of his lowly incarnation. If she was dishonored by her first transgression, she has this honor, that the Incarnate One was the "*woman's* seed."

It would be no small gratification to exemplify these general observations by a reference to some of the more distinguished of women whose names live on the pages of secular and Christian biography, had we time for such a reference. Though the biography of woman is not often written, for the obvious reason that she seeks not the public eye; yet, such is the redundance of materials for female biography of the richest kind, that the most classic and Christian author would be at a loss to make selections that would do justice, even to himself. He might conduct you to the thrones of princesses, and to the cottages of peasants, and there show you woman in her loveliest virtues. He might point you to her counsels of wisdom as treasured up in volumes alike endeared to the wise and the unwise. He might direct you to halls where science has baptized her thousands by female hands. We are not ambitious of this arduous, though delightful work; yet is there this one thing of which we are ambitious,—to elevate the standard of female excellence. We would fain have you dwell upon those inimitably beautiful touches of female character delineated by the writers of the Old and New Testament. We would ask you to inspect, with us, the records of churches from which the young and the beautiful have gone forth to be the adornment of heathen lands. We might go with you to the graves of the departed, and there where mothers sleep, and the cypress mourns, spell out names that were the glory of their sex. We might pass with you to the ever-varying scenes where woman lives not for time, but for eternity; and you might visit, with us, scenes where many a faithful servant of God complains not of the cross, because he bears it with such a helper, and no longer deems his way rugged and tedious and mournful, because he is travelling with such a comforter and friend. Let woman put on the whole armor of God, and true soldiers of the cross will not be wanting. Their armor will be bright, as hers is embellished; and as is her valor, so will be theirs. God has given woman beauty, loveliness, and self-denying courage; we have nothing to ask for her but consistent piety. Let *woman be pious*, and how will man feel the impulses of her piety! how will this ungodly world feel the constraints of redeeming mercy, and how soon would it realize the vision of the Holy City, the New Jerusalem, coming down from God out of heaven, prepared as a bride adorned for her husband!

CHAPTER VI.

The First Marriage.

THERE are few subjects the Scriptures treat of more instructively, or even with greater solemnity, than the subject of Marriage. They reveal to us its origin, its sacred intimacies, and its great design and object. They speak of the matrimonial bond as constituting a union of the highest order, as the most exalted and inviolable of all earthly relations; and in order to put upon it the most emphatic seal of the divine approbation, they compare it to the union between Christ and his church, and consecrate its endearment and tenderness by the love which exists between the Redeemer of men and his own redeemed people. "We love him," says the apostle, "because he first loved us." It is the order of nature and of God, that the man should first love the woman, and that the woman should respond to the affections of the man. I find nothing in the Bible about marriages of mere expediency and interest. There are such marriages; as calculating as an algebraic equation, and as cold as the moonlight on the frozen sea. And though such marriages sometimes turn out well, the history of the domestic feuds that have embittered our world would form an instructive comment on the words, "from *the beginning* it was not so."

Among the *first things*, after the narrative of the completed creation, we have an account of the marriage of the first parents of our race. It had the sanction of God himself, for He was its immediate author. The halls where these holy nuptials were celebrated, were the primeval Paradise, overhung by the clear, blue heavens. The happy pair were the first man and the first woman. God himself was the Great High Priest. Attending angels were the witnesses; while these morning stars sang together, and all the sons of God shouted for joy. Ancient mythology seems to have had some traditionary and indistinct inkling of this beautiful transaction, when it represented the reciprocal attachment of the sexes as the offspring of the zephyr and the rainbow. How much more beautiful was the simple reality, as narrated by the sacred historian! "And the *rib* which the Lord God had taken from man, made he a woman, and *brought her unto* the man!" Adam did not take his newly-created bride until she was given to him by his and her Creator. She *was* God's gift, and she *is* God's gift; it is still a truth, that "a prudent wife is from the Lord."

It is worthy of remark, that such were the arrangements of unerring wisdom in regard to the human family during the period of their unfallen integrity. But how much more important in its influences upon a race that is fallen! With the foreknowledge of their approaching apostasy, and a far-reaching wisdom and purpose, the benevolent Deity here laid the foundation of the domestic relations. And they embosomed those restraining, conservative, and hallowed agencies destined to act on the successive generations of men, and effectively coöperate with that wondrous method of redeeming mercy which as yet lay undisclosed within his own benevolent mind, and which time, and all the institutions and events of time, exist only to unfold. This great work of mercy was to be a progressive work. It was pre-arranged for a race, not called into existence by a single act of creative power, but that sprang from a *common pair*, and whose progeny were to cover this outstretched globe, as the sands cover the sea-shore. The arrangement might have involved a promiscuous intercourse of the sexes; it might have been a divinely authorized polygamy to the end of the world. But it was neither of these; it was *marriage*—the marriage of one man with one woman, inseparable but by death, or conjugal infidelity.

And who does not see the wonderful goodness and wisdom of God, in making this arrangement at the outset, and thus ordaining the descent of the race?

We have but a single object before us, therefore, in the present chapter; it is to *present a scriptural account of the institution of marriage, and with special reference to the religious influence of the domestic relations.*

The sacred writers greatly honor the institution of marriage. "Marriage is honorable in all, and the bed undefiled." From the equality of numbers in the different sexes, to which we referred in our last chapter, it is not unnatural to conclude that it is the duty of *every man*, whose condition in the world justifies the belief that he is able to sustain the responsibilities of wedded life, to become a married man. I say, whose condition in the world justifies such a belief; because no man, and no woman, has the warrant to rush heedlessly into these responsibilities, unless, with the ordinary favor of providence, there is good reason to believe that they can be sustained. Depression, poverty, crime, dishonor, mortification, and death, are too often the fruits of precipitate matrimonial alliances, not to sound the note of alarm on the ear of those who never look beyond the present moment. There are doubtless exceptions to this universal obligation to the married life, arising from the employments to which men are devoted;

from the disturbed and warlike, or persecuting age of the world, like that to which the Apostle Paul's advice referred, suggesting the inexpediency of marriage to the early Christians under the bloody reign of Nero. Nor do we deny that they may also arise from those melancholy providences which bereave them of the object of their first love, and leave them desolate and beyond the reach of a second attachment. But they are exceptions only; the law itself is too wise and benevolent a law to be disobeyed with impunity.

The revealed motive for the creation of woman was a beautiful motive. "And the Lord God said, it is not *good* that man should be *alone;* I will make an *help*, meet for him." With all his lofty faculties, and all his divinely imparted dominion, he was *alone.* Amid all the fertility, and fruits, and beauty of an unsullied Paradise, and all the charms and splendor of this exterior world, unveiled and unobscured by sin, he was still *alone.* His Maker had so formed him, that there were high and holy sympathies in his nature which solitude could not satisfy. The air would be more sweet, the fruits of Eden more delicious, the melody of its groves and the murmur of its streams the more exquisitely enjoyed, if shared with one who, with like hallowed and affectionate sympathies, could maintain a correspondence with him in thought, and language, and emotion, and, with him, could become the grateful and happy partaker of the divine bounty. Even in his solitude, the first man was created the happiest of the race. He was happy in the tranquillity of his own mind, and in his earthly inheritance; more than all, was he happy in his delightful and delighted fellowship with his Maker. But even the services and joys of a sinless piety would be augmented and more joyous by woman's fellowship, because it would be a twofold piety and a twofold joy. There would be another being like himself, reflecting back upon his own joyous thoughts, new admiration of the wondrous Deity; another mind uttering its responsive impulses, and at the same time, by its tenderness and susceptibility, exercising a refining influence on his own. Piety may, and often does solicit retirement. Sweet and almost unearthly are its hours of solitary communion with God and things unseen; while its purest and highest joys both in earth and heaven, are the most exalted and pure, where thought responds to thought, and love commingles with love, and praise is in sweet harmony with praise.

Paradise was no monastery. The spirit and joys which our first father drew from religious sources were too full for his own single heart to hold. He would have mistaken his calling if he had been a monk; and that fair and newly-created woman, taken from his side, would have been unmindful of her high and sacred destiny, if, in accordance with the ascetic teachings of a later, and certainly not a purer age, she had taken the veil. Of all men in the world, it is not good for religious men to be alone. The Creator foresaw this in relation to the first and purest of men; and provided him an associate, meet and every way fitted to share his responsibility and his joys. The man and the woman are mutually necessary to each other; the latter to soften the sterner attributes of the former, the former to fortify and ennoble the character of the latter. Nor were it an easy matter to say which has the greater need. The vow of celibacy, either in man or woman, is a wicked vow; and is as truly the bane of piety as of joy. Although the subsequent history of the first man shows that solitary piety may be ensnared by woman's importunity and loveliness, it does not show that it is not more pure, more safe, and sweeter than the piety that dwells alone. No man is secure from temptation by becoming an anchorite, nor does he find repose by merely retiring from the noise and bustle of the world. Solitary man we do not envy. No, "it is *not good* for man to be *alone*." In youth, woman is his charm; in manhood, his protection; in old age, his comforter. In youth, he turns from a deceitful and sickening world to her, as his garden of delights, and knows no solitude. In manhood, she is his refuge from the storms which agitate and overwhelm. While in old age, the love which, amid the perplexities of middle life, was sometimes agitated and disturbed, is found to have been all the while striking its roots the deeper. Under a wise and kind ordering of God's providence, it has become like that which gladdened the day of his espousals; and he still finds that the zephyr breathes upon the rainbow cloud, and that under life's waning moon, he knows no solitude so long as he is with her he loves.

Man was not created a simple unity; nor yet a trinity, but a *duality.* "In the day that God created man, male and female created he them; and blessed them, and called *their* name *Adam.*" The one was constituted of the two, and the two were one. The perfect man is made up of twain. Adam was not complete without Eve; when he awoke from that deep sleep, he must have had something like the consciousness that he was but *half a man.* Nor did he feel that he was his whole self, until God restored the rib, and he could say, "This is now bone of my bone and flesh of my flesh." Thus do the Scriptures honor the marriage bond. The name of the married pair becomes one; their rights and privileges, their hearts, their persons are one. Nothing may sever them but the blow which dissolves the union of the body and the soul. "Therefore shall a man leave his father and mother, and cleave unto his *wife*, and they twain shall be one flesh."

As we before intimated, there are great *moral reasons* for this arrangement. What are these reasons, and how much importance is to be attached to them, and to what extent may they be regarded as elevating and sanctifying the domestic relations? These are inquiries of interest, and deserve more than a few passing remarks. "And did he not make *one?*" demands the Prophet Malachi. "And yet had he the residue of the Spirit. And wherefore *one?*" Mark and digest the answer, "*That he might* SEEK A GODLY SEED." The first pair became pious without this parental training; God was their immediate Father, and they were taught of him. But they were to transmit this heaven-imparted legacy to their children; and therefore he made them *one.* He had the residue of the Spirit; he could have made millions. But he made *one common pair*, from whom all the rest should proceed, that he might have a *holy offspring*, and that being the property of *one*, they might be cared for, and educated in his fear.

The object of this arrangement is to *preoccupy* the mind of the rising generation in favor of truth and goodness. It is no marvel that infidels and socialists have complained of this as an invasion upon human liberty. Why, say they, should our fathers bind us, and we bind our children, and thus make religion little better than an hereditary bondage? Why should not intelligent beings, before their minds receive any religious direction, reach those adult years, in which they are capable of judging and acting freely for themselves? Religion implies the exercise of reason and assent; of personal liberty, one of the dearest branches is liberty of conscience, and this no one can exercise till he comes to years! To all such appeals as this, we have only now to reply, that they are opposed to the whole spirit of *the Bible.* The method which the God only wise has selected for carrying into effect his purposes of mercy is a very different method. The Scriptures regard the blessings of the great salvation as the most precious legacy, and speak of those as most distinguished in spiritual privileges, who enjoy the earliest and best religious training. In defiance of such infidel sneers, they regard it as the shortest and safest way, to *preoccupy* the youthful mind with religious truth, and before the Enemy has the full and unresisted opportunity of sowing tares. It never occurred to the writers of the sacred volume, that it is any encroachment upon natural rights, for the God of love to bring the rising generation into such relations as are designed to counteract the evil tendencies of their own depraved nature, and to forestall their consciences in favor of truth and heaven. Their professed object is, so to direct the youthful mind, that as soon as it begins to open the eyes of thought and intelligence, one of the first impressions of which it is capable should be, that the God that made it has a claim upon it prior to that of the Prince of Darkness. It is a delightful feature in the gracious government God has established, that it thus consults the nature of man as a social being; puts his seal upon the domestic relations; and makes use of those ties of blood and kindred, of love and tenderness, by which the heart of the parent is bound up in the child, in order to give it a heavenward tendency. Nor is there any agency so important as this, to be employed in perpetuating moral rectitude in the earth, and elevating the countless families of which it is composed to a companionship with the angels of light.

When we look into the Scriptures, we find several important facts on this subject, which ought never to be lost sight of. One of these is, that *no parent acts for himself alone.* The legal consequences of one man's conduct may be felt not only by himself, but by others. One may suffer for the sins of another, or be benefited by another's righteousness. Another may be appointed to stand in his place; may represent and bind him, and entail upon him consequences of conduct that is not his own. Whether this truth forms a part of our theological creed or not, we cannot help discovering it in the framework and various compartments of society. The world is full of it; the ordinary intercourse of men could not exist with it. The husband acts for the wife, the master for the servant, the guardian for the ward, the ruler for his subjects. And it is emphatically true of the parental relation. The mere *law of nature*, in a multitude of instances, constitutes the parent the representative of the child; so that the character and destiny of the child, through the operation both of physical and moral causes, is affected by the conduct of the parent. The first man was constituted the representative of the race; his character was the pivot on which their destiny turned. He acted for them; his apostasy was virtually their apostasy. God has ever acted thus toward the human family as a whole, and nowhere is this feature of his government more distinctly observable than in the domestic relations.

In these relations, this principle is of twofold aspect. The language of his law is, "I the Lord thy God am a jealous God, *visiting the iniquity of the fathers upon the children* unto the third and fourth generation of them that hate me; and *showing mercy unto thousands of them that love me*, and keep my commandments." So long as this law is in force, children will be disobedient, and will suffer on account of the disobedience of their parents; and they will become obedient, and receive blessing on account of their parents' obdience. And what are the *facts*, but that wherever you look over this wide world, you see that the piety and virtues of parents affect the well-being of their children, while their evil-being is as truly affected by their parents' impiety and vices? The history of the church and the world reads affecting lessons illustrating this great fact. In the communications of his grace, God has regard to Christian families; while he pours his wrath upon the heathen and upon the families that call not upon his name. However, in the exercise of his sovereignty, he may go out of these limits, and here and there abandon the incorrigible of Christian families, and reclaim those who are not incorrigible from the families of the ungodly; the instances of this sort are comparatively rare. And who does not see that it is of great practical importance, that, in promoting the interests of rectitude in such a world as this, the God of rectitude should give this distinguished token of his complacency to moral and Christian virtue, and at the same time fix this strong mark of his displeasure upon wickedness? What more powerful dissuasive from sin, or more powerful persuasive to holiness is to be found within the compass of human thought, than the consideration that the effects of our piety or impiety tell on the destiny of our children? Men who have little concern for themselves, tremble at wickedness when they think of the consequences of it upon those they most love. When, for their sakes, and for their sins, God threatens to visit the iniquity of the fathers upon the children, his threatenings sink deep. Nor is the promise less affecting than the threatening. It is a most cheering fact, that the blessings of obedience descend from parents to their children; nor is the Christian parent to be found whose heart does not respond to this great promise, as one of the most sweet and one of the holiest on the pages of the sacred volume.

We are not wont, as we ought to do, to appreciate this arrangement of heavenly wisdom. In constituting the population of the earth into a world of families, the Father of mercies has formed it of delicate and sensitive materials. It is a most beautiful moral machinery; a "building fitly framed together;" a net-work so perfect that every cord and filament, and all its thousand knots act and pull upon its sister cords, and one is strengthened, only as it keeps the others in its place. Holy wedlock is the centre of these evolving circles; and the parties by which it is organized entwine themselves with all these sacred influences. What is it that holds in check the boisterous levity and bold wickedness of that ungodly youth, who so lately found his joys only amid the coarser revellings of his own sex, and who, with scorners, delighted in his scorning? A subduing influence has come upon him, because he is a husband and a father. A new world opens to his thoughts, of which he is the head and prince; novel scenes present themselves to his eye, new responsibilities press upon his conscience, new emotions spring up in his heart. And if he be human, he will not break these cords of love, nor cast these bands asunder. The eye of his child is upon him; and though he himself may have been ever so thoughtless, he would not that his children walk in the counsel of the ungodly. And what is it that has produced such a wonderful transformation in the character of that gay and giddy girl, and clothed her with womanly dignity—and cast a sombre shade over her brow, so that she seeks retirement, and often converses with God and heaven? She has been made to feel that she has others to live for besides herself; because the God of all grace has made her the centre of attraction to her husband and children. She, too, occupies a new world of her own, of which she is the adornment and head, and where her gentle, but effective power would fain draw the feet of those she so much loves from the paths of the destroyer.

It is a truth never to be lost sight of, that in the dispensations of his grace, the God of love *does not ordinarily separate the child from the parent.* The principle of *representation* here looms, as one of the great principles of the divine government; and what is more, it looms in the brightness of hope. We see it everywhere—shedding its light upon the past, and gilding the future. We travel along with it, as the men of other times were conducted by the pillar and the cloud in the wilderness; and we look toward it for days to come, as a sun that shall never go down. When, in the patriarchal age, God was about to destroy the world by a flood, he said to Noah, "*Thee* have I found righteous before me in this generation; *therefore*, come thou and all thy house into the ark." And when, in predicting the approach of brighter days, the prophet speaks of a time of which it is written, "I will pour my Spirit upon *thy seed*, and my blessing upon thine *offspring*." How often, how forcibly, and with what inimitable beauty the sacred writers enforce this thought, is best known to those who best know the Holy Scriptures—kindling as they go, and never painting the scene in which "Jerusalem is a rejoicing, and her people a joy;" in which "the wolf and the lamb shall feed," and where there is "nothing to hurt in all God's holy mountain:" without reminding us of the altars and firesides of domestic piety and joy, and without telling us that "the *children* shall be as aforetime," and that they are "the seed of the blessed of the Lord, and their *offspring* with them."

The promise of blessing to the children of the righteous for the sake of their parents, is among the "exceeding great and precious promises." They bring relief to many an anxious and aching heart; thousands have been buoyed up by them, as they passed through deep waters. They encourage the sower as he goes forth to sow; and they shed a calm and summer's light upon the harvest, as the church looks toward the days of her ingathering and autumnal glory.

It assumes a more solemn form too than a bare promise; it is a covenant with an annexed and most impressive seal. That seal was a household ordinance under the old dispensation, and it is a household ordinance still. It does not accord with the analogy of the divine dispensations, that spiritual privileges enjoyed under the Old Testament economy, should be denied or restricted under the New. *We* have the family promise and the family seal. It is still the privilege of parents and their children; children are a part of their parents, and pass under the bond of the covenant. They are no outcasts. They are neither pagans nor Mohammedans, but are under the wings of the same cherubim with their parents. The change in the seal affects no change in the promise; the seal is more simple under the gospel than under the law; but it is not less significant. It is Christian in its form and in its import. And its sweet language is, "Suffer the little children to come unto me, and forbid them not, for such is the kingdom of heaven."

In addition to these specifications, look now at the *general scope and design* of the sacred writings. The honor which the Bible confers on the matrimonial relation is abundant honor. It protects this relation by laws and sanctions, by which no other relations are protected. How often, and with what solemnity is the thought there uttered, that "whoremongers and adulterers God will *judge*;" and that they shall have their part in the lake of fire? There is, moreover, running throughout the whole of the Old and New Testament this household right; the right of the children by inheritance. It is the right in *fee simple* to the same spiritual privileges with their parents. The whole spirit of this sacred book stands forth, as a guardian angel, throwing its shield over these hallowed associations, and giving them preëminence among the selected means by which the designs of the divine mercy are accomplished.

Observe now the *remarkable fitness and wisdom* of this arrangement. Occupied the youthful mind will be; pre-occupied it is, and for evil. How shall the intruder be dislodged, the usurper expelled, and in his place be introduced its rightful proprietor, the God of heaven? There is no relation like that which exists between the different branches of the same plighted household, and which so effectually secures the moral and religious culture of the young. What human society is to be, depends upon what its children now are. One generation goeth, and another cometh, rapidly as the eagle when he hasteth to his prey. Before they are aware of it, the present generation are laid aside as useless, or rest in their graves, and sportive childhood and smiling infancy occupy their places, and exert their authority and influence. It is but yesterday, as it were, and those whose locks are now white with age, were young. The men and the women who, when the sun of life has risen a little higher, will bear this responsibility, are now forming their character; they are an unformed mass, submitted to the control of senior hands, like wax to the seal. The impression now stamped upon it is one which remains. And what is it without those hallowed influences, which flow from the mutual dependence, mutual obligation, and mutual endearment of the domestic relations? Relax and sever the household bond; melt this golden chain, and scatter it on the broad and undefined surface of a loose and licentious socialism; and where are the hopes, either of the church, or the world? Who cares then for the religious education of the young? or who then appreciates an intelligent and virtuous childhood?

Men there are who are the advocates of such a

relaxation of the marriage bond; but what, I entreat them to consider, would the world become in twenty years, were its households broken up, or changed at pleasure, or left in ignorance of God and his word, unrestrained in their vicious courses, and never cheered by the voice of prayer? How long before the scenes of other lands would be realized; infanticide become an act of piety; and parents never more devout than when they caused their children to pass through the fire as an offering to Moloch? If these cruel paths are now untrodden, it is because the God of the Bible preserves to us the integrity and piety, the tenderness, and affection, and preciousness of the marriage bond and the household relations. It is in the midst of these, that religious instruction has influence; that the goodness of God leads to repentance; and that his judgments teach men righteousness.

Yes! his judgments. Let us stop a moment, and weigh this single thought. One of the selected instrumentalities in the conversion of men, which neither the church nor the world can afford to dispense with, are those afflictions which, though not joyous for the present, yet afterwards yield the peaceable fruits of righteousness. Men are accessible to the salutary influence of judgments, chiefly through the domestic relations, because they touch so many chords of tenderness and love. If we have not been unwise observers of God's dealings, we have found those disciplinary dispensations to be, not the striking and the rare—not the more stunning and overwhelming; but those of more ordinary occurrence, and which, though they attract less attention from without, go on their effectual message to the habitation and the heart where they are sent. The solitary tree upon the mountain top may be riven by the whirlwind, and not a bird shall be disturbed in its nestling, because it is not there that the birds build their nests, and utter their song. It is in the domestic grove, and in the green bower, and when the clustering vine is riven, that these cheerful voices are silent, or die away in the lingering and plaintive sounds of the storm. Would you see God's hand as it comes in mercy to the souls of men; go to that home of sorrow where the heart-stricken parents are mourning over blasted hopes. Go where the widow and the orphan vainly strive to dry up their tears, and where a sense of their loss comes gushing over them like a flood. Go where the strong man bows in his agony, and struggles in the grasp of a stronger than he. Go where God has cut down the loveliest and the best, because a father's and a mother's heart had begun to yield to idolatry, and needed just such an admonition to save them from the pit of destruction. Men read such lessons of God's love, and understand and apply them. They come home wnere the track of the pestilence, or the wasting conflagration, or agitating revolutions are unheeded. Yet the effect of this whole class of judgments is associated with the marriage bond, and depends upon the tenderness of the social relations.

We may not, therefore, regard these relations with lightness; there is no view in which their importance may not be magnified. The church and the world will be disappointed in their hopes; generation after generation will live and die in their delusions, just in the measure in which these relations are honored, and the spirit of piety is preserved among the descendants of a pious ancestry. It is no marvel, that in carrying into effect the method of redemption, these purposes of mercy should early entwine themselves with the affections and hopes of the family circle. It is a most beautiful arrangement, and deserves the place which God has given it as the selected instrumentality by which true religion is to be extended and perpetuated among fallen men. The great foe of God and man desires no coöperation more effective than an irreligious and ungoverned family; while, as the great offset to this degenerating process, the God of love has made choice of the domestic relations as the depositaries of his grace, and there laid the deep foundations of that spiritual temple from which the symbol of his presence and glory is never more to depart.

Our desire is, that *youthful families* should appreciate these thoughts. The mutual affection of a young married pair, if not seriously disturbed in the earlier years of its existence, is not often disturbed when that affection is matured by time, and cemented by the same habits and interests. It may, perhaps, be surprising to a youthful bride, to see what a difference one short month makes in the relations she sustains to him who is now her husband. She has been wont to be regarded as the idol; her lover was all devotion; no toil and no self-denial were too great to gratify, and if possible to anticipate her every wish. But she is the wife now; she is as truly the loved one as ever; but she has other wishes to consult than her own, if she would be happy. The change is great, and it is too much to expect that every young woman is prepared for it. She must bear her part in the toil, and burden, and battle of human life, as well as its joys. And it may be she is disappointed. She had treasured up her joys where she does not find them. Her affections and her pride are mortified. The flowers of hope wither in her path, and her prospects seem for a time to be all blighted. A young girl brought up with romantic notions of the married life is very apt to fall into this mistake. And the preventive of the error is found in the instructions which the Bible gives of what a good wife should be. Her sphere is eminently one of self-denying tenderness and love; and not a little depends on her knowledge of the duties of that sphere. If this be disregarded, there may be trouble, and the evil must work its own cure. And if she have good sense and affection, and her husband is generous and kind, it will not be long before the cure is effected. A little mutual forbearance, and she will rest satisfied in being his adviser and comforter. And then she will be happy. They will travel on together, no longer expecting this earth to be a paradise. They will enjoy its sunshine together; together will they breast themselves against its storms; and together will they rove among its flowers and gather its fruit. I have often thought that this is a most critical period of human life; and more especially where the marriage is one of affection. Much depends, in the early part of the married life, upon the "meekness of wisdom." The youthful pair are not always apprised how busily the great tempter is employed in exciting those little contentions, and fomenting those unexpected and provoking feuds which originate in unsuitableness of temper, and in the many cares and inconveniences of domestic life; but which are soon forgotten by an affectionate and generous mind. "Resist the devil, and he shall flee from you." This "Prince of the power of the air" would fain blow them up into storms, and breathe into them the hurricane's blast; while in fact they are a passing cloud. A single gush of tears, a summer shower, and the sky is clear.

The contrast is wide between an ungodly and a godly household. "The curse of the Lord is in the house of the wicked." An ungodly family, what a melancholy picture is this, here in this world of mercy and of hope, and yet a world so full of danger! God is not there; his word has no place, nor does his truth shine as a lamp to their feet, and a light to their path. The voice of prayer and praise is not heard there; nor do tranquil Sabbaths ever visit their abode of plighted love. The young wander there amid precipices and dangers, to whom no guardian angel ministers, and for whom no Holy Spirit has been invoked; and wander in the broad way that leads to death. On the other hand, the sun shines upon no lovelier scene than a godly family. It is recorded of Zacharias and Elizabeth, that "they were both righteous before God, walking in all the commandments and ordinances of the Lord blameless." The blameless pair, what a beautiful sight! I recollect seeing the picture of a child passing over a very narrow path, with precipices on each side, and I wondered at the serenity and hope with which she travelled on, until I saw an angel behind her, hovering over her, and directing her to some bright object in the distance. And I thought of

God's promise to the families of his people, and was reminded of the words, "Are they not all ministering spirits, sent forth to minister to them that shall be heirs of salvation." God "blesseth the habitation of the righteous." It is a verdant island amid Arabian sands. The dry wind of the desert does not scorch it, nor does its beauty wither under its mid-day suns. No; nor do its flowers languish under the western sky. There is a maturity, a richness of affection in those long-wedded minds that have weathered the storm of life together, and together have so often made the Everlasting God their refuge, which may not be compared with the feverish affection of inexperienced youth. There is that perfect repose and confidence which the youthful heart cannot know. The smile of affection is there; nor is it less cheering that it radiates the brow wrinkled by time. It is a "dwelling-place of Mount Zion," where God himself resides, and on whose altars he hath created a fire and a smoke.

We would have these thoughts appreciated also *by parents.* Parents may be unfaithful, and God may visit their iniquity upon their children. Such unfaithfulness, we fear, is too common a sin. Christian parents, beside violating their covenant engagements with God, are rebuked for this unfaithfulness by the tardy fulfilment of all that is cheering in the divine promise, and by that "hope deferred which maketh the heart sick." Parents begin their work of prayer, instruction, and discipline, with the seal of God's covenant in their hands, and under the high commission, "Take this child and nurse it *for me*, and I will give thee thy wages." The infant Moses, of whom this was spoken, was then a weeping babe in the ark of bulrushes, exposed on the banks of the Nile. But he was destined to be the greatest man of his age, mighty in words and deeds, learned in all the wisdom of the Egyptians, and God's inspired Prophet; eminent for holiness and usefulness, and the great legislator of the world. When the proud daughter of Egypt's haughty tyrant, saw this little Hebrew slave, "behold the babe wept." And she had "compassion on him," and "the woman took the child and nursed it." Take heed that *ye* despise not one of these little ones. That child which God has given you has a high and immortal destiny. There is the dawn of intelligence there, which will shine when the sun is turned into darkness. There are capacities of thought there, that are capable of unlimited expansion; and capacities for holiness, usefulness, and joy, whose brightness may hereafter mingle with the glory that constitutes the radiance of the Redeemer's crown. Yet is it born to weep, to sin, to suffer, to die—nay, to perish, but for parental love and faithfulness. O bear it on your bosom. Impel it heavenward.

Bear it on your bosom while it is young; and when you can no longer do this, travel with it, hand in hand, to the city of our God.

Our desire also is, that the thoughts which have been suggested, should not be neglected *by the young.* These domestic relations, my young friends, where you have been so carefully nurtured, and which will never be forgotten, are the pledge of blessing. "You have Abraham to your father;" but you may not forget that "God is able, from the stones, to raise up children to Abraham." It is an affecting truth, that "many shall come from the East and the West, from the North and the South, and sit down with Abraham and Isaac and Jacob, in the kingdom of God, and the children of the kingdom shall be cast out." The piety of your parents will not save you, if you yourselves live without God in the world. There is many a man, and many a woman, early trained up in the nurture and admonition of the Lord, now in the world of mourning. Your perverseness may prove too great a trial for the faith of your parents; you may discourage them too often, and tear from their bosoms their last hope. They may cease to pray for you, because they feel there is no more encouragement to pray. There may be a crisis in your history, beyond which the divine forbearance cannot be extended, and parental faith expires.

But apprehensions like these, though they may be realized, are not so much in keeping with our theme, as the more cherished hopes it inspires. You fill a wide space in the world in which you dwell, and form a link in the chain that takes hold of the destiny of those who shall come after you. They are your natural and rightful heirs; see to it that they inherit from you treasures and honors which this world cannot give. There is enough in the generosity of God's gracious arrangement in regard to the domestic relations, to induce you to put a high estimate upon *them*, and enough that is significant of his grace to induce you to look toward *him and them* with religious hopes. The social bond should constrain you to become Christians. Both the Spirit and the Bride say, Come.

CHAPTER VII.

The First Sabbath.

THE fatal exposure of our race is to be absorbed in the pursuit of the things that are seen and temporal, to the neglect of those that are unseen and eternal. So immersed and engulfed are they in this all-devouring vortex, as to be in danger of being carried down the cataract beyond the hope and possibility of return. The great excuse with the mass of men for not paying that serious attention to the concerns of the soul which their importance demands, is that they have *no time* for this service; and in order to remove and forever silence this excuse, the God of heaven has set apart one day in seven, and thereby one seventh part of every man's life to be devoted to the interests of his immortality.

The thought is an interesting one, that this appointment was coeval with man's creation; and that at no period since, has this world existed without the Sabbath. The Sabbath was literally among the "first things." The material heavens and earth were scarcely called into being; man himself had only begun to exist, and woman to share his existence and joys; when the institution, so full of heavenly forethought, was made known by the words, "And God blessed the seventh day and sanctified it, because that in it he had rested from all the work which God created and made." In this original appointment were included the entire Sabbatical institution, and all those elemental observances that were essential to its influence. The benevolent Creator would not send forth into this new world the intelligent and immortal beings he had made, and give them dominion over the inferior creatures, and the commission to replenish the earth and subdue it; without the illuminating, sanctifying, and conservatory influence of the Sabbath. Sinless as they were, they needed the Sabbath; sinful as they and their posterity would be, the Sabbath was indispensable to their hopes.

Man thus began his earthly career. As under the legal economy, the *first* was to be chosen for God; the *first*-born of man; the *first*-born of beasts; the *first*-fruits of the field; so it was the duty and honor of the first man to devote to God the *first* dawnings of time. Man was created not until the close of the sixth and last day of the creation. So that, reckoning from evening to evening, the *first entire day* of man's life was the Sabbath. He had but begun to be conscious of his existence, and open his eyes upon the marvellous works of God, and upon himself more wondrous, and upon his still more wondrous Maker, than he and the woman God gave him, were embosomed in the quiet atmosphere of God's holy day of rest. The shadows of the first evening were the eve of the Sabbath. The light of the first morning they ever beheld was the morning of the Sabbath. The first voices that greeted them were the song of cherubim and seraphim, as they sang together, and all the sons of God shouted for joy. It was a day of rest. There was no upheaving of the dry land, and no rushing of the waters to their appointed beds. The lights of the firmament were established, their laws prescribed, and they were moving quietly in their orbits. The new creation was finished. The day of rest was quietly bidding welcome to the new-created race; and man, the last of all God's works, began his career in loving, praising, adoring God his Maker. It was not the busy world he first entered, but the temple of God; God's sanctuary—there to worship, and there to listen to the voice from the excellent glory. The first Sabbath was the great preparative for his life of toil; the great preparative, and the emphatic emblem of his immortality.

But we must proceed to sober argument. There are not a few who regard the Sabbath as an institution peculiar to the Jewish people, and who, while they consent to its observance as a wise and benevolent arrangement, and one fraught with great benefits to mankind, at the same time teach that it is not the revealed law of Christianity, but only the conventional law of Christians.* We are by no means prepared to adopt this view; yet is it one which has obtained so extensively, more especially in the continental churches of Europe, that it deserves to be considered with respect.

The first question in relation to it is, *When was the Sabbath instituted?* This question, it appears to us, is answered by the narrative of Moses, to which reference has already been made. There we are instructed, that immediately after the work of creation was completed, "God blessed the seventh day and sanctified it." He commanded his blessing to rest upon it; he sanctified, or set it apart from other days, as the natal day of the world, and as a memorial of that great and perfected work. He foresaw, that there would be ungodly men, and atheists, and that it was necessary there should be some sensible *commemoration* of the fact that it was created by himself in the space of six days. With the recurrence of every seventh day

* Among these writers, are the distinguished names of Calvin and Paley. The reformers were divided in opinions on this question, as may be extensively seen by consulting *Vitringa*, Aphorismi Doct. Christ. It is no marvel they were tenacious of Christian liberty in regard to *days*, just freed as they had been from the superstitious observances of Rome.

of rest from worldly employments, the inquiry would naturally arise in the minds of the young, What means this remarkable observance? Nor would the answer be likely to be forgotten, that God himself set it apart as a memorial of his work of creation. This single fact shows, unless there be some subsequent revelation to set it aside, that the Sabbath, from its nature, was designed to be a permanent observance.

It is no doubt true, that there are religious observances appointed by God, which are of local and temporary obligation, as well as those which are universally and always binding. All *moral* laws possess this universal and permanent force. And there *are positive* statutes which have the same permanent obligation, because they are made binding by the command of God. It is a safe principle to adopt in the interpretation of positive statutes, that when once they are enacted, they always remain in full force unless they expire by their own limitations; unless they are formally repealed; or unless the reasons for their original appointment so obviously cease, that they are no longer called for.

The *patriarchal* Sabbath, or the Sabbath instituted at the creation, differed in some respects from the Jewish Sabbath. It was not instituted, so far as we know, by any *expressed* command. The authority for it is contained in the narrative already given. We have, in this portion of the sacred writings, no other divine authority for it, than that which is implied in God's example, and his setting apart and blessing the Sabbath-day. And this, while it has not the language, appears to us to have the force of law. God may enact *his will* as a rule of action to his creatures, in other ways than by an express command, provided he makes his will intelligibly known. Have we not a right to conclude, from this early notice of a seventh day's rest, that it was God's *pleasure* that it should be observed? For *whom* was it instituted? Not for God himself. He did not require the repose of the seventh day, either for physical or spiritual refreshment. He did not take that repose; but was employed in upholding and directing the world and the creatures he had just made. "The Sabbath was made for *man*." God's example in instituting it was for man; he thus made known his will to man; his example was man's law. And if this be thought to be loose reasoning, I can only say, it appears to us to be reasoning which ought to satisfy every fair mind, and which is adopted by the Scriptures themselves. It is the reasoning which is adopted by the Great Lawgiver in the command requiring the observance of the Sabbath in the Decalogue; and it is the reasoning of the apostle in his epistle to the Hebrews, where, the fact that "God did rest the seventh day from all his works," forms the premises to the conclusion, "There remaineth therefore, the keeping of a Sabbath to the people of God." It was the Sabbath of heaven and the Sabbath of earth; it was the Sabbath which so many failed of enjoying through unbelief; it was the Sabbath which was the prefiguration, the example, and the law, and the early heritage of man.

There is a difference between the binding obligation of those positive statutes which were given during the patriarchal age, and those which were enacted under the Mosaic economy. The Mosaic dispensation includes that entire period which intervened between the giving of the law, and the resurrection of the Son of Man from the dead; the patriarchal age includes the entire period between the Creation and the giving of the law. If the claims of the Sabbath cannot be supported except as a part of the Jewish ceremonial, it must share the same fate with the sacrifices and new moons of that dispensation. All Christians agree in the conclusion, that whatever was purely positive and ceremonial in the Jewish dispensation has passed away, and was superseded by the "simplicity that is in Christ." They were obligatory upon the Jewish nation alone; and on that nation only until the Christian dispensation.

Yet are there positive institutions which cover the

whole duration of time, because they were of prior origin both to the Christian and Mosaic dispensations. Such, for example, was the patriarchal law concerning the murderer, "Whoso sheddeth man's blood, by man shall his blood be shed." It binds the race; it was given to men, not as Jews, nor as Gentiles, but as *men*, as God's creatures. It never has been repealed; nor has it expired by its own limitations; men ever, and everywhere are bound by it. And such is the institution of the Sabbath. It is confessedly a positive, and not a moral institution. It is a moral duty that men should worship God; but it is a positive and not a moral duty, except as the enactment renders it moral, to worship him socially one day in seven. But made up as it thus is of a positive statute and moral duty, we affirm that it is, from its origin, of perpetual obligation. Like the law concerning the murderer, it is not of Christian, nor Jewish origin; but was proclaimed in an age that represented the race, and was dictated by the great Creator and Lawgiver to all mankind long before either the Christian or Jewish dispensations were in existence, or the distinction between Jew and Gentile was known. It is human and not national merely; universal and not merely local. It is God's law to men; his wise and benevolent arrangement for humanity, and for man everywhere. The same reasons which existed for the original institution in Paradise, and before man fell, exist in no diminished force now after he has fallen. Whatever be the facts it commemorates, the lessons it teaches, the obligations it confers, and the influence it exerts, they are not more necessary for men in one age and one portion of the world, than for men in all ages and all places. In the original appointment of it, there is no intimation that it had reference to one people, or one age of the world more than another. It has never expired by its own limitations, and has never been repealed. The peculiar positive institutions that were commanded to the Jews have been formally abolished, or superseded by others that have a relation to the race. The Jewish sacrifices, the Jewish passover, the Jewish hierarchy, as well as all those Mosaic rites and ceremonies which were merely typical of Jesus Christ, and which, from their purely ecclesiastical or political nature, were designed to separate the Jews from other nations, have been abrogated. But there is no abolition of the Sabbath. There is no reënaction of it under the Christian dispensation, for the obvious reason that no reënactment was necessary; it remains an unrepealed, a permanent, and standing institution, and of perpetual obligation.

The objection against this reasoning is somewhat peculiar. It lies in the acknowledged fact that from *the time when the Sabbath was first instituted*, *there is no mention made of it in the Scriptures until a period of about twenty-five hundred years*, and when the manna fell in the wilderness. But it must not be forgotten that the history of this early period of the world is, beyond parallel, a crowded history, in which a single paragraph often includes the events of centuries. "The silence of history with respect to the continuance of a rite, or custom, well known to have been instituted or adopted, is no argument against its continuance, provided the reason on which the institution was founded remains the same." There is no mention made of the Sabbath throughout all the wars of Joshua, and the revolutionary period of the Judges, a period of some hundred years; while it is conceded that it was instituted long before in the wilderness. No mention is made of sacrifices, from the birth of Seth till the flood, a period of fifteen hundred years. Nor is there any mention made of the rite of circumcision from about the time the children of Israel took possession of the land of Canaan, under Joshua, until the days of Jeremiah, a period of more than eight centuries; while this does not prove that it was not of earlier appointment. It may be, that the Sabbath was not scrupulously observed during the patriarchal age; there was great forgetfulness of God, great ignorance and great wickedness in that infant age of the world. They were a thoughtless race—men of gigantic iniquity; they were marrying and giving in marriage, and spending their days in folly and sin, until the day that Noah entered into the ark and the flood came and swept them all away. They had few religious teachers; no part of God's word was then published, and they had very little instruction of a religious kind. It is not wonderful that they lost sight of the Sabbath; for if they had not lost sight of it, they never could have been so vile. Yet amid all this abounding iniquity, there are some notices of what seems to be, by fair inference, a seventh-day observance; for we find a seven-day division of time, well known by Noah and Jacob and Laban. The probability, too, is, that during the severe and protracted bondage of the Hebrews in Egypt, the Sabbath was greatly neglected; during a portion of that period, we know it was neglected altogether. And when that people, after they came out of Egypt, were *reminded* of its obligations, it was in such a way that it is difficult to avoid the conclusion that it was a *forgotten* institution, and not one then for the first time instituted. This was in the wilderness, and *before* the giving of the law, which some contend was the first statute requiring the Sabbath observance. They were about to gather manna on the Sabbath-day, and Moses checked the unhallowed work, and said unto them, "This is that which the Lord *hath said*, To-morrow is the Holy Sabbath unto the Lord. Six days shall ye gather it, but on the seventh day, which is the Sabbath, ye shall not find it in the field."

It was not until fifty days after they left Egypt that the law was given, in which the Sabbath holds a prominent place. So that it was not the Jewish Sabbath, as such, to which Moses here referred, but the Sabbath of the Patriarchs, and which was binding upon the Jews before the specific enactment in the fourth commandment. It is an error to suppose that the fourth commandment originated the obligation to observe the Sabbath even among the Jews. It did but confirm a prior law. The friends of the Sabbath have lost ground by endeavoring to defend this position. When, after their fifty days' wandering in the wilderness, God gave the children of Israel the ten commandments, the language was, "*Remember* the Sabbath-day to keep it holy." It is not, "Sanctify the Sabbath;" but "*remember* to sanctify it." The day was something to be remembered; it was no novel observance first given by Moses, but one long before known and of ancient date. And the reason for it runs back to the creation and entwines itself with the original institution and blessing: "*Remember* the Sabbath-day to keep it holy; for in six days the Lord thy God *created* the heavens and the earth, the sea and all that in them is, and rested the seventh day: wherefore the Lord blessed the

Sabbath-day and hallowed it." God himself spake these solemn words amid scenes never to be forgotten, and twice did he write them upon two tables of stone. AFTER SIX DAYS' LABOR, THERE WAS TO BE A SEVENTH DAY'S HOLY REST; THIS WAS THE LAW OF THE SABBATH. It was the law for the world. It was preserved in the ark of the covenant, was embodied within that Propitiatory which was typical of the Christian atonement, and forms an integral part of that great moral code, "THOSE TEN WORDS" which bind all nations, and which the Saviour affirms he came not to destroy, but to fulfil. There was *nothing ceremonial or Jewish* about these *ten words*, nor about the particular precept here enforcing the observance of the Sabbath. It was all moral, and all of universal and perpetual obligation.

If the question be asked, *Was there then no Jewish Sabbath, and no ceremonial scrupulousness in its observance incumbent on the Jews, which is not binding on other nations, and which was abrogated by the coming of Christ?* I answer, there were; but they are not contained in the fourth commandment. There was a subsequent law given to the Jews, which bound them and no other people, which consisted of fifty-seven precepts given immediately after God had "talked with them from heaven;" and given, not by God to *them*, but to *Moses* privately, that "he might set them before the people." These ceremonial injunctions were from time to time, increased; some of them respected the Sabbath; and all of them were abol ished by Christ. These peculiar Jewish observances formed no part of Sabbath religion, or Sabbath morality for other nations. Other days were called Sabbaths by them as well as the seventh day. The Pentecost was so called, whatsoever day of the week it was; because no servile work was to be done in it, and on it there was to be "a holy convocation to the Lord." The first day of the Passover was a Sabbath. On the Passover week in which the Saviour suffered, there were two Sabbaths. There was the convocational, or festival Sabbath, the first day of the Passover week; and there was the ordinary weekly Sabbath, which was the next day. It is not the ceremonial of the Jews which we advocate; nor any of the peculiarities of their Sabbatical observance which the law of God requires. They were appendages to the day, and not the day itself; the shadow and not the substance.

The Sabbath, *for substance, and freed from the Jewish ceremonial*, God has bequeathed to the world. It is delightful to know that other portions of the earth have an interest in it beside the Jews. As proof of this, we find it frequently spoken of in the Scriptures as extended beyond the Jewish dispensation. The prophet Isaiah, speaking of the day when God's house "shall be called an house of prayer for *all people;*" when Jews that were disqualified by bodily infirmity, and Gentiles who were always disqualified, should bring their sacrifices, and they should come up accepted on God's holy altar; when the wall of partition between Jew and Gentile should be broken down by the all-levelling and all-elevating influence of Christianity; when the Jewish dispensation should be abolished and superseded by the more comprehensive claims and privileges of the world's gospel; speaks of the "eunuchs who keep *God's Sabbaths*"—of the "sons of the stranger that keep *the Sabbath* from polluting it"—of those who "call the *Sabbath* a delight, the holy of the Lord," honorable—and of those who, in the days of the yet coming glory, "from one new moon to another, and from one *Sabbath* to another, shall come and worship before God." Nor do we see how the conclusion from these predictions and intimations can be avoided, that there is a divinely authorized and a divinely honored Sabbath after the Jewish dispensation is passed away, and therefore of more permanent obligation than the ceremonial or civil code of the Jews.

It is certainly a fair question in this argument, To what extent has a religious observance of every seventh day been known among the different nations of the earth? We have already adverted to the reasons for believing that the early patriarchs divided their time into *weeks*, or periods of *seven days;* nor do we see any reason to believe that during the twenty-five hundred years before the Law given on Sinai, there was no Sabbath. The Hebrews divided their years into seven, and into seven times seven; every week had its Sabbath, every seventh year its Sabbath, and every fiftieth year its Jubilee. To what extent this septenary division of time has obtained among nations who were contemporaneous with the patriarchal age, as well as among those pagan nations which flourished after the giving of the law, we have not the means of ascertaining to such an extent, as to warrant the sweeping assertion which has sometimes been made, that it is a universal observance. If, as we have seen, the Sabbath is an institution of high antiquity, it must have been known to those ancient Eastern nations which sprang from the sons of Noah. And so the fact was. The ancient Assyrians derived their origin from Ashur, the son of Shem; and they divided their time into weeks of seven days. The ancient Egyptians, who sprang from Mizraim, the son of Ham; the ancient Indians, and also the ancient Persians, whose origin is traced to Joktan, the grandson of Shem; and the ancient Arabians, who descended from Ishmael, all observed this division of time; and so far as this observance goes, it indicates, that however the Sabbath may have fallen into disuse, it was once known. The more ancient inhabitants of Greece and Italy had a different division; the Greeks dividing their months into decades or periods of ten days, and the Romans into the three divisions, calends, nones, and ides. But it is to be remarked, that in the early period of their history these nations had very little intercourse with the Eastern nations; and that as soon as they became acquainted with the calendar of the East, they divided their time into weeks of seven days. The origin of this usage cannot be doubtful; nor does it stop short of the ancient Hebrews and the patriarchal age. Learned men inform us that there are few languages that are not found to contain a word synonymous with our English word week, signifying seven days. With the Hebrews, the number *seven* was the sacred number. We read of the *seventh* day, the *seventh* month, the *seventh* year, the *seven* altars, the *seven* lamps, the *seven* seals, the *seven* thunders, the *seven* angels, and the *seven* crowns. Nor does this fact distinguish the religion of the Hebrews alone. A modern writer, in a late number of the Westminster Review, though he impugns the sacredness of the Sabbath with infidel scurrility and bitterness, is constrained to acknowledge, that "throughout Hindostan and all the dialects of India, the word *seven* is a mystical number." This writer has put us in possession of some facts which are by no means favorable to his own conclusions. The Hindoos observe a seventh day as a religious festival; and they call it Sunday, or the sun's day. They also observe every seventh lunar day; and they call it Monday, or the moon's day. In the forms of prayer used in their temples, the word *seven* occupies a conspicuous place. It is also a fact of interest, that the word Sabbath is adopted by pagan nations, not a few, to denote the day of religious convocation. So far as the light of history shines from different eminences, during the long course of years prior to the coming of Christ, it discloses to us this extensive observance.

Facts of this nature, which might be collected to a great extent, interest us, because every other method of accounting for them is unnatural, except the original division of time by God himself into periods of seven days, and the consequent institution of the Sabbath. Other divisions of time are marked by the diurnal and annual revolutions of the earth and the moon; while there is nothing in the solar system to mark this division into weeks; nor is there any historical trace of the origin of this usage in any of the memorials of antiquity, unless we find it in the tradition of the creation of the world in six days, and a subsequent day of rest. Here we find it. It was revealed to our first parents, that the one only living and true God created the universe; and this revelation prepared them for the appointment and the delightful service of this first Sabbath. What a day was that which thus first celebrated the mysteries of nature's birth; and with what radiant robes did this queen of days descend to dwell with men, while creation lay around her "wet with its first dews," and man, as its high-priest, offered up the incense of his grateful heart! Never did the rising and setting sun utter speech of such truth; nor have they done uttering the instructive lesson. It is solemn and expressive silence, but it speaks to the mind and heart.

"In reason's ear, they all rejoice,
And utter forth a glorious voice,
Forever singing, as they shine,
The hand that made us is divine."

When we come to the Christian era, the question assumes somewhat a different form. There is no express command in the New Testament for the observance of the Sabbath. Why should there be? The command originated with God's example at the creation; was solemnly embodied in his law from Sinai; and has not been repealed. The blessed Sabbath is no less God's witness for him, to the Christian, than to the Jewish and pagan world. It began with time, and with time only will it end; like all other commemorative institutions, it is coeval with the event it commemorates, and will terminate only with the consummation of this material world. Hence we find that the early Christians observed every seventh day as a day of holy rest. They honored it by assembling on that day for social worship, for the celebration of the Lord's Supper, and for taking up their charitable collections for their poor brethren. And the Saviour himself honored it. It was on the regular return of the seventh day, that he appeared to his disciples to bless them, and that he poured out upon them, after his ascension, the pentecostal effusions of his Spirit. And hence we read in the New Testament of "the Lord's day," a day separated from all secular time, distinguished as his own, as a holy Sabbath unto the Lord. This example, connected with the primeval institution of the day, and the fourth commandment, is the law of Christianity.

Nor is there any good reason for perplexity in regard to the *change of the day* from the seventh to the first day of the week, which is the Christian Sabbath. Our own mind is satisfied on this vexed question in something like the following way. God has set apart *one seventh portion of time* for sacred purposes. A literal simultaneousness in this observance no one contends for, nor were it easily practicable from the elliptical form and rotatory motions of the earth. What is dawn to one portion of the earth is evening to another; and what is noonday to one is midnight to their antipodes. The spirit and substance of the law is for one seventh portion of time; whether it be the last day of the week, or the first, and whether it begins with the rising or the setting sun, is of minor consideration, so long as every seventh day is sacredly observed. Time was when, at the command of Joshua, the sun stood still for a whole day, and when the shadow went ten degrees backward on the dial of Ahaz; and who will undertake to *demonstrate* that either the first, or the seventh day of the week is the exact and astronomical return of the seventh day from the creation? Different systems of chronology also are so various, and so many ingenious methods have been adopted for improving and establishing the calendar; so various have been the methods of computing time; and the beginning of the year has been so often changed, that no living man can now *prove* that any one day of the week corresponds with its numerical counterpart in the days of the creation. We hold therefore, that so long as there is a uniform and conventional observance of *every seventh* day as a day of holy rest, *after six days of labor*, the law of the Sabbath is complied with.

If it be said that these general observations are not applicable to that period of the world when Christianity was promulgated, because its chronology was then well understood, and the days of the week well known; and that there was confessedly a change then from the seventh to the first day of the week; we answer they are applicable so far as it regards the difficulty of identifying any given day of the week with its corresponding day of the creation. There *was* a change then, and there were good reasons for it. The change in the Sabbath falls in with the changes that were introduced in the external organization of the church of God at the introduction of Christianity. Everything was changed by the example and authority of the divine Author of the Christian dispensation. What was Jewish was done away, because the Gentiles were now called into the kingdom of Christ, and all monopoly of religious privileges was abolished. The rites and ceremonies of the Levitical law were repealed; the prefigurations of that whole shadowy system were superseded by the reality; while all that could be permanently valuable was modified. The Jewish priesthood was superseded by the Christian ministry; the Jewish Passover by the Lord's Supper; the rite of circumcision by baptism, and the Jewish Sabbath by the Lord's day. And is there not quite as much evidence that the first day of the week, now that it combines in its commemoration the greater work of redemption, is as distinctive a memorial of the great work of creation as was the original seventh day? The Lord's day is in honor of Him, "by whom are all things, and for whom are all things;" who is "head over all things to the church;" who is "Lord also of the Sabbath-day," the Author of a new and regenerated world, the Maker and Builder of the "new heavens and new earth wherein dwelleth righteousness," and in comparison with which "the first heavens and the first earth shall not be remembered, nor come into mind." The Psalmist, in anticipating the deliverance of Jesus Christ from the grave, well exclaims, "This is the Lord's doing; it is marvellous in our eyes. *This is the day* the Lord hath made; we will rejoice in it and be glad." Jesus Christ is greater than the Temple. He has power over all ordinances; he is not a servant, but a Son over his own house. The first creation had its Sabbath, and so has the new. It was the old Sabbath still, but in new and brighter vestments, the witness of new and brighter things, the servant of the redeeming God and King. We hail this distinctive honor of the Son of man and this distinctive badge of Christianity. It is meet that the Christian church be thus distinguished from the Jewish, and the Christian from the Jew.

What are the facts in relation to Sabbatical observances as they now exist? With very few exceptions,* the whole Christian world observes the

* The Mohammedans' Friday. Aside from these, and the Jews, who still profess to observe the seventh day, I am not informed that this latter

first day of the week. We observe this day; so did our fathers; and so did generations that preceded our fathers. How is this fact to be accounted for? We trace back this usage until we find it sanctioned by the churches in the early centuries of the Christian era,* by the apostles, and by our infallible Lord himself. We go back until we reach the period when a new and most gracious Dispensation first marked the moral history of man, and find that the introduction of it was commemorated by the observance of this same day. We go back farther still, and find the Jewish prophets anticipating this same observance; and are satisfied, that so far from detracting from the importance of the original institution, this Christian memorial gives magnitude and emphasis to the primeval Sabbath. It is scarcely credible that the King of Zion would have suffered his church, the very church which the Scriptures teach us is to exist in her greatest beauty under the Christian dispensation, and which is to extend her light and glory to the Gentiles, to have re-

observance extends beyond a few congregations in England proper, and these are chiefly confined to two in London. In our own country, it is limited to secessions from the Anabaptist churches, called "Seventh-day Baptists," or Sabbatarians.

* *Ignatius*, who was a companion of the Apostles, *Justin Martyr*, who flourished at the close of the first, and the beginning of the second century, *Irenæus*, a disciple of Polycarp, *Dionysius*, who lived in the time of Irenæus, and *Tertullian* and *Petavius* of the second century, all bear testimony to this observance of the first day of the week.

mained in darkness for eighteen centuries, in relation to the day on which she is to celebrate her religious festivals. It was of no small moment that her external institutions and ordinances should be rightly maintained; nor would the all-wise and all-gracious Founder of Christianity have left the weekly Sabbath, its great guardian and bulwark, without its proper place in the earth.

There is a single remark more in relation to the change of the day. It is not at all improbable that the *seventh day* Sabbath was confined to the *Jews alone.* Learned men have maintained that the Patriarchal Sabbath was the *first day of the week.* It was the *seventh* day, reckoning from the first of the creation; but it was the first day of time, as reckoned by man—the seventh day after God's six days' work; but it was the first day of the week from man's creation. Man, as before remarked, was not created until the close of the sixth day, so that the seventh from the creation, as reckoned by *him,* would be the first day of the week. We would not hastily endorse this representation; nor would we hastily reject it.* We can only say that if there be good reasons for it, the Christian Sabbath, according to the received chronology, occurs on the same day with the Patriarchal. There

* See Bedford's Chronology—Smith's Doctrine of the Church of England concerning the Lord's Day—Dr. Kennicott on the Offering of Abel and Cain—Jennings' Jewish Antiquities, and Belfrage on the Shorter Catechism in loc.

has been *no change* of the day, except that which began and ended with the Jewish dispensation. The Patriarchal Sabbath degenerated into idolatry; men became worshippers of the sun and moon and stars of heaven, and gave the name of their idols to the days of the week. The same divine wisdom that separated the race of Abraham from these idolatrous nations, also changed their Sabbath from the first day—the Sun's day, or Sunday, to the seventh day, that this peculiar people might have no sympathy with idolatrous nations. Nor is the thought an unpleasant one, that if the weekly Sabbaths which were observed before the time of the Mosaic law, were observed on the first and not on the seventh day of the week, the Christian Sabbath professedly occurs the same day of the week with the first Sabbath in Paradise.

There is one objection to this whole course of remark, and it is the same which perplexed the minds of Calvin and some of the reformers.* We

* We regret to find the name of John Calvin in favor of this error; yet it is quite obvious that the fact is so. In his commentary on Col. ii. 16 and 17, speaking of the discrimination of days, he says, "Talis partitio conveniabit Judæis, ut dies præceptos sancte colerent, ab aliis segregando. *Inter Christianos talis divisio cessavit.*" To make his meaning perfectly explicit, he states and answers the following objection. "Atque dicet quispiam, *nos* adhuc retinemus aliquam dierum observationem. Respondeo, Nos dies *niquaquam servare*, quasi inferiis aliqua sit religio, aut quasi *fas non sit tunc laborare;* sed respectum haberi politiæ et ordinis, non dierum."

will not now quote at length the passages in the New Testament to which it refers. The apostle Paul, both in his epistles to the Romans and the Colossians, appears to relax the obligations to this observance, and to leave it to the option of every man's conscience to observe it, or not, without being condemned by others, either in regard to the feasts of "the new moon, or of the *Sabbath-day*." In regard to this objection we say as follows. The phrase, the *Sabbath day*, in the language of the New Testament, uniformly denotes the Jewish, and not the Christian Sabbath. In the discussions

Calvin was imbued with the notion which I have heard half a century ago defended by a few New England divines—that all time is holy, and that what it is lawful to do on other days, is equally lawful on the Sabbath. In his Institutes, Lib. ii. ch. viii. p. 132 and 133, Editio Hackii, in his exposition of the fourth commandment, he says, "Cæterum non dubium, quin Domini Christi adventu, quod ceremoniale hic erat abolitum fuerit." It had been well had he stopped here. But he proceeds, "Ipse enam veritas est, cujus presentiæ figuræ evanescunt; corpus cujus aspectu, umbræ relinquuntur. Ipse, inquam, verum Sabbathi complementum.—Sabbathum umbram fuisse reifuturæ alibi scribit Apostolus; corpus extare in Christo, hoc est solidam veritatis substantiam quam illo loco bene explicavit. Ea *non uno die contenta est*, sed *toto vitæ nostræ cursu*, donec penitus nobismet ipsis mortui, *Dei vita impleantur*. A Christianis ergo abesse debet superstitiosa dierum observatio." In a subsequent section he says, summing up his views, "Summa sit; ut sub figura Judæis tradebatur veritas, ita nobis sine umbris commendatur; *primum*, ut perpetuum *tota vita* Sabbathismum meditemur a nostris operibus, quo Dominus in nobis per suum Spiritum operetur; *deinde*, ut piu operum Dei recognitione privatim se quisque, quobis vacat, diligenter exerceat; *tum etiam*, ut omnes simul legitimum Ecclesiæ ordinem, ad verbum audiendum, ad sacramentorum administrationem, a publicas orationes constitutum observemus; *tertio*, ne nobis subditos inhumaniter premamus." We take this last concession thankfully, while we differ from Calvin as to the conventional and orderly ob-

between the Jewish and Gentile converts, the great points of difference referred to by the apostles, related to *meats* and *days* that were peculiar to the ceremonial law. In addition to their weekly Sabbath, the Jews observed thirty-five days in the year, as sacred days, and some of these occurred on their weekly Sabbath. If the apostle here has reference to these numerous sacred days, he does *not* refer to the Christian Sabbath; or if he refers to their weekly Sabbath, it is *not* the Christian Sabbath of which he speaks. There were Jews converted to the gospel who kept the Jewish Sabbath; they did not neglect the Lord's day, but

servance of the Sabbath merely, and number ourselves with those who "diei sanctitatem animo retinere."

The same views are substantially expressed in the catechism of the Genevan church. See Opera Calv. tom. viii. p. 18 and 19.

M. Jubetne sex diebus laborare, ut septimo quiescamus?

P. Non simpliciter: verum sex dies hominum laboribus permittens septimum excipit, ut quieti destinetur.

M. An quemvis laborem nobis interdicit?

P. Hoc præceptum separatam et peculiarem rationem habet. Siquidem quibis observatio, pars est veterum ceremoniarum: itaque Christi adventu abrogata fuit.

M. Dicesne præceptum hoc ad Judaos proprie spectare, ideoque temporarium duntaxat fuisse?

P. Nempe: quatenus ceremoniale est.

M. Quid ergo? *Subestne aliquid præter ceremoniam?*

P. Tribus ex causis datum fuit.

M. Cedo mihi eas.

P. Ad spiritualem quietam figurandam; ad conservationem politiæ ecclesiasticæ; ad servorum sublerationem.

This whole subject has been discussed by Dr. John Owen, at great length, and by our distinguished countryman, Dr. Dwight, in his system of theology.

they kept the Jewish Sabbath also. All that Paul says in these passages is, Let them keep it, if they will. Let them not be disturbed in their prejudices. He allowed them this observance; but in so doing, relaxes not the permanent obligation of the Christian Sabbath.

But we are more concerned about the due *sanctification* of this day, than about the particular day of the week which ought to be thus sanctified. At its original institution, God "blessed the seventh day and sanctified it." Time has no holiness, except for the purposes for which it is consecrated, and in which it is employed. God has given it all the holiness of which it is capable; which is to be consecrated to his service. It is a rest from worldly labors for man and for beast, for the master and the servant, the mistress and the maid. It is a rest for kings and beggars, for men in power and meaner men; nor is it less a rest for the stranger than the home-born. They are quiet waters which flow from the sanctuary; tranquil scenes and verdant banks through which they flow, where there is no galley with oars, neither gallant ship shall pass thereby. Vitringa has a beautiful description of the manner in which this day is to be observed; it is contained in three words, and though in a foreign tongue, I may be allowed to repeat them. It is to be observed, says he, "cum *lœtitia*, *abstinentia ab opere*, aut *penitentia*:"—joy, rest, and piety. They are not days of idleness and listless repose, but days of thought, days of self-inspection, of devout and spiritual study of God's word, of meditation and prayer, and of the sacred observance of those domestic, social, and public institutions which are so indispensable to true religion. Nor are they days of gloom and sadness; nor yet of sport and pleasure; they are cheerful days, and days when the heart is lighted up with smiles. The objects and pursuits of the Sabbath are delightfully congenial with man's wants as a sinner and a sufferer; they bring peace to the troubled and balm to the bleeding bosom; they tune the harp that would otherwise be hung upon the willows; and because they tell of him who is the resurrection and the life, and the first-fruits of them that slept, they pass silently over the earth strewing flowers upon the grave.

It is greatly to be regretted that the teachings and the example of some of the best of men have left so deep an impression that a cheerful spirit is not in keeping with the design of this sacred day. There was a rigor required of the Jews in their observance of this day, that was altogether ceremonial and peculiar to themselves, and as we have already seen enjoined, not in the fourth commandment, but in subsequent requisitions. The fourth commandment requires simply that it be regarded not as one of the working days of men, and as a day inseparable from religious reminiscences, and sanctified and blessed of God. The later Jews had put an erroneous construction upon the exaction it made upon them, and these errors were more than once rectified by the Saviour. It was an error in the Puritans of New England, not that they observed the Sabbath too religiously, but that they threw over it the unnatural and factitious gloom of blue habits and blue laws. It was more natural for them to do so than for any other men in the world; because, in the land from which they were exiled, they had been scourged and driven by cruel and sacrilegious laws to unseemly mirth and public sports on this God's holy day. Human nature is prone to extremes; if we ourselves were bound by royal proclamation, like the "Book of Sports," in the reigns of James I. and the first Charles, requiring us, on pains and penalties, to profane the Sabbath, we should verge to the opposite extreme, and do just as the Puritans did. But it is an error. Why a sombre cloud should be superinduced over the hours of this gladsome day, I cannot tell, unless it be a trick of the devil to render it a weariness and make it unwelcome to the young. If we cannot make God's claims palatable to the unrenewed heart, we need not clothe them with uncomeliness. If the voluptuary smiles in the indulgence of his sensual pleasures; the avaricious in the accumulation of his wealth; the men of ambition in their honor and elevation; why may not the Christian indulge in smiles of complacency, and delight in this day of joy and triumph? There are trains of thought awakened in the Christian mind on the return of this delightful day, which are sometimes so full of love, gratitude, peace, hope, and joyous expectation, that if he were told he might not *smile*, he would feel that he must stop his ears against the gladdest tidings that ever greeted fallen humanity; close his eyes on one of the bright spots in the wilderness; and turn from the sacred and cheering fragrance that had been shed upon his weary spirit, and made him long for heaven. While the Sabbath is the most sacred retreat from the noise, and bustle, and folly of the world, it is the most glad retreat. The feet that tread it, and the hands that open the doors to its altars might well drop with myrrh and their fingers with sweet-smelling myrrh.

God has been liberal to men of secular time. Six days out of seven he allows them to employ in the pursuit of things seen and temporal. There is no earthly want, or sympathy, or secular relation and anxiety, which may not then be regarded and cared for with interest and diligence. It is but one out of seven that he asks for himself, as separated from the pursuits of earth. Time is his, and men are his creatures; nor may his right be questioned to prescribe the portion which they shall employ in his service. He claims the Sabbath as his own; he calls it "The Sabbath of the Lord thy God." Men may not encroach upon it for their own purposes without robbing him. The whole of it belongs to him from beginning to end, claimed by his law, consecrated by his example, devoted to his glory, and distinguished by his blessing. No man, and no body of men, no human policy or power, either by their laws or their usages, may ever countervail the appointment or the objects of this day of holy rest. God has marked it in the history of the world, as a blessing to our race. Whatever is instructive in his truth, and urgent in the motives to holiness which that truth presents; whatever is winning in his love, and constraining in his authority, is thrown into the influence of this sacred day. All that is effective in the means of grace and salvation which he has revealed; all that is beautiful in the simplicity, the symmetry, the harmony of this divine arrangement for the salvation of men; all that magnifies and honors this redemption, is inseparable from the Sabbath. Where the Sabbath is not found, these things do not exist; where the Sabbath is perverted, they are the savor of death unto death. The pivot on which this moral machinery turns, the shaft that impels it is the Sabbath. Everything secular is put at rest by it; everything that is spiritual is set in motion. The church militant and the church triumphant—parents and teachers and ministers—men and angels, are then awake and in earnest in urging the claims of holiness on this lost world; while God the Spirit, who breathed on the first chaos, and put his seal on the first Sabbath, bows his heavens to dwell with men.

We plead for a sacred observance of this day, and these are the grounds on which we rest our plea. Permanent reform cannot be secured except by religious principles and motives. There are *temporal* advantages arising from this observance; but they hold a secondary place. If God's authority and love do not influence men and communities to keep the Sabbath holy, nothing will influence them.

This land, though exemplary in this observance compared with other lands, is not guiltless. There are individual, domestic, and social violations of this day, for which there is no excuse; and they are the more aggravated by the great goodness of God toward us as a people, as well as by the fact that inviolate and blessed Sabbaths were the heritage we received from our fathers. We regret to say there are violations of this day sanctioned by law, which are "reproach to any people." They are of long standing, and deliberately persevered in, in opposition to the respectful and urgent remonstrances by the friends of the Sabbath throughout the land. The legalized transportation of the mail on the Sabbath, the opening of post-offices, the consequent disregard of public worship, and the attendant and increasing flood of immorality which rolls over the land, are national sins which still stand registered against us.* And it is a sin for which there is no excuse. There never was any excuse; but since the introduction of telegraphic communications, fitted to meet special emergencies, one would think there is no apology left for this national desecration.

Whether this sacred day is destined to contempt by the great mass of the inhabitants of this land, is yet a doubtful problem. It is by no means improbable that the voice of God and the voice of

* In the year 1829, *four hundred and sixty-seven* petitions were presented to the Congress of the United States, from every part of the Union, signed by individuals of different religious denominations, and containing the names of the most active, enterprising, and intelligent of our citizens, praying for a repeal of the law which sanctions the transportation of the mail on the Lord's-day. There never was a more delightful union of sentiment and feeling than was expressed in these petitions; nor is it easy to find in any of the more elaborate dissertations upon the sacredness and importance of the Sabbath, stronger reasons, or reasons expressed with greater sincerity and earnestness in favor of the proposed reform. The prayer of the memorialists was not granted; God's day is not yet rescued from this national desecration. Extracts from these memorials may be seen in "An account of Memorials presented to Congress by numerous friends of their country and its institutions; praying that the mails may not be transported, nor post-offices kept open on the Sabbath," printed in New York, 1829. This valuable pamphlet lays before the public a list of places from which memorials were received, extracts from the petitions, selected names of petitioners, and a few concluding remarks. It is an anonymous pamphlet; but came from the pen of the late Jeremiah Evarts, of Boston.

experience may be disregarded. There are some bright signs of the times in this particular, and there are some dark ones. The successful efforts to induce the proprietors of steamboats and railroads to honor this day of God, are full of encouragement, and demand our thanks; while there are encroachments upon its sacredness, especially in our cities, which fill us with concern.

The danger to which we are exposed, is to convert the day, after the morning service of the sanctuary is concluded, into a day of pleasure and amusement. We are told from the press that it is a *holiday;* that it has no more *solemnity* than other days; and that its only peculiarity is rest from toil, a festival, and a day of pleasure.* We have been publicly appealed to, to fall in with the usages of Continental Europe, and after the hour of prayer to resume the business of the week, and more than its secular pleasures. We have been told that the rigid opinions concerning the Sabbath are not entertained by Christians, "if we except English Protestants, Scotch Presbyterians, and their American descendants;" that "Sunday fairs and markets are customary on the other side of the channel, and were so in Britain before the time of Cromwell;" that "the Sunday abroad is usually divided between the services of religion, the duties of labor, and the objects of

* See Westminster Review for Oct. 1850.

recreation;" and that, "even in the city of Calvin, Geneva, the theatre is open on a Sunday evening." This able writer must have received a large *bonus* from some Sabbath-breaking establishment in order to have embodied so much sophistry and weakness on the wrong side of the question. We can only now reply to these ensnaring temptations to evil, that they indicate no small alarm at the efforts that are making on the other side of the water to restore the influence of the Lord's day; and that if a cheerful and religious observance of it is one of the peculiarities of this land, we glory in the peculiarity, and humbly pray that it may be perpetuated. We wish it were so uniformly, and everywhere. But we have our fears for the rising generation, lest they should become a generation of Sabbath-breakers. And should this exposure increase, this one thing is left us; and it may be the only thing that is left us—it is FOR THE CHURCH OF THE LIVING GOD TO REMAIN FIRM, CONSISTENT AND EXEMPLARY FRIENDS OF THE SABBATH. Whoever else may profane it, and for whatever purposes, let the professed disciples of Jesus Christ *with their families*, show the world that they have a strong sense of the obligation to obey the command, "Remember the Sabbath-day to keep it holy!" I say these things as one whose sun is going down, and I would respectfully ask that they receive solemn consideration. Disobedience to this command will incur God's displeasure; obedience to it will receive his marked approbation. Augmented wickedness, desolating calamity, and gloomy foreboding on the one hand, and public virtue, prosperity and happiness on the other, will mark our future history, as we obey or disobey this precept.

Good principles and good morals can no more exist without religion, than religion can exist without the Sabbath. Blot out this sacred day, and in a quarter of a century we become pagans. An infidel literature and a cultivated taste may preserve us from abjectness and degradation; but our iniquity will be full. Such apprehensions are to the last degree painful. As any man values his immortality, let him not profane the Sabbath. There is no one external observance that exerts so powerful an influence on moral character and immortal hopes as a sacred regard to the Sabbath. It is the salt of the earth, and the light of the world. Its price is far above rubies.

Little do we know how to value this day of God, with all its quiet and heaven-like serenity, and its attractive summons to the assemblies of his saints. Sweet type of that rest which shall never pass away till it is superseded by its glorious ante-type, where the nations of the saved walk in the light of his countenance! Delightful thought! that the dawning of the *first Sabbath* was a light that shall never go down. From generation to generation it has transmitted, and will yet transmit its joys, until the joyous praise of men on the earth unite with the sweeter harps of men in heaven, ascribing everlasting honor to the God of the spirits of all flesh, and the Lord of the Sabbath-day.

CHAPTER VIII.

The First Revolt in Heaven.

Men who "live and breathe in the lighter literature of our age," are very apt to imbibe a disrelish for the more weighty truths of God's word. In the series of thoughts which we are called on to present, there must be truths from which the human mind naturally revolts; because there are truths humbling to the pride of man. If in exhibiting some of these, we find fewer enchanting scenes to look upon, and fewer stimulants to an excited imagination, we shall find *God's truth*, and find it in its own heavenly dress.

Those great events by which the more weighty truths of God's word are enforced, lose none of their importance in their ascending series; rather is the importance of them increased as they remount even beyond the history of our own race. In the present condition of the universe, its inhabitants, so far as they are known to us, consist of angels, men, and devils; there was a time when there were no devils. It is not permitted us to know how early the angelic race came into existence. This much has been revealed, that there was such a race prior to the race of man, whom the all-wise and sovereign Creator was pleased to regard, in some respects, with distinguishing favor. They were the elder family of the universal Father, the first-born sons of light, the first expressions of his infinite power and love. When this material universe was created, they were there; and when the Eternal and Omnipotent One "stretched out the 'line" upon this earth, and fastened its foundations, and raised the dome of this wondrous temple, they were probably the spectators of this wondrous work. They were a superior order of beings; not formed from dust like the first man, but spiritual in their nature and advanced to glorious dignity. They are styled "thrones, dominions, principalities, and powers," because they are the ministers of God's providence in the government of this lower world, princes under him, ranged in different orders, and each class acting within its appropriate sphere. It was no infected parentage from which they sprang. They were streams from a pure fountain; rays from the "Father of lights;" stars that reflected the purity and brightness of the uncreated sun.

And because they were thus exalted and holy, they were happy. Their inheritance was rich and unfading; it was the heaven where they dwelt; the love and fellowship of their Creator, and unrestrained access to this fountain of joy. Employed in services that elevated them in knowledge, holiness, and enjoyment, as high as their created natures would admit, they lived only to love and serve God, "swift to do his will, hearkening to the voice of his word." They were more than servants; they were sons. More were they even than sons; they were princes and courtiers of heaven—illustrious and immortal spirits—attendants in God's own chamber of presence. We have no knowledge of their numbers, except that "thousands" ministered unto the Ancient of Days, and "ten thousand times ten thousand stood before him;" and that "they are all ministering spirits sent forth to minister to them who shall be heirs of salvation."

In proportion to the magnitude of God's plan, it was important to make an early disclosure of the great principles of his moral government. The angelic race were created under liabilities inseparable from their nature. They were to pass through a process similar to that through which all intelligent creatures pass, and stand or fall, as they sustain this appointed ordeal. They held their existence *under law*, and were subjected to a probationary course, on a larger scale than that subsequently appointed to man; and their starting-point was " the high and holy place." Exalted as they were, it was the prerogative of the sovereign Lawgiver to give law to them as his subjects; and, in the event of their disobedience, to punish them according to their desert. The divine government is, and must be impartial, and impose its obligations on every class of intelligent beings. Could we " make the tour of the universe," we should not find a race of beings who are not bound to love God with all their hearts, and their fellow-existences as themselves; and who, in default thereof, are not subjected to penalty. It does not appear that the angelic race mingled with any other portion of the population of the universe; nor that they were freighted with any other hopes than their own; nor that in making shipwreck of their own, they involved any others beside themselves. Multitudes of them were obedient to the law, and retained their integrity; others, and great multitudes, sinned and fell.

It is a fact of some interest, that sin was not introduced into the universe by man. Fearful was the responsibility of the first sin. Man, in the progress of time, was induced to join in this foul revolt; but it was not first concocted in the human bosom. Man did not exist when the order, beauty, and blessedness which reigned throughout the divine empire, were first disturbed, and the arm of rebellion was first raised against the government of the Most High. This primeval revolt was the beginning of sorrows, and aimed at a radical revolution in the empire of the rightful Sovereign; but it was the work of another race. Says the Apostle Peter, "God spared not *the angels* that sinned." The Apostle Jude also speaks of the *angels*, who "kept not their first estate, but left their own habitation." The particular act of sin by which they fell, is not revealed. Very many are the conjectures in relation to it; but the most we know is contained in that representation of the Apostle in which he speaks of the danger of being "lifted up with *pride*, and falling into the condemnation of the *devil*." But whatever may have been the particular act, it was disobedience to the will of their sovereign Creator, and a transgression of his law.

There were several things that greatly aggravated their crime. They "could not sin at a lower rate," than of set purpose and wilfully. They were angels, and there was no weakness or ignorance in their nature. They were too intelligent to have been imposed upon and deceived. They were their own tempters; for there was none to tempt them, as they afterwards tempted our first parents. There was no stumbling-block in heaven; God had made them exalted, holy, and happy; nor was the service required of them hard and unreasonable; nor could they ever do too much for Him who had made them what they were. God had not been a wilderness to them, but the dispenser of their comforts, their portion, and joy; nor could they have rebelled against him from any other spirit than a desperate determination to have their own will in opposition to his, to raise the standard of revolt, and at all hazards to establish a kingdom of their own. They forsook their Father's house, merely from a revolting and proud spirit. They "sinned in heaven, the last place in the universe where there was any excuse for sin." They sinned as proudly, as enviously, as obdurately, as maliciously as it was possible to sin. And they sinned in view of the most fearful con sequences, without the least expectation of reprieve or hope of pardon, and with no other design than that of perpetuating their hostility to God through the succeeding ages of time, and the unwasting ages of eternity.

Such was their first revolt,—the first revolt in the universe of God. Probably there is no world in which a revolt could have taken place with more fearful results, and which could have made more exacting demands of the resources of the all-knowing and all-sufficient Deity. It was a revolt which would hold on its course for countless ages; which would be an example to all worlds; the consequences of which would be seen and spoken of in the endless future; and from whose unfathomable depths, the voice of instruction would go up that would make the ear of him that heareth it to tingle. Well did the prophet exclaim, "How art thou fallen, O Lucifer, son of the morning!" When Babylon fell, the merchants of the earth wept and mourned over her, and the kings of the earth stood afar off, and said, "Alas! alas! that great city Babylon, that mighty city! for in one hour she is made desolate." Thus might the intelligent universe, standing afar off, have lifted up their voice and wept over the fall of this mighty and exalted race—these bright and morning-stars, displaced and wandering throughout the vast expanse, disregarding the law which binds them to their Great Centre—falling promiscuously, and sinking to "the blackness of darkness!"

The *consequences* of this revolt were serious. It was a fearful fall, and a fearful punishment. God measures the punishment of sin by its true and proper demerit; and therefore we are told that "he *spared not* the angels that sinned." Though *angels*, he did not spare them. Though his first-born children, though so munificently endowed and highly exalted, though so holy and happy, he could not endure such a revolt as this. Though they were the most exalted of his creation, and the noblest image of their Creator, and though, if any creatures can be dear to God and the objects of his love, they were so endeared; yet sooner would he abandon his throne than not exact from such deliberate, scornful, and malicious rebels, the utmost they deserved. He was the God of love; but there were others to be cared for beside these reckless traitors to his government. He had no malice in his bosom, no spirit of revenge to gratify, and no pleasure in their death; yet well did he know that any departure from strict justice in this early instance of rebellion, would be an impeachment of his rectitude, a blow against his government which it could never survive. His truth, his justice, his holiness, and all the glory which illuminated heaven, would have vanished into night, had he hesitated to execute his law, and reward these early and invincible offenders, every one according to his deeds.

The process with them was summary and decisive. He began the work of punitive justice by *banishing them from heaven.* Distinguished as they were, since they would be disobedient and rebellious, heaven was no place for them; they could no longer remain in that holy and happy world, and companions of that holy and happy society. Their sin was a complete and everlasting forfeiture of all the blessedness of that glorious state and place. Heaven was too pure and holy to contain such offenders; for there shall in no wise enter into it anything that defileth. They must go out. They must depart accursed. They could not be suffered to be there to awaken disgust and abhorrence, nor to become the tempters of the unfallen. And this decree was executed without delay. There was no inquiry instituted; no trial, and no defence. God saw the crime, and he cast them out. He gave them no space for repentance; for the first sin he cast them out, without allowing them time or opportunity for a second revolt this side their everlasting retribution.

Not only did God banish them from heaven, but he *cast them down to hell.* There was no such place as hell in the universe, until the fall of the angelic race. Then it was the mighty Architect laid the foundations and built the walls of this lurid, fiery prison, and there treasured up his magazines of wrath. Far away, where the light of mercy never shines, did he fit up those dark and melancholy regions—that wretched state of existence—that world of desolation and despair, the very thought of which awakens anguish, and fills the mind with horror.

This horrid, everlasting *hell* now became the habitation of these fallen spirits. They left their own habitation of holiness and joy for this deep dwelling of pollution and wickedness, of mourning, lamentation and woe. They were driven from the face of God into the burning lake; and now, that many a thousand century has passed away, there they still lie engulfed in flames, and the smoke of their torments ascends forever and ever.

This may seem to us a severe sentence. But God will vindicate this procedure in that day when he shall judge the world in righteousness. We are told in the Scriptures, that he "delivered them to chains of darkness to be reserved unto *judgment*." What the judgment is, to which they are thus reserved, we learn from the more explicit representation of the apostle Jude, "The angels which kept not their first estate, but left their own habitation, he hath reserved in everlasting chains under darkness unto the judgment of *the great day*." Creatures may not hold the great God accountable; but the great God holds himself accountable even to creatures. His plans are vast and comprehensive plans. The fact here revealed is, that the fallen angels are bound over as criminals, and reserved to take their public trial at the day of judgment, when the sentence will be openly pronounced, and finally executed. I say finally executed; for, though their doom is inevitable, for wise reasons God defers the extremity of their punishment. Other parts of the sacred writings instruct us, that these apostate spirits are still invisible agents in this world; that they are conversant with men; exert their power and influence upon the human mind; and as "roaring lions, go about seeking whom they may devour." God is pleased to enlarge the bounds of their prison, and give them, for a time, the opportunity of employing their power and malice in opposing the purposes of his love to men, and in attempting their destruction. But they cannot go beyond the length of their chain. They are prisoners of justice, and bound over to the judgment. On that great and last day, when the mystery of God shall be finished, and that Saviour, whom these apostate spirits refused to acknowledge, shall be exalted and glorified; when the trumpet shall sound, and the voice of the archangel shall awake the dead; God shall call them forth to receive their doom, to be judged and sentenced to woes as fearful as was the distinguished rank from which they fell.

Such was the first revolt in the universe, and such its penal consequences. And while it is among the "first things" recorded in the sacred volume, it was recorded for our instruction. The first great moral lesson it inculcates is, that *sin produces a great and deplorable change in the character and condition of its perpetrators.* This is not mere theory, based upon the nature of sin and the character of a perfect moral government; it stands out before us in melancholy history. The angels who kept not their first estate, once belonged to the highest, holiest, and most happy order of beings in the universe; now, they are the most abject, the most base, and the most miserable.

Once, they were amiable and lovely, worthy of confidence, the ornament and comfort of a pure society, and resplendent jewels in the bright crown of heaven; now, they are malevolent spirits, lying spirits, unclean spirits, tormentors, murderers, and foul devils, roaming over the earth like so many ravening wolves, or shut up in their impure and odious prison. Once, they were the examples and patrons of all that is holy and excellent; now, they are the subtle, indefatigable, and vile tempters to evil, spreading sin, misery, and destruction, as far and wide as the length of their chains permits them to rove. From angels, lovely and honored, refulgent with the beauties of holiness, and happy as their Maker's love could make them, they have become horrid, hateful, miserable devils. "Fools make a mock at sin." Yet this is its accursed work. It never, in the end, does better than this. The man who trifles with sin would do well to think of the guilt and punishment, the horror and despair which are its consequences and punishment.

Another lesson plainly taught by this revolt is, that there *is no inconsistency between the perfect goodness of God, and the everlasting punishment of all who revolt from his authority.* Not a few have thought that the infinite goodness of God would not allow him to make even the vilest and most ill-deserving of his creatures eternally miserable. Instead of this, would it not be more logical to say, that if God is good, then whatever he does is consistent with his goodness? All objections against his conduct are objections against his goodness. His character and his conduct must be in keeping with each other; so that when once facts teach us what his conduct is, we cannot avoid the inference that it is consistent with his character. It does not appear to us a difficult matter to show *à priori* that goodness punishes; but the *à posteriori* argument is still stronger when we can show that goodness has punished. The man is a fool whose logic leads him to quarrel with facts. If we inquire whether a being of perfect goodness can inflict endless suffering on the incorrigible; our inquiry is answered, not by theory, but *by facts.* One fact outweighs a thousand theories. The fallen angels are lost. There are no devils in heaven. God has already cast them into hell, there to remain forever. I say *forever*, because when time shall be no more, the sentence will be pronounced, "Depart from me, ye cursed, into *everlasting* fire, *prepared for the* devil and his angels." There is not an argument in favor of the doctrine of universal salvation, which is not repelled and refuted by this *solemn and affecting fact.* Is it said that no sin can deserve eternal punishment; the assertion is *contrary to fact.* Is it said, that God is too good thus to punish; this is also contrary to *fact.*

Is it said that his mercy will not suffer him thus to punish; this is also directly in the face of this *plain fact.* Is it said that these apostate spirits sinned with peculiar aggravation, that they became real devils, and though *they* may be eternally punished, this affords no proof that any of the *family of Adam* will fall under a like condemnation? This is giving up the whole argument, and conceding at once to the position that it is not inconsistent with the perfect character of God to punish *some* of his creatures with everlasting destruction. And if not inconsistent with his character to punish *them*, why should it be inconsistent with his character to punish the incorrigible of our fallen race? Did he "not spare" these once exalted, once lovely, once beloved attendants on his throne; and will he spare abject, rebellious, incorrigible men? Did he cast these once glorious and glorified inhabitants of heaven down to hell; and will he not cast into hell incorrigible man who is a worm, and the son of man who is a worm? What a death-blow is such a fact as this to all the presumptuous hopes of impenitent men! The truth has been revealed, and it must be proclaimed, that "the wicked shall be turned into hell, and all the nations that forget God." Those who live and die in sin, cannot hope to be spared, if God did not spare the angels who fell. Though they were dear to him as the bright seraphs who were once around his throne, he will cast them down.

Another lesson taught by this first revolt is, *that no being is safe unless he is upheld by God.* It is very difficult to conceive how angels fell, unless they were dependent on God for their continued integrity. And did not God mean to teach us this truth, by their fall? Who may affirm that his power was not as necessary for their preservation as for their original existence? What were they unsupported by him? and what power but his could perpetuate their integrity? They were not incorruptible, though once uncorrupted. Nor let the truth be forgotten, that their melancholy fall teaches us that no created mind and no created holiness in the universe can live without God. God alone exists, and is holy, uncaused and unsustained. Left to themselves, the holiest are unsafe. So long as they retained their integrity, angels were kept by divine power. It is this that has kept Gabriel from falling, and keeps him now. It is this that kept Paul and keeps him still. Angels and saints are kept in holiness only by the effectual power of God. Proud man boasts of his free agency; but there is no free agency in the universe that is safe, unless it is in God's keeping. Man's is safe only when he is humble. His dependence on all-powerful grace is one of the sweetest truths of the Bible, and is most deeply felt when he has most of the spirit of that sacred book. Take from us our dependence on God, and we must despair. Who can hope to *become* holy without him, if, without him, angels fell? Who, without him, can hope to be preserved in holiness, if angels were not thus preserved?

Another lesson taught by this revolt, is the *inscrutable sovereignty of God in the dispensations of his grace.* All the angelic race were probably created at the same time. They had great capacities for holiness and happiness, were all perfectly holy and happy, and equally beloved by God. And in this high, holy, and happy state, they remained for a period of time unknown to us. But there was a moment when they began to differ, and some of them remained angels and others became devils. And in these two different characters they have remained ever since, and will remain, throughout eternity. Who does not in this single fact *see and adore the inscrutable, and yet the holy sovereignty of the Most High?* Why this difference? Why were some upheld, and others left to themselves and permitted to fall? And after they had fallen, why was a Saviour provided for an inferior race, and not provided for those who were once so exalted, and holy, and happy, and honored? O, it is past finding out! Why was it? Hell asks the question, *Why?* Earth responds to the dark inquiry, *Why?* And heaven answers; and says to all the unhallowed curiosity of the created universe, *Be still and know that I am God! Have I not a right to do what I will with mine own? Hath not the potter power over the clay of the same lump to make one vessel unto honor and another unto dishonor?* I veil my face here, and bow in silence at his throne. This is his royal prerogative as the Creator and owner of angels and men. "Who art thou, O man, that repliest against God!" The sovereignty of God, therefore, is not only a doctrine that is taught in Scripture, but is founded in fact, and acted out in the history of a race besides our own. It is no theory, but a series of *facts*, designed to wake up the slumbering minds of men, and fix them upon his deep designs, manifold wisdom, and wonderful government. Nor is it a mere theory with which so many contend, but a series of facts, with which, when they contend, they are only fighting against God.

Another lesson which the revolt of angels inculcates is, *the high vantage-ground occupied by the human family under the Mediatorial reign of Jesus Christ, compared with the purely legal economy to which the angelic race were subjected.* We are sometimes tempted to complain that we were not created angels. Let us be thankful that we are *men.* How long the period of probation allotted to angels continued, God has not been pleased to reveal. It is not, however, until after the resurrection and ascension of Christ, and after his exaltation to "be head over all principality and power," that we hear anything about "elect angels." And are we not justified in concluding that God stands pledged to keep those who did not join in the first revolt, from falling at some future time. Their confirmation was the reward of long-tried obedience. For four thousand years it is probable they thus remained *probationers*, and during the whole of this period, *one sin* would have exiled them from heaven, and cast them down to hell. Nor was the issue of their probation dependent on the integrity of some one of their number, less likely to fall than others; each individual of that angelic race was to stand or fall *for himself*. Where then is the man who, under a clear view of these responsibilities, does not see that he has privileges above the angelic race?

More than this. When the angels fell, they fell irrecoverably and without hope. No mediator was found to "take upon him the nature of angels." No Saviour was thought of, and no glory of the Lord shone round about that fallen race to soothe their fears and tell them of the mighty Deliverer. But he who "took not on him the nature of angels," in boundless condescension and love, clothed himself with the "seed of Abraham." The dark and immeasurable ruin that spread before our race after the fall, was lighted up, not by some faint and twinkling ray of hope, but by the "Sun of Righteousness" rising with "healing in his beams," and in full-orbed glory. The door of life, shut by the first man, was opened by the second. The condemnation is for one offence, the justification is from many.

Nor is this all. The angels, though created holy, had, as we have already seen, no promise that they should not fall. But man is *confirmed in holiness from the hour he first believes in Jesus Christ*; and from that hour is in an infinitely more safe condition than angels before their apostasy. They held all their holiness and happiness by an uncertain tenure; while believers in the gospel hold theirs upon a surer covenant and upon "better promises." The irrecoverable fall of angels is the only instance of irrecoverable falling from grace on the records of the universe. Man fell, but man was restored; believing man has the promise that he shall never so fall as finally to be cast away. "If when they were enemies they were reconciled to God by the death of his Son, much more, being reconciled, shall they be saved by his life." When God gave them to his Son, before the foundation of the world, the guaranty was given to him, that they "should never perish" —that "none should pluck them out of his hand" —and that of all which he had given him, he should "lose nothing, but should raise it up again at the last day." Who then will utter the inconsiderate wish, O that I had never been born of woman! So thought not the proud seraph who fell. No work of God interests the angelic race so much as this great work of redeeming mercy. They were astonished spectators of the creation and fall of man; and they are admiring spectators of his recovery. Let the reader be reminded, that the tidings of mercy denied to fallen angels, are proclaimed to *man.* We may not say to angels as we may to sinners of this fallen race, that there is One who is able and willing, and faithful to save them. *Men* have a *birthright* to the offers of this redemption, because they are men. Like Esau, there may be those who profanely "sell that birthright" for a "mess of pottage;" and hereafter, like angels that are fallen, seek a place for repentance, and never find it, "though sought carefully and with tears." O then, by the terrors of that day in which they shall be judged; by the glories of that heaven which they despised, and can never regain; by the riches of that grace never offered to them, be entreated to fall down before that Saviour, and own him as your Lord and King.

What suppose ye those fallen spirits think of *man's* rejection of such offers of mercy? And what, suppose ye, those *unfallen* ones think of *man's* hesitation and delay to accept the mighty Saviour? Were they permitted to stand in the place of those of us who are ambassadors for Christ, how would they plead with the infatuated sons and daughters of men, by all the folly, and ingratitude, and eternal agony of their apostate and lost companions, to beware how they "neglect so great salvation!" And do they not thus minister? Happy in being humble and obedient, like their divine Lord, they are even "now in the midst of this fallen world as one that serveth." They hover over the pillow of the thoughtless sinner, when he sleeps; they hover around the sanctuary where he worships; they hover over the volume that he reads, to see if there be no repenting prodigal that may be setting his face toward his father's house. Even now, as the reader closes the present chapter, they wait to see if they cannot discover some victory of the cross over ignorance, sorrow, and sin—some sighings of a broken and contrite heart—some dawnings of hope—some babe-like lispings of the new and everlasting song—some one returning sinner, whose repentance will fill *them* with transport, and *heaven* with praise.

CHAPTER IX.

The First Deceiver.

Up to the events of which we speak in the present chapter, everything on this earth was bright and gladsome. Infinite all-sufficiency and loveliness had called into existence this vast and beautiful creation, and by the same infinite power and goodness, formed a race holy as God is holy. We have seen him instituting and consecrating the domestic relations, and giving to this new-created world, that day of rest, of light, and of fellowship with heaven; thus setting this earth in motion under influences which may well be supposed, would secure its progress and its perpetuity in holiness. Heaven itself could scarcely present a scene of more exquisite beauty and loveliness, than these bright outlines of this early and unsullied creation.

But in an evil hour, a dark and heavy cloud is superinduced over all this matchless beauty; its light fades, its varied and splendid coloring becomes obscured. The "six days' labor of a God" is spoiled; and from that hour to the present, every successive generation of men bears witness that some foul enemy has done this.

Among the "first things" therefore, which we are contemplating, is this First Deceiver. We have already adverted to the apostasy of a part of the angelic race; it was the great head and leader of this revolt who became the tempter of man.

We are not now about to enter into any philosophical disquisition upon the origin of man's apostasy. The researches of men into the cause of this lamentable fact are almost as many as they are useless. Their explanations are profound and ingenious; but very many of them, instead of relieving the subject of difficulty, render it more complicated and embarrassed. The Mosaic narrative is intelligible to a child; if God had desired we should know more, more would have been revealed. So far as that narrative instructs us, the thought of man's rebellion is one which originated in the mind of another; one to which he was tempted. Our object is to speak of the tempter.

It has been remarked by a learned commentator upon the book of Job, that "men who do not believe in the existence of the devil, do not believe in the existence of God." With those who receive the sacred writings as the rule of their faith, there can be no doubt of the existence and agency of this Evil Spirit. It is no uncommon thing for writers, both of a philosophical and an imaginative cast of mind, to speak familiarly of "the principle of evil," of the "genius of destruction;" as though by these, and such like designations, they conveyed some intelligible and well-defined thought. The Scriptures never utter themselves in this mystic language; they speak of the inciting cause both of evil and good; but they lead our minds to distinct and responsible *personalities*. The account which they give of the common enemy of mankind is as explicit and intelligible as that which they give of any other person, or agent. They give us his origin and history; they delineate his character, and set before us the great objects he is pursuing; they premonish the world of his subtlety and wiles; and they distinctly foretell his overthrow, and the triumphs of the mighty Conqueror by whom he is to be cast down. They give him his distinctive names and appellations, every one of them marking his distinctive qualities. "There is no characteristic property, or feature of distinct personality, and nothing which constitutes personal individuality in any case," which they do not attribute to this great author of wickedness. The teachings on this subject in the book of Genesis alone are as explicit as language can make them. It were to make a romance of the Bible to call them allegory. If the representations in the third chapter of this book respecting the serpent and the woman be a mere allegory, then is the Saviour there promised an allegory; the whole revelation of God is an allegory; man's apostasy is an allegory; his redemption an allegory; the final judgment, heaven and hell, are allegories.

Great as are the power and influence which the adversary exerts, they are mainly dependent on his subtlety and craft. "Now the serpent was more *subtle* than any beast of the field." His *character as the Deceiver*, and the *extent of his deceptions*, are the two leading thoughts, therefore, to which our remarks are now directed.

In turning our attention to HIS CHARACTER AS THE DECEIVER, we may not venture into the fairy land of conjecture and imagination. The sacred records alone furnish the clue by which our pursuit may be safely governed; and with these lights, we may ferret even the tortuous and slimy path of the serpent. These infallible records speak of him as one who "goes forth to *deceive the nations*;" as "the devil, and Satan, which *deceiveth the whole world*." The character of this prince of darkness is to deceive; to mislead the mind; to cause it to err; to induce it to believe what is false, or disbelieve what is true; to impose upon it by stratagem and artifice.

In proof of this position, we advert, in the first instance, to the fact that *his agency is concealed.*

For this concealment he is peculiarly fitted, as he belongs to that class of beings, who, from their spirituality, are invisible. He is the head of those high and apostate spirits "who kept not their first estate." With the exception of those instances in which, to answer some wise purpose of a righteous providence, he assumes a material form, he is as invisible to men as those angels who never fell, and all of whom are "ministering spirits to them that shall be heirs of salvation." It is not the open assault of a manly foe that men encounter when they enter the conflict with this "angel of the bottomless pit;" but the stealthy assassin whose step is in the dark, and whose presence is indicated only by the blow he strikes. The best, as well as the worst of men, are not always aware of the subtlety with which he is lurking about their path. There is no bosom so pure, but in an evil hour, he may insensibly invade its tranquillity; no sanctuary so holy, but he may pollute it with sacrilegious, though unseen hands. And what is true of himself, as the head and chief of all evil spirits, is true of the "legion," who act in concert with him. They are all perpetually employed, but with impervious silence and secrecy. We live on the verge of the world of spirits; good and evil angels are always hovering about us, though unperceived. It is the treachery of this arch deceiver, that he should persuade multitudes who are themselves the victims of his treachery, that his agency is visionary and unreal; so that, although his influence is so extensively felt, it should not be suspected. Amid the noise and bustle of the world, and amid the retirement and silence of the closet; at home and abroad, on the land and on the ocean, by day and by night, he is exerting his power; yet no touch feels, no ear hears, no eye sees him. Behind every scene of iniquity, he is the dark mover. His stratagems are often discovered; we find the gin, but we cannot detect the fowler. Millions writhe under the wounds they receive from his hand, but the hand that inflicts them is undetected. The pit itself may sometimes be left uncovered, but never the foe that digs it.

Nor is it his *agency* only that is concealed; he conceals *his object.* What this is, his deep malignity leaves us at no loss to determine. When he fell from his primeval integrity, from a pure spirit in the heavenly court he became a reprobate in the world of darkness; from an angel, he became an incorrigible, irrecoverable fiend. Every development of his character has been indicative of his fell malice and revenge. We have become acquainted with his object, not from himself. From the beginning to the present hour, he has kept his own secret; nor has so much as one note of alarm escaped his venomous tongue. Yet has his aim been steady and single. It were a dark chapter in the history of our race, that should recite even a few of the more prominent instances in which men have been beguiled by him to their undoing, and in which to have dealt honestly and have avowed his purpose, would have been to have defeated it. It matters not on whom he practises this deception, nor upon what scale; his object is alike concealed. It was concealed from Adam and Eve; it was concealed from Cain, when he made him the abhorred of his race, and brought upon him a punishment greater than he could bear. It was concealed from the antediluvian world and from Sodom, when their blind credulity in his promises was answered in the rushing waters of the Deluge, and in fire from the Lord out of heaven. It was concealed from Judas, when he "put it into his heart" to betray the Son of Man with a kiss. All the world over, those who yield to his temptations, find, when it is too late, that they were a lure, and that while he flattered them with the expectation of good, his object was evil. "The tree was *good for food*, and *pleasant to the eye*, and a tree to be desired *to make one wise*"—this is the whole story of his stratagems. It is an artful appeal to the three vulnerable points of humanity—"the lust of the flesh, the lust of the eye, and the pride of life." And in making it, the devil excels all other deceivers—never unfolding the flower without concealing the thorn; never aiming to injure, without promising to benefit. The poisoned cup is held to the lips, and while it sparkles and exhilarates, shows no signs of the death that lurks within. Who of all the victims of his treachery are premonished of their overthrow? Not one. It is the voice of the Deceiver which they hear. It is the fascination of the lap of indulgence, where the head of the victim is laid to be shorn of its strength, and then blinded and delivered over to the tormentors. It is the syren song that invites to pleasure, and introduces to death. It is the serpent's breath, carrying its notes to the ear, and instilling its poison into the soul, till the unwary and deluded awake to the struggle only to be bound faster in his coils.

The same artifice is also discoverable in *the means by which his malignant ends are attained.* Of his influence in the physical world we are not able to speak with definiteness or certainty. From the fact that he is represented in the Scriptures as the "Prince of the power of the air," learned and sensible men have believed and taught, that it is not beyond his province to "produce winds and storms, and other natural evils to afflict mankind, and carry on his malignant opposition to Christ and his kingdom." Some instances of this sort occur in the Scriptures. The magicians of Egypt seem to have a limited power over the material creation, when they "withstood Moses," in the presence of Pharaoh. This great Enemy is also distinctly represented as obtaining permission from God to visit Job with various and sore physical calamities. The notion of his power in the material creation was certainly extensively prevalent among the Jews, as well as not a few even of the learned Gentiles. Demons and evil genii were supposed by them to have the seat of their empire in the air, there exerting their influence, and watching their opportunities to harass and destroy. And it is a fact worthy, in this connection, to be mentioned, that in those portions of the world that are unvisited by the light of the gospel, and where the inhabitants are most under the power of the Prince of Darkness, his physical power is most dreaded.

Be this as it may, he has another sphere of action, which, if it be not his own selected sphere, is the one in which he has the divine permission most extensively to employ his subtlety. That sphere is the *human mind*, with all its faculties of perception, thought, imagination and memory. Nor do I know that we are warranted in saying that he has no power over the *heart*. It has been supposed, that if his power extended to the hearts of men, the havoc would be so fearful that there would be no hope for the race. The reasoning would be conclusive, if his power were not watched by an unsleeping eye, and restrained by an unwearied arm, and always effectually countervailed in exact accordance with the counsels of redeeming mercy. There is no more impossibility in his acting upon the minds of men than there is in any other invisible agent's acting upon them. And there is no more absurdity. He "moved David to number Israel," and he "filled the heart of Ananias to lie unto the Holy Ghost." The way in which he influences the thoughts and affections of men may not be known to us, nor may the nature of his communications with them be capable of being explained, or even comprehended; while we see not how those communications themselves can be questioned. If I dared, I would make the appeal to the personal experience of my readers, and ask them to recall some dream of the night, some waking vision, some unwonted and wicked train of thought, some process of false reasoning, some fearful and fiendlike impulse, to which their own habits of thought and feeling were not only utter strangers, but to the last degree hostile and repulsive. I would make the appeal also to their observation. I would ask them to visit the asylums for the insane, and look into the solitary cells of the madhouse. Not a few of these instances of mental insanity, no doubt, are the effect of physical disorganization; but are there not among them those which present mournful instances of *moral* derangement? In tracing their history, is there not as much evidence as the subject admits, that the origin of the mania was cherished wickedness, the cherished tempter; and are there not instances of this sort, which are as truly specimens of demoniacal possession as those we read of in the records of the New Testament?

I have said that the appropriate sphere of the devil's subtlety is *the mind.* And here he practises his deceptions with a skill and subtlety that show that he is no novice. To a great extent, he makes use of men as *their own tempters.* By their want of consideration, and not less by their unsleeping suspicions and jealousies; by their unguarded thoughtlessness and vanity; by their imperturbable sullenness and gloom; by their indifference, and by their over-prying curiosity, they lay open their own minds to his artful and intriguing suggestions. Sometimes he avails himself of the opinions they form before reason can discuss, or the judgment confirm them; and sometimes of that absence of all opinions, that mental vacuity which invites his cultivation. Where the prepossessions and prejudices are wrong, however dreamy and absurd they be, he leaves them undisturbed; while, if they are right and true, he spares no pains to agitate and disturb them, to assail them with sarcasm, abuse, and sneers, until these great outposts of truth and duty are, if possible, broken down. The mind of man is an apostate and depraved existence, while all its operations are most narrowly watched by the adversary. Its very *excitability* is one of those frailties of which he very often takes great advantage, and under which he urges men to say and do what, but for this excited state of feeling, they never would have thought of. Whence is it that such multitudes so unreluctantly abandon themselves to impulse and passion rather than be governed by cool reason and sober judgment, unless it be from some practised delusion? Moral depravity here goes beyond its calculations, and supreme selfishness misses its aim. There is no characteristic of the mind more marvellous than the preference it is prone to give to the joys of the present moment. Nor can it easily be accounted for. This rude recklessness, so incorrigible in the young, and with such difficulty eradicated in the old; this utter disregard of consequences, so often condemned and never controlled, so often rebuked but rarely amended, so often held in check but not always subdued even by the grace of God, indicates the power of the charmer. Every man, too, has his ruling passion; nor is the tempter ignorant either of its nature or its power. If it be the love of money, he aims to bind the soul in fetters of gold; the love of power, he aims to dazzle it with the splendor of dominion; the love of pleasure, he aims to incite those "fleshly lusts that war against the soul." And even where it is the love of God, he aims to quench its ardor, or inflame it by a misguided and headlong zeal; and as melancholy facts show, even instigate it to deeds of wickedness under the semblance of doing God's service. Not only does he know the temptation that is fitted to address itself to the predominant disposition and habits, but the one that is suited to the existing state of the mind, whether that state arise from its outward circumstances, or its inward spirit. It may be the state of prosperity, or of adversity; of hope, or fear; of severe toil, or of relaxation, leisure, or idleness; of presumption, or despondency: and in either case, he fits the snare to the path in which the unwary pilgrim is travelling.

If you now advert to a few of those extraneous influences he employs, you will see that they partake of the same artful character. Sometimes they are those whom men love most in the endeared relations of human life; sometimes those in whom they have the deepest interest and confidence in the relations of business; and sometimes those who are most revered as the teachers of religion, as the makers of their laws, or as the leaders of a party. All those *associations* which have a tendency to taint the purity of the mind, or to familiarize it with men and scenes where God is dishonored, the authority of his word called in question, the peculiar doctrines of Christianity ridiculed, or the obligations of morality regarded with loose indifference; present opportunities of which he is not slow to avail himself. There is an exposure to moral assimilation amid such scenes which he most artfully promotes, and by which his malignant ends are too often secured. Some he persuades to phrensied activity, that they may sin without reflection; and some he persuades to eat the bread of idleness, that he may have the better opportunity of employing them in his own work. Some he stupifies by their ignorance, and some he misleads by their knowledge. Some he infatuates by pride, and some he inflates by "a voluntary humility." Some he ensnares by their ingenuousness; and others by overspreading and obscuring their minds by a web of sophistry. Some are led astray by an overweening attachment to their own rights and prerogative, others by a tame surrender of them; some by a sense of honor, and others by the fear of shame and reproach. Very rarely, if ever, does he carry his point by assuming the garb and showing the hideous face of wickedness, or by any such means, the just view of which stings the conscience and awakens disgust.

Another evidence of his deception will be found in *those artful insinuations by which he tempts to evil by slow degrees.* When a man has taken a single step in wickedness, he is very apt to take another; and when he has taken a few more in the downward path, he is hurried onward with such accelerated and fearful velocity, that it is impossible to predict where he will stop. The stone has gone out of the sling, and no man can tell where it will alight, or what mischief it will do in its course. We may not doubt that the subtle agency of the Deceiver is employed, both in the first impulse, and in the subsequent and rapid progress. The history of Ahab, Jeroboam, and Judas; of Nero, the bloody Mary, and Voltaire, furnish melancholy exemplifications of the truth of these remarks. Nor are they less applicable to large bodies of men, than to individuals. Large bodies of men are indeed less apt to yield to the restraints of conscience, and more liable to be driven and hurried on, from small beginnings to courses of headstrong and unresisted iniquity. It takes time for a nation that was once moral and virtuous, to become immoral and vicious. They are drawn into the snare of the devil little by little. Some nations had their origin in an illustrious and noble ancestry; and could they have foreseen at a single view the downward course they would travel, they would have looked upon it with abhorrence, and have trembled to anticipate their destiny. Others had their origin in ignorance, superstition, idolatry, and blood; and even *they* would have scarcely thought it possible that their subsequent history would have been marked with the obdurate degradation which attended it. It was by slow degrees and smaller sins that the world began to be corrupted after the flood; yet in about half a century after the death of Noah, the earth was overrun by abounding iniquity. In the person and family of Abraham, the Hebrew nation was planted "wholly a right seed;" while according to the testimony of their own historian, "never was there a time from the beginning of the world more fruitful in wickedness," than in remoter periods of their history. When Ashur, and the few adventurers who shared his fortunes, founded the Assyrian empire, they little thought that the early pride of Nineveh would lead to the luxury in which so many generations slumbered, and finally kindle the fire by which an empire which had existed 1400 years was subverted in a day. It was not in a moment that "the iniquity of the Amorites became full;" nor that Babylon, "the glory of kingdoms, the beauty of the Chaldees' excellency," became "as when God overthrew Sodom and Gomorrah."

The evils which many portions of the earth now suffer, and the wickedness to which they are in bondage, were the offspring of a barbarous age, of which the adversary was the author. The time was when these unmitigated enormities were a novelty in the history of our race, and were all concentrated in the devices of his teeming bosom. There was no tumult of alarm at the first suggestion of them; they crept in with a snail-like progress. The Old Serpent is too great a veteran in the arts of deception to allow men to conjecture the course in which he means to lead them. It is enough for him to know that they will be carried beyond their own expectations in sinning. His policy, his subtlety is not so much seen in what the sin is in its first encroachment, as in what he designs it shall be. It was but the entering wedge of destruction, but drove home by an experienced and dexterous hand. It was but the unnoticed trains and associations of thought, that sprung up almost imperceptibly; but which gradually increased like the stream that flows from a fountain of water, till it has become like the torrent of the wilderness, swollen and impetuous by the bursting of the storm. It was but the unobserved flake of snow, floating under the control of the "Prince of the power of the air;" now it is the avalanche tumbling upon the plain below. It was but the invisible vapor, secretly struggling to find its way through some subterranean crevice of the sulphurous mountain; now, it is the dark exhalation from the bottomless pit, and "goes up like the smoke of a great furnace."

Add to these one other thought, and his character as the Deceiver is complete and entire. I mean *his bold and unblushing falsehood.* We do not slander him when we say he is an impudent liar. Falsehood is inherent in his very nature. If he ever speaks the truth, it is but to give emphasis to some greater falsehood. He never made a sincere declaration to men, save with the view of carrying into effect some sinister and base design. Truth, that eternal and unchangeable reality which forms the indissoluble tie, the sacred connection between God and man, and between all virtuous minds in the universe, and which animates their confidence, and secures and promotes their everlasting tranquillity and joy, is to him unknown, except to be hated and opposed. There is no degree, form, or color of falsehood with which he is not familiar, and which did not originate, and is not fostered within his own false bosom. His whole character and history are distinguished for treachery and lies. The Saviour, when speaking of him, says "he abode not in *the truth;*" and in the same sentence he not only calls him "a liar," but "the father of lies." He is false, not from inconstancy and fickleness; not from the instability of passion; but from cool reflection and settled principle. "He was a liar from the beginning;" and what he was in the beginning, he is now, and ever will be, world without end. As God is immutably and forever true, Satan is immutably and forever false. False declarations, false names, false reasonings, false quotations of Scripture, false promises, and hopes of impunity in sin which he knows are refuges of lies, are his ordinary, if not his universal and uniform resort.

It is worthy of remark, that in his influence upon the minds of men, he is wont to assail the most demonstrable truths. Mr. Locke observes of a certain class of propositions, that "they are those clear truths, that either their own evidence forces us to admit, or common experience makes it impudence to deny." This shameless effrontery is the true character of the great Adversary. There is no truth more fully established than the indissoluble connection between sin and suffering. This is the great ordinance of the divine kingdom, and on this depend all its order and harmony. The laws of the physical creation are not more firmly established than this great law of the moral creation. It were just as rational to believe that heavy bodies do not fall, that light does not shine, that cold does not contract, that heat does not expand, and that fluids do not seek a common level, as that sin does not engender suffering.

Yet has the Deceiver set himself from the beginning to disprove and disallow this fundamental principle of the divine government. Scarcely had this great law been pronounced by the lips of unerring truth, than he had the shameless effrontery to call it in question, and give it a bold and flat denial. Thou shalt "*not* surely die!" Wonderful discovery! and found only in the depths of those deceptions which are nourished in the bosom of the "crooked Serpent." His first, and with the exception of his menaces and terrors, his last resort, is to inject this delusion, either in unmingled, or diluted forms. His great strength lies in his powers of deception. With all his gigantic intellect, he would accomplish little without these artifices. This is his character; this is his nature; this is his work; the work for which he has the talent and the heart.

CHAPTER X.

The Extent of the Deceiver's Snares.

THAT we may perceive somewhat of the assiduity and success with which this arch-Deceiver has cultivated his powers, we propose in the present chapter to advert to the EXTENT OF HIS DECEPTIONS. The Scriptures speak of "the depths of Satan," and of his amazing power. They represent him as a "roaring lion going about seeking whom he may devour;"—as "going to and fro in the earth, and walking up and down in it;" and as "deceiving *the nations*," and the "whole world."

His powers of locomotion are not known to us, nor are they to be comprehended by human organs. As a spirit, he is possessed of wonderful activity. Milton well represents him as an "archangel ruined." The angel Gabriel flew from the supreme heavens to this world, a distance far beyond the starry firmament, during the time that the prophet Daniel was employed in uttering a short prayer. Nor is there any reason to believe that the activity of infernal spirits is less than that of these celestial beings. He who "maketh his angels spirits, his ministers a flaming fire," has given to these invisible ones of the world of darkness, powers of moving from place to place, which, while we have no means of ascertaining, are so great, that when combined with their subtle artifices, would render them still more fearful engines of evil, but for him who restrains the wrath of devils as well as men. Not only are the measures of this common foe planned with wonderful adroitness, but from his amazing activity, laid out upon a large scale. He is the great moral juggler of the universe. This earth is spread out before him like a vast chess-board, every part of which he has been studying for 6,000 years. There is not a square of it which his eye has not surveyed; not a king, nor bishop, nor knight, nor castle, nor pawn, nor the meanest figure that has a part in the great game of life, with the power and value of which he is not acquainted, and which he knows not how to make use of to the best advantage, both for the purposes of defence and attack. If there were but less proportion between his skill and the value of the stake for which he plays, his indefatigable assiduity would not excite so much alarm. The stake is infinite; the skill, blessed be God, falls short of that which is infinite; he is a *creature*, though probably the greatest of creatures. Yet though a creature, it is no ordinary place that he occupies; no common powers that he possesses. It is no small game that he is seeking after. His aim is to blind and infatuate men by millions, and make his victims as the sand of the shore. He does not indeed overlook individual and isolated man; nor suppress his exultation when he circumvents the poorest and meanest of our race. But his eagle eye is fixed upon *the nations*, and for nothing does he utter a louder shout of triumph, than when he has them hoodwinked in his hands, degraded and enslaved.

Among the various ways in which he aims to do this, we will direct our attention, in the first place, *to the extensive prevalence of those institutions and customs by which large portions of the human race are held under his dominion.* If every age is distinguished by some peculiarity of moral character, it is for the most part a peculiarity in wickedness. Any one who has observed the amazing power which corrupt institutions and customs exert upon the character of the world, will not doubt that they constitute a part of that moral machinery by which this Deceiver retains the minds of men in inexorable bondage. Men and nations who would recoil from a sinful act, are cheated into upholding a sinful custom. Institutions and customs which, proposed for the first time, would strike the mind with horror, cease to be revolting when, by their long standing, men have become familiar with them. If they are handed down to them from their ancestors, they venerate them, because they are slow to believe that those whom they have been accustomed to respect could do wrong. No matter how absurd the usage, if it comes to them under the sanction of great names, and universal adoption, and by-gone ages. It is enough that it is inwoven with the framework of human society, and comes to them under all the force of a prescriptive law; they have no settled opinions about it, except that change would be an inroad upon the past.

As a general fact, the customs and institutions of the world belong to a concern in which the great Adversary traffics in wholesale deception. This invincible attachment to long-established usage, is the principal reason why, in most of the countries of the East, the *female mind* is so degraded. Woman holds too important a place in human society, fills too interesting a sphere, and is fitted to exert too wide an influence, to be overlooked by the common enemy. There, her place is the harem; the light of day may scarcely look upon her; her mind is unimproved, and her office is that of a pet-slave. Yet, strange to say, such is the power of custom, that even if the long-imprisoned bird were let loose, it would return to its cage.

This also is the principal reason of the division of *castes* throughout India, by which a large majority of the inhabitants are reduced to the most hopeless state of humiliation. No advantage results from it to any one order of society; the humbled classes are by far the more numerous, and might easily become the more powerful; but they have been so long accustomed to the yoke, that they know not how to live without it. Here is a territory containing one hundred and fifty millions of inhabitants, where this wretched system, primarily a religious, but so inwoven with the social and civil institutions of the country, and indeed with the entire life of the Hindus, not only precludes all improvement in their secular affairs, but so enslaves the minds of the people as to present the most discouraging obstacles to the propagation of Christianity, and their consequent elevation.

The same delusion attaches itself to the *feudal system.* The most striking features of this system were its landed aristocracy, the absolute subjection of the vassal to his lord, the tenure of land by military service, ecclesiastical nobility, and the independence of the peers and barons of the crown. The two great evils of this system, furnished the great adversary with the most effective instruments of destruction to the souls of men. They were the personal servitude of the greater portion of mankind during the dark ages, and the elevation of the profession of arms, to the absolute contempt of the more honorable, virtuous and peaceful occupations. *Chivalry*, too, was the proud and restive associate of the feudal system. And who does not see, that, that passion for arms, that reckless spirit, that honor of knighthood, those rewards of valor, that splendor of equipage, those romantic ideas of justice, that love of wild adventure, and that affability and gallantry, so artfully inwoven with all its dissipation and blood, were but the false glare thrown around it by the prince of darkness?

The religious frenzy of the *Crusades* is another feature of this strange delusion. It is no extravagance to say, that in these military expeditions Satan himself bore the banner of the cross. Under the pretence of recovering the Holy Land from the power of infidels, he has by this device immolated millions on his own altar. So absolutely did this wild fanaticism take possession of the mind of Europe for several centuries, that not only sovereigns, princes of the blood, dignitaries of the church, and a countless multitude of the common people, but women and children enlisted by thousands under its colors. Ninety thousand children, commanded by a child, were once engaged in this adventure, only to be murdered, or starved, or sold as slaves. "So many crimes and so much misery have seldom been accumulated as in the three years of the first crusade." It is not enough to confess that these expeditions were the result of a misguided enthusiasm; they were the result of marvellous delusion, and led on by the angel of the bottomless pit.

The long-established custom of *war* is also one of the artifices of the great adversary. The moral perceptions and sensibilities even of Christian men and Christian nations, in relation to this fearful scourge of humanity, have actually been blinded and blunted by his subtle influence. As a source of crime and misery, this unnatural, absurd and barbarous custom stands out beyond every scourge of the earth. Yet is it a perfect illusion. There is no reason for it in the world. No good comes of it. There is no such enmity between nations as war intimates. Men do not *hate* those they kill, for they do not *know* them. No; there is strange delusion here. It was inwrought into the habits of society by their greatest foe. It was among the earlier lessons instilled into the youthful mind, both in the brightest and in the darkest ages of the world's history. The maxims, the laws, and the policy of nations have been founded upon it; and it has been sustained by the talent, the poetry, and the enthusiasm of the world. But the devil is at the bottom of it. Nor is his deception yet fully detected and abhorred. When I see the enthusiasm which excites the thirst for military glory; when I observe the almost universal admiration of military talent which is so fatal to the souls of men; when I hear mothers chanting the praises of warriors in order to soothe the sobs of the cradle; I have evidence which I cannot resist, that the wise and the good,—nay, the loveliest and the best, are sinfully heedless of the extent of his subtlety who "goeth about seeking whom he may devour."

This same attachment to customs and institutions is also one of the reasons for all those *corrupting amusements* by which the deceiver has obtained such power over large masses of men, and drugged their cup of pleasure. The early amphitheatres at Rome, and especially its gigantic Coliseum, so long the arena of games, and spectacles, and gladiatorial shows, cannot now be contemplated without horror. Those scenes of carnage and blood, and licentiousness, could never have obtained the sanction of princes, and men and women of noble birth, and been made the favorite pastime of the people, but for a miserably deluded state of mind. The Greeks were more refined and civilized; yet their festivals, noted for folly and sin, were in honor of a heathen god and goddess, and their athletic games were celebrated in honor of Jupiter, Hercules, Apollo, and Neptune. Both their festivals and games confirmed one of the noblest races of men in all the atheism and vices of idolatry. The Bacchanalian orgies, celebrated in Greece, Egypt and India, consisted of horrid and unnatural rites, and were distinguished by every kind of lewdness and extravagance. And what were the tilts and tournaments of the dark ages but the stimulus to magnificence and luxury, to those false notions of honor which have deprived society of so many bright ornaments, to passions which agitate, and to manners, habits and principles, which degrade and destroy?

If from amusements of this barbarous character, we advert to the *dramatic exhibitions*, both of ancient and modern times, we cannot fail to discover indications of their dark origin. Whether in the form of opera, farce, pantomime, comedy, or tragedy, its tendency is to tempt men to sin, and then harden them in the commission of it. Strange to say, they were first introduced at Rome to appease the wrath of the gods on account of a prevailing pestilence. It were difficult to find a more convincing proof of the diabolical auspices under which they came into being. In Greece the theatre was notoriously dissolute; and historians have recorded that the fondness for theatrical representations was one of the principal causes of the degeneracy, corruption, and decline of the Athenian republic.

Nowhere has wickedness so systematically assumed the names of virtue as in the *drama*. Nowhere is vice exhibited in more harmless, not to say bewitching colors. And nowhere, when visited with its native consequences and just reward, is it so surrounded with incidents, and palliatives that secure it sympathy. Honor and sublimity are here attached to deeds and motives which religion shudders at; nor are there wanting instances in which woman is here seen as not the less lovely because she poisons, or assassinates her husband, nor the son the less detestable because he is a parricide. The most captivating ingredients of the drama are its incentives to evil, adorned by all the charms of painting and poetry. Music herself, the native daughter of heaven, with all her enchanting harmony, is here pressed into the service of the devil. And as though this were not enough, under the auspices of the church of Rome, the drama has been profanely *spiritualized*. Moses and the burning bush, the Virgin Mary, and the infant Jesus, the holy sacrament, and the Eternal Father have in turn been produced upon the stage, and in inventions and language of the lowest farce. Nor are we greatly surprised to learn, that the infidel world has caught the spirit of holy ecclesiastics, and in our own day, and when "men's hearts were failing them for fear," the judgments of Almighty God have been grossly ridiculed, and his pestilence actually personified upon the stage, amid scenery and decorations that were fit emblems of the dark and invisible world where the first sketch was drawn.

There are other amusements too, far less corrupting indeed than these, against which the voice of the pulpit has often been lifted in vain. I regret to say it, but there are scenes, even in embellished society, among ourselves, where when the "sons of God appear, Satan also comes among them." And what is most deeply to be regretted, they are so interlaced with the modern systems of education, and unhappily form so essential a part of our social organization, that it would seem that nothing can root them out. Some of them are innocent and harmless in themselves, but from their nature so liable to abuse and perversion, that they become snares, and at best give no proof that those by whom they are sanctioned, "abstain from the appearance of evil." And whatever may be said or thought of them now, few I think will doubt that they will have no place in Christian families and in a Christian land, when that day shall come in which Satan shall be bound, and no more go forth to deceive the nations.

Institutions and customs like these indicate the subtle influence of a subtle foe. They spread through great masses of men; their action is insensibly and incessantly going on, and their effect is to blind the mind, sear the conscience, harden the heart, and produce indifference, if not contempt of all that assimilates the soul to the character of heaven.

We take then a second thought, and it is certainly one not destitute of interest; I refer to *the extended power which the adversary exerts in the education of the young.* He is not so destitute of knowledge and art as to overlook the rising generation. Give him the training of the youthful mind, and he asks no better opportunity of satiating his malignity upon the race. Give him this, and you invest him with power to do more to advance error and ungodliness, to corrupt and destroy the world, than can be accomplished by any other means. That resistance to parental authority, that disregard of truth, those habits of self-indulgent idleness, that companionship with fools, that laxity of morals, that insidious intemperance, and that wide-spread infidelity, which mark the character and conduct of so many of the young, are all indications of his artful training. The examples of piety, the force of truth, the power and tenderness of parental love, have no such formidable enemy as his indefatigable subtlety. He well knows, that as a general law of the human mind, what the child is the man will be; and that in a few fleeting years the boys and the girls that are now overlooked by the risen generation, will themselves constitute the only effective portion of human society when the risen generation have descended to the tomb. We need not then be surprised at his zeal and artifices to control the education of the young. He begins his work early, and lays the axe at the root of the tree.

It is a fact well fitted to excite suspicion and alarm, that in his efforts to carry this foul device into effect, he has so extensively corrupted *the literature* of the world, and thereby poisoning the sources of human knowledge, has poisoned the community at the fountain-head. In few things is the cunning craftiness of this dexterous intriguer more apparent than in controlling literary men and literary institutions. The most important of these institutions were founded by his influence; while not a few of those founded "for Christ and his church," have been wrested from them by his artifices; and for the few that remain pure he has already set his snare. From the school of Plato to the Royal Academy of Paris, the most renowned seats of learning have been sources of infidelity, or false religions.

Since the invention of the art of printing, he has also spared no effort to control the *press*. To a lamentable extent, it has dazzled only to blind the youthful inquirer. It has possessed so much genius and so little piety; its splendid intellect has been the vehicle of so much irreligious sentiment; it has so greatly abounded in caricaturing true religion, and in "daubing with untempered mortar;" that the marvel is that the fabric of the best organized communities has not long ago crumbled to its foundations. Natural science and the fine arts, the researches of history and chronology, have been prostituted to the designs of the base Deceiver. The popular tales of fiction and romance, to say nothing of their positively demoralizing tendency, are for the most part distinguished for total absence of moral and religious principle, and especially amid scenes where moral and religious principle are demanded and looked for. No mind that indulges itself in this kind of literature, and especially the young mind, unwary and unarmed as it is, can be safe. Its talent and enticements constitute its danger. Artful is that device which thus entices so many thousands into the enemy's country without any suspicion of the perils that await them. Of all the faculties of the human mind to which the Deceiver has the most ready access, the *imagination* is probably the most exposed. And here it is trifled with and polluted to a degree that renders it familiar with scenes of wickedness, progressively indifferent to sober reflection, and even decidedly averse to those teachings of practical wisdom which are its only security.

In adverting to the absence of religious and moral principle in the education of the young, I cannot repress the remark, that the growing disuse of the Holy Scriptures, in the system of instruction in common schools, is a blow aimed at the rising generation by the prince of darkness. It is a vain effort to conduct the youthful mind into the paths of light, while it shuts out the sun. It is nothing else than an attempt to educate a generation of human beings, born for immortality, without the knowledge of God. It is leaving them, amid all the lights of science, to feel their dark way to eternity in lonely gloom. I do not know that it is in the power of the devil to direct a more malignant, or more subtle blow against the best interests of men than this. If there is intelligence in the universe, it is in the word of God; if there is moral truth in the universe, it is found there. If there are treasures of thought which reason and philosophy could not acquire by the patience and toil of centuries, they are there. If the youthful mind is ever expanded, and its lofty faculties made more lofty; if its powers of will and feeling are ever wisely controlled; and if the true sources of intellectual and moral enjoyment are ever opened to it; this is the source of them all. Science and literature, and the social affections, the rights of conscience and the rights of man, his holiness and his hopes are all rooted in this consecrated soil. It is not the master intellect of the universe merely that is the author of the Bible; it is the all-pervading and infinite love of the universe. It is no marvel that the prince of darkness should endeavor to cut off the youthful mind from all access to this fountain of light and love. Who, but this "arch thief," and those who are led captive by him at his will, would steal away this heavenly treasure? "Woe to that generation by which the testimony of God shall be abandoned! But woe also to that generation which is preparing the seed of evil-doers that shall perform the accursed work!"

There is another view of the general thought I am endeavoring to illustrate. I allude to *those master-strokes of the devil's policy, by which he involves large masses of men in the sin of a single individual.* Such is the organization of human society, that when one man sins, others not only feel the consequences, but in very many instances, sympathize with the moral turpitude of his wickedness. They do it by treading in the footsteps of his example; by refraining to reprove his conduct; by justifying and vindicating it; and by neglecting to use all proper means for preventing future offences and reforming the offender. Hence the apostolic injunction, "Neither be ye partakers in other men's sins." One sin, also, often produces associations of wickedness, and gives vice a currency and a name. The dissolute conduct of Charles II. and the Duke of Buckingham stamped their own dissoluteness on large masses of the English nation; and the licentious court of Louis XIV. and XV. corrupted the mass of the French people.

One sin also not unfrequently promotes combinations in wickedness, just like combinations in trade; men grow rich by it, and make it a matter of speculation and gain. The distiller of ardent spirits thus fabricates iniquity; so does the opium dealer; so does the railroad corporation that profanes the Lord's-day; and so does the purveyor of luxury in every form. The gaming-table, too, and the brothel, and the vile wretch who lives to pander to the lusts of men, sins that his own sin may become the sin of thousands.

Virtue weeps at this clustered wickedness. Some little spot, otherwise unnoticed, has become as famous in the annals of mankind as the palaces of kings, and not less fatally the slaughter-house of men, than many a bloody field of battle. The scythe of the Destroying Angel thus takes a wide and fell swath, and by a single sweep cuts down and throws together every green thing. If you inspect the corrupted character of men who congregate in large masses, and investigate their history, you will often trace their corruptions to some characteristic delinquency, some single sin of one man, little thought of on his part, but craftily devised by the adversary. The disobedience of Saul, and the rebellion of Absalom, were felt by other men and other times. By consulting the Sacred Records, it will be found that the vile character of Jeroboam, the son of Nebat, extended its corrupting influence to twenty kings in succession, and demoralized the nation of Israel for nearly two hundred and fifty years after his death. The apostasy of Julian, and even the errors of Constantine, were felt by unborn ages. The horrors of the French Revolution may be traced to that depraved, unprincipled, and fallen nobleman, Mirabeau, who, to reinstate himself in the salons of Paris, secretly planned the destruction of the monarchy, the regeneration of the state, and sacrificed his country to his ambition.

There are artifices practised by the great Deceiver which never take effect without vitiating everything with which they come in contact, and producing in the end a portentous amount of evil. Every reader of history will easily recall facts by which this remark is illustrated. It is illustrated by the influence of men of great talents and great vices: such were Voltaire and Chesterfield. It is illustrated by the power of princes and princesses, who, though they have shed lustre over their reign, will, from their profligacy of principle, be remembered for nothing more, or longer, than that they were the models of ambition and injustice: such were Alexander VI. and Catharine II. of Russia. And a corrupt legislation illustrates it, "framing iniquity by a law;" enlisting the popular voice in favor of transgression, and giving it emphasis and permanency by the solemnity of its deliberations, and the force of its enactments.

But this is not all. In adverting to the policy of the adversary in involving multitudes in the sins of others, there is more than the mere natural and associated tendencies of wickedness. Such is the moral constitution under which God has placed the human race from the beginning, and such the arrangements of the divine government, that no man sins for himself alone. "The iniquity of the fathers is visited upon the children to the third and fourth generation of them that hate God;" the iniquity of one age of the world is visited upon another; and unless arrested by Him who came to arrest the current of human woes, will flow on to the end of time. On this great principle of the divine administration, the Deceiver has engrafted many a device of his own. If men inherit the sins of their fathers, he corrupts the parent stock; and if one generation is held responsible for the wickedness of previous generations, his stratagem is to corrupt the generations in their origin.

Among the exemplifications of this fact, the present condition of the Jews may not pass unnoticed. With some incidental variations of unbelief and suffering, their condition has been stationary for eighteen centuries. They are a dispersed people, but an undivided nation; a nation scattered throughout all nations, and intermingling with none; a people, with some honorable exceptions, bearing the ignominy of the world's contempt and heaven's reprobation. And all this is in fulfilment of an ancient curse, and for an ancient sin. Their ancestors crucified the Son of God, and uttered the fearful imprecation, "His blood be on us and on our children!" The Scriptures inform us that the great Deceiver was the prime mover in this deed of horror, as well as the secret instigator and sustainer of their present unbelief. "The veil that is upon their hearts is yet untaken away." They constitute the greatest phenomenon in the world, not merely for their national peculiarities, but because they are a living witness of the truth which they themselves deny. Obstinate prejudice, inflexible resistance to all inquiry and argument, national pride, and a deeply imbedded hatred and scorn of Jesus of Nazareth, form the citadel within which they have entrenched themselves, the keys of which are hung up in the hall of the adversary, and among the trophies of his subtlety and conquests, who "blinds the minds of them that believe not."

There is a large portion of the earth that is occupied by the descendants of Ishmael. This race originated in unbelief of the divine promise to Abraham; and, to the present day, bears the burden of the sentence, "Cast out the bondwoman and her son!" A bold manœuvre of the adversary, practised upon Sarah, upon Abraham, and upon an Egyptian slave—a deep-laid plot, early concocted in the councils of the prince of darkness, severed this powerful people from the people of God, perpetuated the disunion, and branded the tribes of Ishmael with their characteristic features of enmity to God and man.

From the descendants of Ishmael, go back to a crushed, broken, and deserted people, the descendants of Ham. Facts show us that, thus far in the history of the world, the wrath of God has come upon this people. They were sold as slaves to the Hebrews as early as the days of David; and from that period to the present, the commerce of the world has been, to no small extent, a commerce in the Canaanitish race. And in this commerce of themselves, strange to say, they themselves have been in a great degree the participators. With wonderful infatuation, they have, from age to age, perpetuated this inheritance of crime and misery. It is calculated that Africa has thus annually been drained of no less than 150,000 of her own native inhabitants. We sigh over the wrongs of the colored man, and reprobate the slave-dealer with unsparing severity; and well we may. There is no land where, according to the unvarying narratives both of ancient and modern travellers, the great Deceiver holds such an undisputed and horrible supremacy. And if we would know by what avenue he entered those desert plains, and how it was that his throne is so firmly established there, we learn from authentic records. What became subsequently "the first commandment with promise," was then the law of nature, and nature's God. The benevolent Author of the social relations would have the precept respected, "Honor thy father and thy mother," and gave that obligation an emphasis at that early dawn of the world that should never be forgotten. It was just after the flood, and the three sons of Noah contained the germ of all succeeding generations. To strike a death-blow at the root of one of these great branches of the human family, was the deep policy of the foe; and it was by instigating *Ham* to a flagrant violation of this great law. He had tempted Noah, and "he drank of the wine and was drunken; and he was uncovered within his tent. And *Ham*, the father of Canaan, *saw* the nakedness of his father, and *went and told* his two brethren without." And when Noah awoke from his wine, he awoke in the spirit of prophecy, and said, "*Cursed be Canaan, a servant of servants shall he be to his brethren!* Blessed be the God of Shem, and *Canaan shall be his servant!* God shall enlarge Japheth, and he shall dwell in the tents of Shem, and *Canaan shall be his servant!*" Thrice was this emphatic curse repeated, in order to make it sure. The Deceiver had sprung the snare, and this thrice-repeated curse sealed the fate of the Canaanitish race.

Now go to the garden of Eden. "God created man upright." Integrity was never more exalted, nor innocence more pure, nor happiness more unalloyed, than when the first parents of our race came from the forming hand of their Maker. But it was fit and proper that as the creature of God, and as the subject of a moral government, humanity should be tried and proved. For the wisest and best reasons, it was tried in the person of its great progenitor, who stood, not for himself alone, but by divine appointment, as the federal head and representative of his race. Since the character and condition of untold millions was thus suspended upon his perfect obedience, if the adversary could but inoculate the primeval stock, the poisonous taint would be transmitted to the end of time. Nor did his purpose fail. Through the foulest treachery, the venom took and poisoned every heart of man. This "prince of the power of the air" called up the storm, and wrecked the bark in which the race was bound for eternity. "By the offence of one, judgment came upon all men unto condemnation." It was a mournful day, for it was the Deceiver's hour, and the power of darkness.

There is one more thought by which our general position may be more forcibly illustrated, at least to some minds. It has been often said, that man is a *religious* being. Not that he possesses, by nature, anything like the spirit of true religion; but from his own immortal aspirations, and the demands of conscience, he is not satisfied without a religion of some sort. Temples he will have, and sacrifices, and a worship, and ministers of the sanctuary; and if they be not consecrated to the true God, they will be consecrated to gods which are "the work of men's hands;" and if they be not the ministry of the true sanctuary, they will be an antichristian, or pagan priesthood. So long as natural conscience has a place in the human bosom, some religion men will have, even though it be false. Blot out the true, burn its Bible, demolish its temples, annihilate its worship, starve, or extirpate its ministry, and the generation now on the earth would not be long in their graves, before some false religion, with its false ministers, would spring up in its place.

No being is more aware of the importance of availing himself of this all-pervading sentiment of the human bosom, than the wary adversary. This, of all other principles of action, it is his policy to control; for if in the matter of their *religion* he can practise deception upon men, his work of destruction is accomplished. "There is a way that seemeth right to a man, but the end thereof are the ways of death." Men never sin with so high and strong a hand, as when they sin from a perverted and blinded conscience. Never was there a more fiend-like plot, and never was a more tremendous engine wielded for the ruin of the nations, than when their *religion* is under the direction of the prince of darkness.

We need not go far for appropriate illustrations of these thoughts. The whole system of *paganism* is the natural offspring of the "father of lies." It had the same leading features in Greece and Rome, that it now has throughout the heathen world; everywhere, and at all times, "changing the truth of God into a lie." Preposterous and absurd as are its rites, and impure and sanguinary as they are; the most melancholy feature of them is that they are not only virtually, and from their intrinsic wickedness paid to the great adversary, but to a great extent, professedly paid to him. The Scriptures teach us that "the things which the heathen sacrifice, they sacrifice *to devils*, not to God." Some they worship, that they may do them good, and others that they may not harm them. The object of religious sacrifices among the Magi of Persia, the Celtic tribes of Britain, and the savages of the western wilderness, was professedly the devil himself. We do not say that such devotees of false religions are not *sincere*; for we have no doubt they were, and are so; and for this reason, is their whole system so much the worse; for it is scarcely necessary to inquire what the character of that man, or nation is, that is a sincere worshipper of the devil. And whence is such a religion? It could not have been the unaided work of man. Wise as he is to do evil, paganism is too preposterous and silly ever to have entered the human intellect, but for the influence of some such invisible agent as the great Deceiver. The fact cannot otherwise be accounted for, that bright and illustrious minds—minds that were the adornment of the classic world in a classic age—minds to whom the wise and great of after-times have been wont to appeal as the great masters of thought and language—minds that have worn their literary honors untarnished, and whose laurels are still green on their brow, actually bowed down to gods of wood and stone! It is a stupidity and sottishness altogether below the human intellect, even in the mass of the people, unless that intellect be degraded, and subdued by some potent spell.

It were no marvel that the state of the world called for some modification of these gross absurdities. It has called for such modification; nor has the author of all evil been inactive in producing them whenever he has seen that it best suited his own designs. Events have occurred, in the progress of which, a few reflecting minds or some one controlling mind, has been restive under this yoke of pagan ignorance; and from mercenary, or ambitious views, or both, has meditated reform. And when opportunity and the times favor it, the Deceiver stands by and moves the fitting instrument. A striking example of this agency is found in the fabrications of the *Arabian impostor*. The Roman empire was attacked on every side by barbarians; the pagan mind was unsettled, and the Jewish mind miserable; while the plot to circumvent them was so artfully formed as to take in a portion of them all. Such was the wild impulse under which Mohammedanism began its career, that although obstructed at the outset, in less than a century it diffused itself throughout Egypt, Palestine, Syria, and Persia. It has subsisted in vigor for more than eleven hundred years; and even now, like some wayward and wandering planet, it casts its dark penumbra across the sun and shuts out a large portion of the earth from his healing beams. Nor is any satisfactory solution of this moral phenomenon to be found, save in the Scriptures; and there it is attributed to the agency of the devil. The revealing spirit, who well knows and watches all the designs and movements of the subtle foe, foresaw and foretold it; and that we may not mistake its origin, he compares it, in its obstructed and yet rapid advances, to the smoke that came up from the bottomless pit, and "darkened the air and the sun."

But they are not false religions alone in which the craft of the adversary is discoverable. Among the most subtle, as well as the more effective of his devices, are to be found his corruption and perversion of the religion that is true. Nothing has escaped his polluting touch. You may turn over the pages of almost any dictionary of religious sects, and from the Adamites of the second century to the Universalists of the nineteenth, and from the beginning to the end of the alphabet, you will discover indications of his unremitting subtlety and zeal.

To begin with Rome: her radical error consists in denying that the sacred Scriptures are a sufficient and infallible rule of faith and practice, under the pretence that they are rectified by her wisdom and illumined by her superior light. The deception was artful, and had the effect which the adversary intended. It jostled the planet that was receiving its light from the Sun of Righteousness so far out of place, as to come into collision with the Sun itself, and produce almost total darkness. The delusion took the nations first by surprise and surreptitiously, and then by force. It was the path of the sorcerer, who, while he held his way amid the mystic and secret rites of Paganism, professed enough of the words and charm of truth, to conceal his aim, until his spell-bound victim rejected the evidence of his own senses in order to abandon himself to deceit and falsehood. If we accredit the Scriptures, Romanism is Christianity metamorphosed into the "doctrine of devils." They inform us, in explicit language, that the "great Dragon," that old serpent, "gave power to the beast." They speak of the papal antichrist as one whose "coming is after the working of Satan," as the full-grown progeny of the world of darkness, as the very "son of perdition."

Now mark the cloven foot, sometimes in the sudden, and sometimes in the gradual transitions from the absurdities of Romanism to other and substituted errors. It would not be surprising, if when men come to see the absurdities and impiety of this system, they should be tempted to reject Christianity altogether; and this the great Deceiver led them to do in France. Elsewhere they satisfied themselves with baptizing radical error with the Christian name; this was the case with the German rationalists and the whole brotherhood of Socinianism. They bear witness to the truth, but propagate lies. "And no marvel; for Satan himself is transformed into an angel of light; therefore it is no great thing if his ministers also be trasformed as the ministers of righteousness."

And what shall we say of the whole system of *religious persecution?* was it from heaven, or from him who "was a murderer from the beginning?" When Pope Innocent VIII. proclaimed that the true method of converting heretics is to burn them—to tread them under foot as venomous adders—to exterminate them; who was his counsellor but the devil? And whence was it that while this doctrine of devils was rampant in Italy, Spain, and France, the spirit of the age was so imbued with it that it infected protestant Switzerland; and that the very Puritans who escaped from it in the old world, did not wholly escape from it in the new? And when the spirit of *exclusiveness* in some departments of the church of God, by which the ministry and ordinances of other departments, that do not suffer in comparison with those who thus proscribe them, are denied their "divine authority?" Such doctrines can hardly be expected to make any very deep impression upon the minds of thinking men. It is difficult to perceive how they can be seriously inculcated, did not melancholy facts teach us that the mind of man is subject to unaccountable *delusion*. It is lamentable *delusion*—delusion that has been silenced, again and again silenced by sound argument—and yet it remains. It is a castle in the air. It has no more foundation in the word of God, than Pool's fancied dragon had in the clouds. I pray that the subjects of it may be "kept from falling," and that God would deliver them from the snare of the fowler. Whence, too, the epidemic terror of witchcraft and sorcery that has left such a stain, not upon Rome only, but upon the fairest portions of Protestantism; but from that dreadful hallucination to which the adversary has been permitted sometimes to incite the superstitions of the best of men?

Nor is this all. Our own day has witnessed the Deceiver's power, by the misdirected zeal of good men, and the machinations of those that are bad. He has endeavored to prescribe rules and a moral machinery for the work of God; and by his oft-practised artifices, has got up those unhallowed excitements by which the unwary and unstable have been misled to their own undoing. One piece of fanaticism has thus very naturally succeeded to another, until there are not wanting those who boast of their sinless perfection; and other some are led away by the ravings of an insane prophet, who prates of that of which he knows nothing, and of which the omniscient Saviour has said that angels themselves are ignorant. To these we might add those latitudinarian doctrines, by which such multitudes are "carried about by the cunning craftiness of men whereby they lie in wait to deceive." The religion of forms without the power of godliness ever has been, and still is the religion which flourishes only under the auspices of the Deceiver. That disheartening stupidity, too, which, in defiance of returning Sabbaths, and the faithful instructions of God's ministers, and the admonitions and rebukes of divine providence, has superinduced the sleep of death in the world, and a dreamy, lifeless inaction in the church; what is this but the work of the Enemy?

We could easily extend this tragical survey. The adversary has always had a well-fortified kingdom in this world, and it is now lengthening its cords and strengthening its stakes. Evidence is not wanting of his character as the Deceiver, and of the extent of his deception.

If there is any one thought which has filled my own mind with solicitude in the course of the preceding illustrations, it is the fear that men would throw the criminality and responsibility of their wickedness on this great Deceiver, rather than, in all self-reproach and humiliation, take them upon themselves. This is just what he would have them do; it is one of his own cherished sophistries. It is not easy to make an impressive representation of his power without seeming to furnish something like a palliative for human wickedness. "The serpent beguiled me, and I did eat!" But the excuse is no extenuation of the crime, plausible as it may seem. While it is no crime to be tempted to sin, unless men themselves solicit the temptation, yet is there emphasis in the words, "Resist the devil, and he will flee from you." A conscientious fear and hatred of iniquity, and an humble reliance on God, will quench all the fiery darts of the fowler. We may have no truce with an enemy who is so alert in the arts of seduction. One there is who is not only able "to keep us from being tempted above what we are able to bear," but "with every temptation to make a way of escape;" who "knoweth how to deliver the godly *out of temptation*," and who has himself taught us to pray daily, "Lead us not into temptation, but deliver us from evil." The counsels of heavenly wisdom are, "Be sober; be vigilant; for your adversay, the devil, goeth about like a roaring lion, seeking whom he may devour." Be sober, lest you tempt the tempter; be vigilant, because your foes are subtle, and aim their envenomed arrows in the dark. To those who are the people of God, the days of temptation will soon be over; nor should it surprise them if the enemy should yet "come down in great wrath, knowing that his time is short." It is but a little longer, and the issues of the conflict will be announced in the exulting gratulation, "Thanks be to God who giveth us the victory, through our Lord Jesus Christ!" With those who are not the people of God, time is also urging its rapid flight, and if the chains of temptation and the bonds of iniquity be not speedily broken, they will feel the bondage forever.

Are we not also called upon by the previous thoughts to appreciate *the importance of moral and religious truth as the great and appointed means whereby the power of the adversary is to be successfully resisted?* There is nothing this Deceiver has so much reason to fear as the truth of God. Plain, honest truth, Bible truth, is the only successful antagonist to a system of measures and efforts whose only success depends on subtlety and deception. Truth penetrates those dark chambers of the human mind which have so long been the lurking-places of this foul fiend; dispels the mists in which he remains enveloped and undetected; discloses his hideous and ugly form; drives him out from all classes of human society, and ultimately destroys his influence in the world. The devil cannot long retain possession of the heart, or the community, that loves the truth of God. His element is darkness, or dim and misty speculation. He shrinks with instinctive repulsiveness from a pure atmosphere, and a sky beautified by the illuminations of heaven. It is frightful to see what a space in an ignorant mind one false notion can fill, and to what a series of errors, and what active power of mischief it can give rise; and on the other hand, it is delightful to see how wide a place one great truth can occupy, and to what a train of truths it gives birth, and what elevating and reforming influences it exerts.

How constraining, then, are the obligations on the church of God to extend his gospel to every creature. This thraldom to the great Deceiver is to be broken in no other way. O when shall the time come, that the polluting errors of the nations that know not God shall be superseded by the purifying counsels of heavenly wisdom; the noxious, though poetic, dreams of heathen mythology be forgotten in the messages of truth and love, and these victims of delusion and misery be made joyful in the glad tidings of great joy! How many more circles shall this planet of ours accomplish round the sun before these dreadful caverns of iniquity shall be invaded by the truths of God, there to combat and conquer the powers of darkness! Vigor, wisdom, courage, fidelity, self-denial, prayer, never were put in greater requisition than by the existing enterprise of Christendom to wrest these usurped domains of the adversary from him, and restore them to their rightful owner and Lord.

And how full of encouragement is the thought, that notwithstanding the deceptions of the adversary, and the extent of his power, *we may triumph in his final and certain overthrow!* In defiance of the convictions of our better judgment, a sort of superstitious dread comes over us, when we call to mind that we live in a world where he who "was a murderer from the beginning," goes "to and fro in the earth, and walks up and down in it." There is one view in which this alarm is causeless. One there is of woman born, who is "stronger than the strong man armed," and wiser than the crafty serpent. Perplex, tempt, ensnare, and depress the people of God he may; but his power over them extends not beyond this partial and temporary injury. "God shall bruise Satan under their feet shortly." Extend his ravages over this fallen world he may; but never to final conquest. "Thou shalt bruise his *heel*," is the utmost limit of his power. It is a great and glorious truth, that "for this purpose was the son of God manifested, that he MIGHT DESTROY THE WORKS OF THE DEVIL. The very curse which the tempter provoked upon the woman, enveloped the germ of her hopes, and contained the foreshadowing of that "promised seed" who should "bruise the serpent's head." The adversary was caught in his own snare. That vilest and most artful of his machinations, the death of the Son of God on the cross, was the most fatal to his hopes, and the surest presage of his defeat and shame. After three short days of seeming triumph over the sleeping Son of Mary in the tomb of Joseph, the manifesto was published and the war began, which is to terminate not until the "devil and his angels" are consigned to "their own place," to go no more out. Even now he durst not venture beyond the length of his chain; nor will many centuries pass away ere he is shut up within the fiery walls of his prison, and bound forever in chains of darkness and wrath.

With joyful lips, therefore, do we proclaim the supremacy of our redeeming God and King. "Dominion is with him!" The very hostility of Satan to his great design and work, is in itself a guarantee of his triumphs. It is a contest of no doubtful issue, in which the King of Zion is engaged with the great Deceiver. "He shall reign until all enemies are put under his feet." In councils far back of the ages of time, this great question was decided; and amid scenes far beyond this changing world, and to be hereafter realized, the triumphs of the Great Conqueror shall be proclaimed in the song, "He loved us, and washed us from our sins in his own blood, and hath made us kings and priests unto God, and we shall reign with him forever and ever!"

CHAPTER XI.

Man's First Sin.

It is something more than romance, that we cannot help feeling an interest, and even a deep sympathy, in that melancholy chapter in the history of our first parents, that narrates their apostasy. Whether it be from the wonted and cherished contemplation of those truths which their apostasy presents; or whether it be that the penal consequences of this first transgression have come upon us, and, in defiance of all our philosophy, we have an instinctive and resistless consciousness of the circling chain that binds our destiny with theirs; or whether it be that for the honor of humanity, we cannot suppress the wish that they had preserved their rectitude; certain it is, that we never read this tale of woe without becoming partakers in their blighted expectations.

The time was, when, above, without, within them, there was nothing to detract from their joy. Sin had not sullied them, nor had its turbid waters mingled with the pure current of their thoughts. There were no bodings of suspicion; recrimination and reproach had not poisoned their lips; remorse had not begun to prey upon their conscience, nor had a shade of apprehension settled upon their brow. They had no conflict with themselves, none with one another, none with the creatures around them. And what is more, nothing disturbed their sweet fellowship with their Maker; they were happy in his love; with uplifted eye and adoring heart, they beheld, praised, and enjoyed him. So beautiful is the picture, that it seems almost like fable. We can scarcely believe that we ourselves are the progeny of such innocence and joy, and that our parents were once the possessors of an inheritance so bright and unsullied.

This primeval Paradise was of short endurance; how short, God has not seen fit to reveal to us. Our first parents were not *confirmed* in this holy and happy state, without a previous trial of their integrity. Nor was it a severe or unwise arrangement, which thus put them upon their good behavior, placed them literally in a *state of probation*, and suspended their destiny upon their perfect obedience. They enjoyed the immediate and miraculous teachings of their benevolent Creator, and all those means and motives to obedience which could be furnished by the supreme authority, the instructive wisdom, and the persuasive tenderness of infinite love. The world they occupied was full of God; every scene was illumined with his presence, every sound vocal with his voice, every object spoke his praise, and every part of this material universe was constructed for their enjoyment. Never, until the manifestation of the Son of God in the flesh, have there existed so many and so affecting appeals of the divine goodness to the heart of man, as were made to these, the first created of the human family; and never have there been found among their descendants those whose intellectual and moral constitution was so fitted to respond to these appeals in every act of filial love, holy fear, and uniform and unremitting obedience.

It was, therefore, in every view, a fitting arrangement, and one suited to their character, condition, and relations, that they should be the subjects of God's moral government, and placed under law. Although it was not a written law, it was written upon their consciences; nor had they any desire to question its obligations, nor could they question them without blotting out from their bosoms those strong conceptions of right and duty which are found in the minds of fallen men, and in so much greater strength and purity in the unfallen.

To this great rule of action they had been obedient; but, in process of time, there was revealed to them *another law*, a special and positive statute, as a *test of their integrity.* It was a prohibitory statute, and is in the following words: "And the Lord God commanded the man, saying, Of every tree of the garden thou mayest eat; but of the tree of knowledge of good and evil thou *shalt not* eat of it; for in the day thou eatest thereof thou shalt surely die." The law was absolute. It was given to our first parents only; no others were present, no others were in existence, no others were bound by it, no others could transgress it; and when the specific object for which it was given was accomplished, it was repealed. It was intelligibly revealed; and revealed with as much precision and exclusiveness as the command given to Noah to build the ark, or the command to Abraham to sacrifice his son. There was also this strong peculiarity in this test of their obedience. They had committed no other sin; and against every other they were fortified by the consideration, that this prohibition obeyed, they were in no danger of committing any other. On every other point of duty they were safe; their only point of danger was centered in their liability to transgress this single interdict.

The *penalty* of this law was expressed in the words, "In the day thou eatest thereof, thou shalt *surely die.*" The language is significant, and denotes that the death here threatened should be executed thoroughly, intensely, and in the most perfect manner. As we use the word, there are three kinds of death, temporal, spiritual, and eternal.

Temporal death, or the separation of the soul from the body, certainly came upon Adam, and has come upon all mankind, in consequence of his first transgression. The first man became a dying man, from the hour of his apostasy. Temporal death constituted a part of the penalty. The separation of the soul and the body, when viewed in all its visible concomitants and consequences, is the most natural and impressive image, or emblem of the true and proper death of a moral and accountable agent. And this is probably the reason why it is called *death;* that by the very name, the true and proper idea of death might be habitually held up before the minds of men. Those few theological writers who have expressed the opinion that the death threatened to our first parents was temporal death, affirm that this is the primary and most natural meaning of the word death. But it is to be borne in mind, that our first parents had no experience and no observation to guide them in determining its import. This threatening is the first paragraph in the Scriptures, and the first time in the history of our world in which the word is used. There is certainly no evidence that this is its primary meaning. There is much more reason to believe that the dissolution of the soul and the body is the secondary and figurative, rather than the literal and primary meaning. The mere separation of the soul and the body does not constitute the true and proper death of the moral and accountable agent. When, immediately after the apostasy, temporal death was denounced, it is not called death, but simply the "returning of the body to the dust." Temporal death may be more properly viewed as one of the appendages of the penalty, rather than as constituting the entire penalty itself. A temporary separation of the soul and the body takes place as a sequence of the first transgression; nor would it ever have taken place without it; it is a standing and impressive evidence that all men are sinners. But whether the mere separation of the soul and the body be itself the original curse, is more than doubtful; and whether the curse could not have taken effect without it, may not be hastily decided. We are disposed to believe that if it had been executed upon our first parents, and no method of mercy had stayed the stroke of justice, temporal death would have been unknown, and these first transgressors would have sunk, body and soul together, under the wrath of God. Mere temporal death is not a sufficient punishment for sin; it is not such a punishment as it deserves. If the body were merely separated from the soul and returned to dust, and the soul, the corrupted and sinning agent, were received to the divine favor; there would be no evidence that the punishment is commensurate with the crime. God must *punish* sin; yet does he not inflict more or less than is implied in his threatenings. If the penalty of the law of paradise be commensurate with the ill-desert of disobedience; something far more dreadful than temporal death must have been implied in the threatening to our first parents.

By *spiritual death* is meant a judicial abandonment to a state of unmingled moral depravity. This death came upon our first parents the day they sinned. And a grievous punishment, a most dreadful curse it is, that for one act of disobedience, the transgressor shall be given up to unremitting and eternal disobedience; that when he has once crossed the line which separates sin from holiness, he shall have no opportunity and no power of returning; and that his evil propensities shall become so strong and violent, and his habits of sinning so inveterate, that nothing shall ever reclaim him. The Scriptures often allude to such a divine procedure as this. "My Spirit shall not always strive with man." "So I gave them up unto their own hearts' lust." "Therefore he gave them over to a reprobate mind." "Ye shall die in your sins." "They shall utterly perish in their own corruption." There is no greater evil than to be thus abandoned to an eternal course of sinning. Nor does this, as has sometimes been said, involve any more confusion between natural and moral evil, or sin and suffering, than necessarily exists. Such a course and state of sinning is itself calamity; it is suffering and pain. To no small extent, all sin carries suffering with it; suffering is, in the nature of things, inseparable from sinning; it is *mental suffering*, and ever will be so, from the intellectual and moral constitution which God has given to men. Men know, from experience, that there are sins which are attended with the most acute mental distress, while this distress is indicative of God's displeasure. "A voice from heaven could scarcely declare more clearly, and certainly could not announce more impressively, that there are certain mental affections which God would brand with the stigma of his severest reprobation." Nor is there any absurdity or confusion in the fact that one sin is often the punishment of another. Men feel this to be true, when they recoil from the first step in the course of transgression, because they know that it will be followed by a second, and that they are on the brink of a precipice. Nor is there any force in the often-repeated remark, that such a course of sinning, as it is the act of the sinner, cannot be the act of God as the punisher. The utter withdrawing of divine influences, and the judicial abandonment of the transgressor is everywhere represented in the Scriptures as God's act. Nor is there any force in the reasoning, that the course of sinning to which the transgressor is abandoned is his own chosen way, and therefore is no punishment. Sin is misery, and the sinner feels it. And if he does not feel it now, the time is coming when the burden will be greater than he can bear. I would not so impugn the moral government of God, as to harbor the thought, that it is not one of its invariable laws, that a state of mind that is bound by the cords of its own iniquity, is one which is not fraught with self-reproach, apprehension, and horror. Besides, the Scriptures teach us, that spiritual death is counteracted only through the atonement of the great Redeemer, and that the Redeemer's work has respect to the penalty of violated law; and if this be so, spiritual death constitutes a part of the penalty.

The penalty of this law consists also in *eternal* death, or everlasting misery. This is the emphasis of the curse, and is the proper death of an intelligent creature. This is the primary meaning of the awful word DEATH. It is used hundreds of times in the Scriptures to denote the everlasting punishment of sin. "The soul that sinneth, it shall *die.*" "The wages of sin is *death.*" "They which commit such things are worthy of *death;*" and that the declaration may not be misunderstood, the writer informs us that by death he means, "indignation and wrath, tribulation and anguish upon every soul of man that doeth evil." It is called "the second death;" and this is the punishment which sin deserves; these its earnings, this its proper wages.

It appears to us, therefore, to be in accordance with the teachings of the Sacred Writings to say, that the penalty of the law of Paradise was *temporal, spiritual, and eternal death.* There is nothing unreasonable in believing that these three kinds of death were threatened by the same term. Death is a word which comprises *all the evil* which is the fruit of sin. All these evils actually exist, and are the result of the first apostasy. The Scriptures never make needless and nicely drawn philosophical distinctions; they address the common mind, and conscience, and sensitiveness. The due and just punishment of sin falls upon the whole man; it is his everlasting separation from all good to all evil; it is the destruction of both body and soul in hell. This is the penalty of the law given to our first parents; and this is the penalty of that universal law under which all moral beings exist. Nor is there any reason why it should have been different in the case of the first transgressors. When the penalty shall be finally executed, it will be seen what is meant by the death of the transgressor. It will be death without mitigation and without reprieve, and without hope.

If our first parents had preserved their integrity, the covenant into which God entered with them secured them from disobedience. They would have been confirmed in holiness: the Tree of Life would have been the pledge and sacrament of their confirmation; they would have eaten of it and lived forever. How under such fearful considerations on the one hand, and such auspices of heavenly kindness on the other, these two holy beings came to transgress this single prohibition, so reasonable in itself, and so intelligibly revealed, has long been, and still is, a vexed question. There are but two theories on this subject to which it is worth our while to advert. *One is*, that it was impossible for God to prevent them from sinning; it is the old notion of the Platonic philosophy, that "evil proceeds from the restriction, or limitation of the divine power." Some modern divines are very bold, and teach that while God desired, in every view, to prevent their fall, and did all in his power to prevent it, the catastrophe was beyond his reach. This theory, if we understand it, asserts that their apostasy is chargeable to the defectible nature of their moral agency, and like friction in a machine, was a necessary evil; that God submits to it of necessity, and that it remains for his wisdom and goodness to so restrain and direct this uncontrollable evil as to produce the least possible mischief. *The other theory is*, that their apostasy was foreseen by God; that it was comprised in his purposes; that he permitted it for wise ends, and in order to bring good out of evil; and that it will eventually be made to answer a most important purpose under the perfect administration of that Almighty Being who will cause all things to work for his own glory, and thus fulfil all his pleasure. Which of these theories accords best with the fact that "the Lord God omnipotent reigneth," it is not difficult to determine. If there be one instance in which he is unable to accomplish his pleasure, who can tell but there may be ten thousand instances, and that the final history of the universe may not be the records of the divine imbecility, and the memorials of a disappointed Deity? How much more truthful is the last-mentioned view of this difficult subject, and how much stronger foundation does it furnish for hope and confidence in God, for prayer to him, for triumph in his government, for the exercise of his adorable sovereignty, and for exulting anticipations in those issues which, while they progressively unfold his unquestioned and infinite all-sufficiency, show that "the wrath of man shall praise the Lord, and the remainder thereof he will restrain." I dare not speculate on this high theme any further than to say, that "our first parents, being left to the freedom of their own will, fell from the estate in which they were created by sinning against God." Their perfect holiness was his gift; it was originally created by him; by him it was sustained; and when left to themselves, they fell. They were holy, but not immutable. The system of which they composed a part was subject to changes, because it was progressive. The fall of angels had already indicated that it was a system subject to moral derangement; the very fact that they were free implied the possibility of their sinning; while that wondrous remedial process, which as yet lay undisclosed in the divine mind had forestalled the otherwise untold evils of the sad catastrophe, and was already preparing to turn it to good account.

We take the divine record on this subject as it is, and are not covetous to be "wise above what is written." We have before spoken of the great Deceiver, "that old serpent, which is called the devil." The first thought of apostasy did not originate with our first parents, but with him. It was his object to countervail the benevolent purpose of God in man's creation. He had left his first estate; from a lofty seraph, he had become the "prince of devils;" from his high place near the throne of God, he had sunk to the regions of misery and despair; and from his glorious employment and immortality in the heavenly courts, he had become the most accursed of all created beings, and hurled down to the lake of fire. Our first parents were the first objects of his subtlety and malice. He hated them, and he hated their Maker. He envied their purity and blessedness, and would fain tempt them to become imitators of his rebellion, and partakers in his doom. This foul fiend was, for wise reasons, allowed to have access to the tranquil, and hallowed, and unsuspecting abodes of Eden. It was perhaps difficult for our first parents to see the reasons of the prohibition which laid its interdict upon the tree of knowledge; and this seems to have been the subtle snare which he first employed to tempt them from their loyalty. It was to the *woman* that this cowardly foe addressed the snare; he found her unprotected and alone; and accosted her with the words, "Yea *hath God said*, Ye shall not eat of every tree of the garden?" God had given them dominion over this entire earth; and he artfully propounds the question, *Is there a tree* of which you are not permitted to eat? She listened to the tempter's voice; he had gained her ear. She consented to reason with him. "And the woman said unto him, We *may* eat of the fruit of the trees of the garden; but of the tree which is in the midst of the garden, God hath said, Ye shall not eat of it, neither shall ye touch it, lest ye die."

Perhaps the thought lingered in her heart, that

the tree belonged to man; that the prohibition may have been misunderstood; and that, if not misunderstood, it held them in bondage. The tempter was emboldened, and "he said unto the woman, Ye *shall not* surely die!" There may have been, at this bold suggestion, a doubt upon her mind as to the nature and certain execution of the penalty. Men rarely sin where there is not some degree of unbelief. Her faith was obscured by clouds; there was a veil cast over her mind, and vague thoughts of escape began to agitate her. Perhaps what he says is true, and we shall not die! And then thoughts, still more impious, injected by the tempter's poisonous breath, began to fester within, and the fearful inquiry passed through her bosom, Can it be *such a giant sin* to eat of this one tree? And then her *curiosity* was appealed to: "God doth know that in the day ye eat thereof, *your eyes shall be opened*." And then her *vanity:* "and ye shall be *as gods*, knowing good and evil." And last of all, her senses were ensnared; she *looked* upon the fruit; the tempter had gained her eye. Reason and conscience were easily blinded then. She tempted her fate. And when "she saw that the tree was good for food, and pleasant to the eyes, and a tree to be desired to make one wise, she took of the fruit thereof and did eat, and gave also to her husband with her, and he did eat." The overpowering temptation to

Adam we do not know. Perhaps the imagination of the great English poet had its antetype in reality; Adam was her *husband*, and, in despair, he linked his fate with hers. And thus did man throw off his subjection to God, and renounce his allegiance to his rightful Lord and heavenly Father. The fearful deed was done. *Evil* they had never known before; but now "their eyes were opened," and new scenes and new histories presented themselves to their view. Eden bloomed in unsinning loveliness and beauty no longer. It was the *first sin*.

> "Earth trembled from her entrails, as again
> In pangs; and nature gave a second groan.
> Sky lower'd; and muttering thunder, some sad drops
> Wept at the completing of the mortal sin
> Original."

It is not for us to weigh the actions of men. The sin of our first parents was a *great* sin, if for no other reason than that it was the *first* sin of man. To pass from a state of perfect holiness to a state of transgression; to cross the line; to sin so soon; to sin in Paradise, and so near to heaven; to sin in God's immediate presence, within hearing of his voice, and while lying within his light as angels lie upon his bosom; to sin after all that he had done for them and given to them; after he had made them for himself and for each other, and to augment and guard their joys, had sanctified for them and blessed to them his holy Sabbaths; to sin not knowing what might be the direful consequences upon their posterity through all generations, or if knowing, thus to trifle with the character and destiny of myriads upon myriads unborn; to sin at the loss of God's favor, and the certain, fearful looking for of his displeasure; to abjure their Paradise, because there was an interdict upon a single tree; to disobey their great Maker at the instigation of him who was a murderer from the beginning, and thus launch forth from the peaceful home of heaven's complacency and joy, upon an ocean of storms; and all that they might know the evil, when they might have known only good; this was a sin which can be weighed in no earthly balance. Melancholy truth!—they fell. How changed the picture, and with what mortification, shame, and fear do we look upon it! What and where are our great ancestors now? They have lost their integrity, and their reward begins to be measured out to them according to their works. It was a day of gloom, and the reign of terror. Dark shadows came upon them like the deep midnight. Never, probably, were beings more forlorn, desolate, bewildered, or whose bosoms heaved more with unavailing sighs, or whose allotment was more drear and melancholy, this side the "blackness of darkness." What a crowd of terrible reflections must have rushed upon their minds, that for violating this *one* precept, they had lost their holy and happy immortality! They have no God to look to but the God they have so wickedly offended, and no refuge from the bitterness of their grief. They sigh, but into whose ears can they breathe their sighs? They weep, and they were the first tears ever shed in this world of sorrow. Perhaps they pray; but who is there to hear, or befriend them! Most truly was it a scene of desolation, anguish, and despair. It was the sting of sin; the bitterness, the hopelessness of those who had thus madly separated themselves from God. If ever despair was written on the countenance of man, it was the despair of that hopeless hour. Fear could not undo the deed; repentance and reform could not undo it. It was too late to think of sinless obedience, and securing the divine favor from the Tree of Life. The cherubim and the flaming sword carried death to every such presumptuous hope.

The CONSEQUENCES OF THIS SIN upon the *transgressors themselves*, are stated by the sacred historian. They had fallen, but they had not become obdurate and remorseless. Conscience did its office; their eyes were opened, and they saw their shame. They were stripped of their glory, and left naked and open, in all their degrading infamy, to one another's inspection, and reproach, and to the searching eye of Him who cannot look on sin. They were confused and confounded, even to weakness, so much so, that they hid themselves amid the trees of the garden. They sought to flee from God. "There was a schism between man and his Maker;" they stood apart. Yet not long; for though man hid himself from God, God did not hide himself from man. They saw the gathering storm, and were filled with agony and alarm.

They themselves were no longer one. That guilty woman, half prostrate with terror and amazement, flees to her agonized husband, himself overwhelmed in horror and despair; but only to encounter his reproach and embittered crimination. "Unto the *woman* God said, I will greatly multiply thy sorrow and thy conception; in sorrow shalt thou bring forth thy children; and thy desire shall be to thy husband, and he shall rule over thee." It was a terrible sentence thus to have her own equality with her husband disturbed, to be made the daughter of suffering and sorrow, and to have her highest earthly hopes withered in their bloom.

And that guilty man, what words does he hear from the voice of God his Maker? Unto Adam, God said, "Because thou hast hearkened unto the voice of thy wife, and hast eaten of the tree of which I commanded thee, saying, Thou shalt not eat of it; cursed is the ground for thy sake; in sorrow shall thou eat of it all the days of thy life; thorns and thistles also shall it bring forth to thee; and thou shall eat the herb of the field; in the sweat of thy face shalt thou eat bread, till thou return to the ground; for out of it wast thou taken; for dust thou art, and unto dust shall thou return." Nature herself had already begun to feel the shock. This fair creation was for the first time clad in mourning; Eden put off its gay attire, and a sickly hue overlay its foliage and flowers. The thunder awoke behind the clouds, and forked lightning darted its streams of terror. The earth was smitten with barrenness, and many a gloomy waste where there were no fountains of water, had begun to appear without tree, or plant, or blade of grass. Sorrow and toil were the bitter inheritance of the transgressors, till they returned to the ground from which they were taken. They were not allowed to remain in Paradise.

> "In either hand, the hast'ning angel caught
> Our ling'ring parents, and to the eastern gate,
> Led them direct, and down the cliff as fast
> To the subjected plain; then disappeared."

We know not the place of their last earthly rest, and only know it was in some far-off land, where flowers of paradise never grow, and the bird of paradise never utters its song. The cypress wept there; for it was the mourner's tribute. Yet faith and hope were there, pointing to a verdant immortality.

The effects of their sin upon their *characters* were even more mournful than these sad effects upon their outward condition. What a loss was that when this newly created pair lost the image of God! *Woman's* beauty, probably never since equalled, how did it fade then, with the fading of her radiant innocence, and how did it wane, and become expressive of her benighted, and waning, and poisoned mind? What has dimmed those bright lineaments so lately on the face of *man*, and chased away that placid smile and lofty bearing, and covered him with shame? The *curse* has overtaken them. They began to *die*. Their very frame is blasted and shrunk, and the freshness of its immortality fled, as though death had passed upon it even in its bloom. And the living soul within was darkened and dead in sin. There was not a virtuous, or holy thought or emotion remaining in their bosoms. "Every imagination of the thoughts of their heart was only evil continually." They were the "seeds of sin, that bitter root," which struck deep into the soil, that but yesterday was prolific in fruits of righteousness. They had broken God's covenant; and that single sin was the knell of their rectitude, and tolled the dirge, "dying thou shalt die"—dying utterly, dying forever.

But the consequences of this first sin were not confined to themselves; others were involved by it in the same condemnation and punishment. The curse pronounced upon the first woman is woman's curse still. To what extent it has been executed, is best known by woman's history, especially in antichristian and pagan lands, where there is so little to alleviate her humiliation and sorrow. It is the history of cruelty and oppression. Women there are slaves, and the mothers of slaves. In countries not a few, she is treated more like a brute than a woman. In others, she is the captive of a capricious tyrant, holding her honor and her life by the tenure of his fitful passions. In others, she is sold to the highest bidder. In others, where public sentiment constrains her to the sacrifice, and makes her life bitter if she refuses his memory this devotion, she perishes by thousands on the funeral pile of her deceased lord. Lands such as these record little else of woman, than that, in all that is dear to woman's heart, she is trodden down and trampled upon. And in Christian lands, alleviated as the curse is, it is a sorrowful history. There are no skies so smiling, no government so protective and generous, no bonds so endearing, where woman is not the sufferer.

And with literal severity, has the original sentence upon the man fallen upon his sons. "In the sweat of his brow he eats his bread." On the earth he cultivates, thorns and thistles have sprung up in vexatious exuberance. Noxious reptiles and devouring insects ravage his harvest fields. Cold and heat, drought and flood, storms and tempest desolate sea and land, and defeat his fondest hopes. Millions are destined to procure a scanty and sorrowful subsistence from the rocky soil and impoverished bosom of that earth which was once watered only by the dews of heaven, and which, now at best, yields its fruits only to painful labor and toil. Toil that is unremitted, and mingled with watchfulness, care, and solicitude; toil that becomes a burden and a weariness to the body and the mind; but which the sun everywhere looks upon as it sets upon millions of the weary and heavy-laden, and as it rises only to urge them on in labor and weariness. It is toil which pervades all classes and orders of men, and all the professions they follow. The rich are no more exempt from it than the poor; nor is the student any more exempt from it than the craftsman and the day-laborer. It is toil which none can shrink from without being the greater sufferers, and which ends only with the decrepitude of years and where "the weary are at rest."

But this was not all. Their sin was the parent sin of the race, as they themselves were its parents. If we look for the source of man's universal sinfulness, we trace it to this fountain-head. If we inquire, Whence is it that every child of

Adam possesses "a carnal mind that is enmity against God;" and why it is that this entire world of intelligent and moral beings, in every age and land, and under all the varieties of their external condition, is distinguished by all the characteristics of wickedness, convulsed by furious passions, rankling with envy, pride, and malice; and how it is, that iniquity in all its forms of ungoverned and unrestrained selfishness, seducing and being seduced—deceiving and being deceived—often gratified and still exacting, and when ungratified still more intense and vehement—always predominating, and yet becoming more clamorous—and unless arrested by heavenly grace, waxing worse and worse; we can only say that our fallen primogenitors begat a posterity in their own fallen likeness. They are born depraved, because this was the character of their depraved parents. "The cockatrice's egg has broken out into a viper."

This first sin involved the race in sin; and sin is as truly characteristic of everything that is human as speech and reason. The youngest infant and the man of gray hairs suffer and die, because they are sinners. "*By one man* sin entered into the world, and death by sin: and so death passed upon all men, for that all are sinners." By an arrangement of heavenly wisdom, and for the best of purposes, Adam was constituted the federal head and representative of his posterity. "By the offence of one, judgment came upon all men to condemnation;" through "the offence of one, many are dead;" the "judgment was by one to condemnation;" and "by one man's disobedience, many were made sinners." The law of Paradise was given to the first man, not only as the root from which all the branches of the race should proceed, and from which they should derive their nature, but as their appointed representative. In the eye of the law, they fell when he fell; his forfeiture of eternal life and his legal responsibilities were entailed upon them; they are his heirs, and the heirs of this attainted inheritance. Every sin, every sorrow, every grave, and every sigh in the prison of eternal despair is not only the fruit of sin in the individual sufferer, but the fruit and expressive memento of that "mortal sin original." The "angel standing in the midst of the sun, did not occupy a prouder position than innocent man;" the foul fiend, confined in chains of darkness, scarcely occupies a more abject position than sinning man immediately after his fall, incurring as he himself did, the wrath and curse of God, both in this life and that which is to come, and, but for God's preventing grace, dragging after him the unnumbered generations of men.

Why he was suffered to fall, we know in part; but we may well wait for the solution of this problem, till we know more of the final issues of that great Redemption of which the "second Adam, the Lord from heaven" is both the Author and the Finisher. It is not necessary to push our inquiries on this point any farther, than to have the assurance, that "high and mighty purposes" have been, and are yet to be thereby accomplished. If man fell from a lofty height, and infinite mercy caught him in his guilty fall, we may be sure that his apostasy is in harmony with the ends of infinite wisdom, rectitude and goodness, and that those ends will be accomplished.

It is much more important for us to leave these problems unsolved than to neglect the great moral lessons which man's first sin reads to us. Sin is a very different thing after it is committed from what men imagine it to be before. To measure the wickedness of that one offence, lies not within the range of human thought. Yet such is all sin. It is always an evil that cannot be measured. It is not possible for the human mind to travel over the immeasurable tracts of misery which it describes. Loud and admonitory is the voice from this first sin. Serpent-like, it charms but to devour. It made Lucifer the "archangel ruined," and the loveliest, happiest pair the most degraded and the most miserable. It is easier to sin than to bear the punishment of sin, or to repent of it after the deed is done.

We need not throw the blame of our own sins

on our great ancestor. It is a crushing burden he has to bear, if he has not found a forgiving God. "If thou be wise, thou shalt be wise for thyself: and if thou scornest, thou alone shalt bear it." We have nothing to cover us from God's omniscient eye; no cloak for our sin; no fig-leaf covering even to hide our shame. It is not to such a covering that we must repair. As well might our first parents have thrown themselves back upon their obedience to the law they had broken, as we, their descendants, have recourse to works of law for our justification before God. This is an unavailing—nay, a preposterous refuge for a transgressor. It is too late now to think of such a hiding-place. Yet is there a refuge even for the transgressor. One there is who is "an hiding-place from the wind, and a covert from the tempest; as rivers of water in a dry place, as the shadow of a great rock in a weary land."

"Go ye that trust upon the law,
And toil and seek salvation there;
Look to the flames that Moses saw,
And shrink, and tremble, and despair.
But I'll retire beneath the cross,
Saviour! at thy dear feet I'll lie:
And the keen sword that justice draws,
Flaming and red, shall pass me by."

CHAPTER XII.

First Interview between God and First Parents, after their Apostasy.

OUR last look at our first parents was immediately after their transgression, and when they were plunged in despair. They fled from the first indications of the divine presence; the very sound of his footsteps whose light and love had never failed to cheer them, now filled them with alarm. They were dark shadows that encircled them, that settled upon them like midnight. In that fearful threatening, "In the day thou eatest thereof thou shalt surely die," they had heard the voice of him who could not look on sin. He was their Maker and their Lawgiver; he was the Lord God omnipotent; and he had expressed his mind and will to execute the penalty they had incurred, in language well fitted to sink them into utter despair of mercy. What now had man to look for? Will the dreadful denunciations of the law have their course? Will the flames of divine wrath break forth upon him, and he himself and the long line of his descendants remain forever the monuments of that spotless rectitude of the divine nature that cannot connive at wickedness? Will his future history be written in mourning, lamentation, and woe; or will it record some new and unexpected manifestations of the all-sufficient Deity, more resplendent even than his infallible justice, and so bright that while they leave his rectitude stainless, they shall still more illustrate his unsearchable mercy?

Our first parents did not know that the invitations of heavenly mercy would ever reach them in their gloomy exile. They had no reason to *hope*, and could not hope to escape the punishment their sin deserved. *Why* the threatened penalty was not promptly executed to the full extent, is one of the difficult problems in theological science, because the divine justice was most solemnly pledged to destroy them. Our only solution of this problem is, that as the supreme Lawgiver, God had a right to remit the penalty of his law, provided there was any method by which it could be remitted consistently with the claims of his punitive justice. Such a method it was not in the power of human reason to devise, though it was not beyond the province of God's unsearchable wisdom and love. He had indeed thought of it "before the foundation of the world;" he had arranged it all in the eternal covenant of redemption with his Son; and therefore, in the interview he sought with our fallen parents, his great object was not to harden them in despair, but to elevate them from the depths of their hopeless depression, and invite them, wanderers as they were, back to their heavenly Father's house. God himself was thus the first preacher of the gospel, and himself proclaimed this first call to repentance.

Before their expulsion from the garden, there was an affecting and instructive interview between him and them, which reads lessons of wisdom and experience to those who are authorized in his name to call sinners to repentance, and to sinning men themselves to whom this divine call is addressed. The more we study this chapter in the early history of our race, the more we shall find it contains those treasures of truth and grace with which we are entrusted as ministers, and in which we all have so deep an interest as sinners. Thoughts are presented here which furnish the means of conviction to the thoughtless, of detection to the disingenuous, of humiliation to the proud, of support to the humble, of alarm to the stout-hearted, and of comfort to the broken in spirit.

The narrative of this interview is in the following words: "And they heard the voice of the Lord God walking in the garden in the cool of the day; and Adam and his wife hid themselves from the presence of the Lord, amongst the trees of the garden. And the Lord God called unto Adam, and said unto him, Where art thou? And he said, I heard thy voice in the garden, and I was afraid, because I was naked; and I hid myself. And he said, Who told thee that thou wast naked? Hast thou eaten of the tree whereof I commanded thee that thou shouldest not eat? And the man said, the woman that thou gavest to be with me, she gave me of the tree, and I did eat. And the Lord God said unto the woman, what is this that thou hast done? And the woman said, the serpent beguiled me, and I did eat."

The interview was a most solemn and serious interview. Our first parents had become alienated from God. The bond which had hitherto connected them was sundered; they had no sweet fellowship with their Maker; they knew that he looked upon them as criminals, and felt that they deserved his displeasure. They were alarmed, but saw no way of averting the judgment they deserved, but to flee from him, and "go forth like Cain with God's mark upon them, and under his eye in all their wanderings." Never were creatures more anxious to put themselves far from the being they had so offended. Left to themselves, they would never have welcomed another thought of God to their bosoms. How different their present state of mind from their wonted affection and confidence! What chilling alienation, what bitter jealousy! What a mournful character to be thus the enemy of the living God! There was that in their intelligent and moral nature, and in their remembrance of the past, which reminded them of what they lost in departing from him; but there was that within their own bosoms which drove them from the divine presence.

In order to reclaim and restore them, and before he would give them any intimations of pardoning mercy, God's first object was to *convince them of their wickedness.* And he did this with so much tenderness, and faithfulness, and heavenly wisdom, that we may well feel that his ways are not as our ways, nor his thoughts as our thoughts. He held up before their minds the mirror in which they might distinctly see their own character and condition; well knowing that they would be strangers to true repentance, if they had no sense of their sin; that they would have no reason for hope, unless they themselves saw that they had reason to fear; and no refuge, unless they had some just view of their danger.

The Lord God came into the garden as though he knew nothing of what they had done, and would know nothing but from these offenders themselves. He did not forestall the convictions of their own conscience by first charging their wickedness upon them; he would rather that they should fill their own bosoms with self-reproach, and voluntarily make an ingenuous confession of their sin, than be driven to that confession by constraint.

He was accustomed by some well-known symbols to manifest himself to them, and most probably at those seasons when they were employed in their more solemn acts of religious worship. The season once more returns when, at the decline of the day, he was wont to bless and accept their sacrifice; but they were not there to greet the approach of their once-loved Maker. Their affectionate and filial character was gone. They fled from the being they so lately venerated, and were filled with dismay as they heard his voice walking in the garden. Even before they had seen or heard anything of God, they had lost all solid foundation for inward peace and serenity of mind, and trembled at the premonitions of his displeasure which they found within their own bosoms. Mournful evidence of their apostasy! Sad indication of a disruption of those ties which had bound them to him who was once their highest joy! He who but yesterday looked upon the Creator as his father and friend, and regarded him with supreme complacency and confidence, now looks upon him as his enemy, and with suspicion and fear. He who but yesterday delighted in acts of grateful homage and loyalty, has now become the first human apostate, and the father of rebellion.

God was not ignorant of the melancholy events that had occurred in the history of his ruined creature; but he condescends to inquire after him, as a father inquires after his lost and wandering child. "The Son of Man" "came to *seek*," as well as to save "that which is lost." And it is a beautiful exemplification of this truth which is thus presented in this first call of God to our first parents. He would have conscience do its office, and leave it for a while unpacified, until "their sin had found them out," and their own convictions testified against them.

But with all this tenderness, there was great faithfulness on God's part, in setting their sin distinctly before their own minds. They had wilfully and criminally gone out of the way. They had voluntarily disobeyed the known will of God, and violated his infinite authority. God designed not only to awaken them to a sense of their lost condition, but to arouse within their bosoms the sentiments of shame and remorse. He designed by the solemn demand he made upon them, to make them see what they had done, and to show them that they were without excuse. He would press the inquiries upon them, What fatal enticement has allured you from your rightful Lord, and affectionate Parent? What strange event has taken place to induce you to shun my lately desired presence? *What hast thou done?* They must be made to feel that they were guilty. They had seen their destiny suspended upon a prohibition that was perfectly intelligible and explicit; the consequences of disobedience had been spread before them; no necessity was laid upon them to sin, but they were free to stand, and free to fall. And they were guilty; there was no cloak for their sin; no apology in the world could exculpate them. These offenders themselves knew this, and felt condemned. A guilty conscience gave force and energy to the first and most gentle accents of God's displeasure; they could not bear the rebuke of injured Deity.

Though God's ultimate design was to call them to repentance, yet he does in fact arraign them before him as their Judge. They had just received law from his mouth, and recognized him as their Lawgiver. They had tampered with the foe, and believed the serpent rather than God; they had broken through the restraints which their rightful Proprietor and Lord had thrown around them; and now, wisdom, benevolence, justice, all combined to bring these bold offenders to feel the force of the authority on which they had so wantonly trampled. They themselves would have secretly reproached their Maker if they had not been called to a solemn account. Nor could he do otherwise than thus make them see the equity of the procedure, should his justice exhaust its rigor on their devoted head. How reproachful the remonstrance, and how cutting to the conscience of this first transgressor, when the God of heaven thus called him by *name*, and required him to answer to the call! With what shame, with what deep confusion must he have been dragged from his hiding-place, and forced to reply to the upbraiding inquiry, "*Adam*, where art thou?"

The *immediate* effect of this call was much the same on their minds, which the call to repentance ordinarily produces upon the minds of their descendants. It was not a prompt return to God; rather did they turn from him with a mind averse to holiness, a defiled conscience, and a face covered with shame. They were conscious of their crime; and the deeper and more painful the consciousness, the more deeply did they entrench themselves within their gloomy retreat. There was also great *disingenuousness* on their part. They hesitated to make a full and frank confession of their sin; nor did they do so, until it was extorted from their lips. An ingenuous and honest spirit would have led them to flee, not *from* God, but *to* him; not to cover their sin, but to spread it all out before him in all its black deformity.

Instead of this, they try to extenuate its turpitude. "The *woman* that *thou gavest* to be with me, *she* gave me of the tree and I did eat." There was something ungenerous and unmanly in this assault upon the woman; while there was more that was impious in the imputation upon God himself, for giving him the woman to be his tempter. Yet how much is this like fallen man! If Adam had not been conscious of what he had done, and had not been sensible that his conduct needed some excuse, he would have laid his hand upon his mouth. Right conduct needs no excuse, and deserves no condemnation. It is only when men know they have done wrong, that they have any occasion for pretexts to excuse their wrong-doing. Our first father's state of mind was not what it ought to have been; nor was he willing to see and confess his wickedness, and abase himself before God; else would he not have allowed himself so dexterously to throw the blame upon others. The tendency of this state of mind was only to fortify himself in his disobedience, and provoke still more the displeasure of God. God did not suffer him to be in doubt as to his real object in coming into the garden, but brought his thoughts directly to the cause of all his trouble. The human heart is "*deceitful* above all things and desperately wicked." This transgressor was not willing to see his sin in its true light. "He that doeth evil hateth the light, neither cometh to the light, lest his deeds should be reproved." He could not bear to look his own wickedness in the face, and fix his thoughts upon the dreadful evils of his presumptuous and reckless deed. He shrunk back from it, and endeavored to wrap himself up in his own delusion. He was not the gainer by his excuses, but the loser by all the turnings and windings of his benighted and deceived mind. His duty was obvious. He ought to have stood speechless, or if he opened his lips, it should have been only to make the ingenuous confession, My Father, I *have disobeyed thee; I have eaten of the tree and am without excuse.* Instead of this, the confession that was extorted from him is prefaced and incorporated with the most flattering extenuation of his crime. And the same is also true of his confused tempter, and the guilty partner of his crime; "The *serpent* beguiled me, and I did eat."

There was much in all this early conduct that evinced obdurate impenitence. Why did they not at once confess and bewail what they had done? and as soon as they heard the voice of their Maker, throw themselves at his feet, and say, "We have sinned against heaven and before thee!" Did they wish to capitulate with God, or suppose that he would capitulate with them, while they were in a state of rebellion? It was no great proof of penitence, that they were fugitives from law and justice; nor that during the whole of this interview, we hear not a word of lamentation from their lips, nor one heart-felt expression of sorrow for their crime.

Yet, wondrous mercy, God's ways are not as our ways, nor are his thoughts as our thoughts. It is ordinarily the method of his grace, to arrest the subjects of it in their greatest obduracy, and when distress and anguish come upon them; that they and others may know and record that it "was not for their sakes, but for his own great name's sake" that he "took them from the horrible pit and the miry clay, and set their feet upon a rock, and put a new song in their mouth, even praise to our God." His way of leading men to appreciate the interpositions of his mercy, is first to make them feel their need of it. Such are the teachings of his truth and Spirit, that they are brought to despair of help from themselves and creatures, before they will be induced to place their hope in God. The call to repentance is never welcome, never indeed well understood, till the sinner feels that he is lost and helpless. The self-righteous, the self-deceived, and the self-hardened, are in no fit state of mind to repent and believe the gospel. It was not until the jailer of Philippi "called for a light, and sprang in, and came trembling, and fell down before Paul and Silas, and brought them out, and said, Sirs, what must I do to be saved," that his anxious heart caught at the answer, "Believe on the Lord Jesus Christ, and thou shalt be saved, and thine house." It was not until the woman of Canaan bowed her proud heart to the reproachful words, "Woman, it is not fit to take the children's bread and give it to dogs," and meekly replied, "Truth, Lord, yet the dogs eat of the crumbs that fall from their master's table;" that the Saviour said to her, "O woman, great is thy faith, be it unto thee, even as thou wilt." It was not until the early Christians saw and felt that "they had the sentence of death in themselves, that they should not trust in themselves," that they "trusted in God." God led our first parents to a just view of their sinful conduct; he made them sensible of the bond between their sin and his own displeasure, before he gave them even the most distant intimations of his mercy. They were overwhelmed in view of what they had done, and God had threatened. It was the hour of alarm. Everything concurred to excite their fears. They knew no way of escape, and were apprehending nothing but death. Thus arrested, tried, convicted, and forced to come forth from their hiding-places, nothing seemed to remain to them, but "a certain fearful looking for of judgment." Well might they feel that "they were naked;" that nothing could cover them from the omniscient eye, nothing hide their shame, and that they had no refuge from the coming wrath.

The time had come, therefore, when with the language of rebuke and judgment, were mingled the whispers of love. Notwithstanding all their vileness, the Father of mercies had thoughts of kindness toward these his ruined children. The Son of God had already taken the initiatory steps to his mediatorial work, and himself interposed to deliver them from going down to the pit. God had been preparing their minds to understand and appreciate those disclosures which, in the fulness of time, would be more emphatically proclaimed as "glad tidings of great joy to all people." And he hasted to unfold his compassionate design, and invite them to repentance. There was some obscurity in this disclosure; it was, but a glimpse of him in whom all fulness dwells; but it was enough to keep them from despair. "To the serpent he said, I will put enmity between thee and the woman, and between thy seed and *her seed;* it shall bruise thy head, and thou shalt bruise his heel." This was an enigma which their darkened minds could not at once solve; yet it threw a beam of light across their future path. They caught the intimation, as a drowning man catches at a straw, and as many a convinced and despairing sinner catches at the first thought of God's pardoning mercy. They were assured, at least, of some suspension of the fearful sentence; who could tell but it might be the plenitude of pardons, and the glad hope of their restoration to the favor of God!

God then proceeds to unfold some of the consequences of their sin; but O, how tempered with mercy! how far short of the curse of a violated law! Enough was denounced and felt to teach them the greatness of their sin, and to impress upon their mind the inviolable claims of divine justice; but enough was disclosed to teach them that the complete execution of the penalty was deferred, and that time and opportunity were furnished them to obtain mercy, through the promised mediator.

Thus in the whole of this solemn and affecting interview, the great object seems to have been, not only thus early to announce to our first parents that there was forgiveness with God that he might be feared, and to reveal the method of forgiveness; but to bring them to true repentance, and to an humble apprehension of the mercy of God in that Saviour who is the serpent's foe, and the sinner's friend.

What the *ultimate* effect of this disclosure was upon their minds, we are not distinctly informed; while from the whole interview itself, from the comprehensiveness of the promise, and from the subsequent conduct of Eve on the birth of her first son, there is reason to believe, that what they had heard about the seed of the woman bruising the head of the serpent, was the means of their saving faith in the promised Saviour; was ultimately the source of consolation and hope, and that they became penitent and pardoned.

It is somewhat remarkable that their history closes here at the termination of this interview with God after their apostasy. We are simply informed, after this, that Cain, Abel, and Seth were their children; and then their names and history, with a bare allusion to them as the parents of the race, are dropped from the sacred record. Their sin had been great; they were the first transgressors; they had covered the world with mourning; and although they found mercy, it was fitting that their history should here be brought to a close, and terminate with the bald record, "All the days that Adam lived, were nine hundred and thirty years, and he died."

Such was the first call to repentance ever issued from the God of heaven to guilty men. There are several important lessons which it inculcates; the first of which is, that *it discloses those great laws of rectitude and of mercy which form the unchanging principles of the divine government.* It was, in substance, the same call which is now made to Adam's posterity, and based on the same great moral principles. In man's redemption from sin and hell, there is a union of those properties of the divine nature, which seem to be irreconcilable. On the one hand, there is a rectitude that is perfect and unerring, and that is the strong support of rectitude in heaven and on earth. There is that even justice which punishes the fallen, and cannot do otherwise than ignite the flame of holy indignation against all wickedness, and express its abhorrence of iniquity in those everlasting terrors which are consuming fire. And on the other hand, there is that mercy and peace, which fully to comprehend, we must dive deeper into the heart of God, and explore the depths of his love more fully than it is for mortals to attempt. There is that self-originating and self-moved mercy which has wrought such wonders in our world, and made so many the partakers of the "exceeding riches of his grace." How these seemingly jarring attributes of the divine nature, and these conflicting principles ever could be reconciled in the government of fallen men rather than fallen angels, is the great mystery of godliness. How to bring about such an arrangement, that a being of inflexible justice could show mercy; that the punisher should become the pardoner; is a problem which could find no solution but in the uncreated Mind. When man had once sinned, everything, in reason and nature, in the divine works and providence, and in the history of other worlds, pointed to the wrath to come, and seemed to demonstrate that the transgressor must perish, or God be unjust.

Yet among the *first lessons* inculcated by the early history of our race, is the fact, that God is just in being the "justifier of every one that believeth in Jesus." Love the most exacting, and justice the most inflexible, were alike satisfied with the first promise. In that early intimation, obscure as it was, were wrapt up the unchanging principles of that mediatorial government, where mercy and truth meet together, and righteousness and peace have kissed each other. The suffering Saviour was there—the seed of the woman, that he might die as a Sacrifice. And the Son of God was there, that he might survive the flames of the altar; that he might impart a consideration to his sacrifice that would render it capable of answering the ends of love that passeth knowledge, and of justice as terrible as ever hurled angels from their thrones, or kindled the flames the smoke of which ascends forever and ever. Behold, therefore, the goodness and the severity of God! thus early disclosed as combining their influence in the government of this fallen world, and thus adorning and giving efficacy to that government till the heavens be no more. "Toward thee goodness, if thou continue in his goodness; otherwise, thou also shalt be cut off."

There is another lesson also to be learned from this early interview between God and our fallen primogenitors: it is, that *no outward condition can make a sinful creature happy.* Our apostate parents were miserable even in the garden of Eden. That garden of delights had not altered, nor were its beauty and loveliness as yet blighted by the curse. Its sylvan scenery was still cheerful, its air soft and fragrant, its ground fertile, its songs and smiles were sweet, and everything was full of God. Yet its once happy occupants were to the last degree miserable. We need not ask why? It availed them nothing now that they still dwelt in Paradise, and that "the Lord God still walked in the garden in the cool of the day." Every path they trod, every tree and flower rebuked them; God's presence only filled them with dismay.

Let us bring the lesson home then, that no man can be tranquil and happy, and live in sin. Crowns cannot make him happy. Wealth and honor, health and friends cannot make him happy, so long as he has a guilty conscience, and an aching, bleeding heart. He cannot be happy even when alone; in the deepest solitude, he cannot forget that he is a dying man; that he is an immortal being, and that there is a God to whom he is accountable. He cannot look up at God's sun in the heavens; he cannot hear his voice in the storm, or in the zephyr; he cannot feel the darkness of the night covering him, without having his existence embittered by fears. He has no almighty Friend, no Father in heaven to whom he can look with the confidence of a child, and of whom he can say, "The Lord is my light and my salvation, whom shall I fear? the Lord is the strength of my life, of whom shall I be afraid?" What is there to be envied in all this world can give, if one view of God, or one retrospective, or introverted thought can spoil the joy? Give a wicked man the material universe; conduct him even to that heavenly Paradise where God dwells in his ineffable glory; and, if still in love with sin, he would be the most miserable of men. Just as our guilty first parents fled from God to hide themselves amid the trees of the garden, would wicked men cry "to the rocks and the mountains to fall on them, and hide them from the face of him that sitteth on the throne."

With what force and tenderness, then, ought these thoughts to *address themselves to all who live in sin.* Their language to them is, "Repent of all your transgressions, so iniquity shall not be your ruin." They utter the gospel call—repentance toward God, and faith in our Lord Jesus Christ. It is not the stern call of justice merely; it is the call of heaven's proffered and tenderest mercy. And what is its language, if it does not say, Dismiss this spirit of alienation from God; away with this disingenuousness, and make a frank and humble confession of your wickedness. You have eaten of the tree, whereof he hath said, Thou shalt not eat of it. You cannot undo the deed; nor can you expiate the justice of a violated law. Yet may you repair to him who "came to seek and save that which is lost," and who has said, "Him that cometh unto me I will in no wise cast out." Flee *to* God, and not *from* him. Flee to the arms of his mercy; flee to the heart of his bleeding Son.

Perhaps the reader *has* fled thither, where grace triumphs and extends its triumphs. Let him learn, then, to *appreciate that goodness of God which has led him to repentance.* After our first parents had fallen, nothing was farther from their thoughts than a true return to the God they had offended. They would have remained strangers to him always—forever undone, but for that condescending grace which pursued them in their flight, brought them forth from their hiding-place, not to confound and destroy them, but to convince, humble, and forgive them. Thus it is that the God of infinite mercy draws the sons and daughters of men with "cords of love, as the bands of a man." We "love him because he first loved us." It is God who first seeks the sinner, and not the sinner who first seeks God. It is only thus that the miserable and guilty exile is brought back to his father's house. No man makes the first advances. God meets him in his wanderings with the treaty of reconciliation in his hands, and counsels him to retrace his steps. Precious truth!

> "Jesus sought him, when a stranger,
> Wandering from the fold of God."

How touching is that memorable appeal, *Adam*,

where art thou? Whence is it that thou hast fled from me, thy Maker, thy Father, thy Shepherd, thy Saviour? What hast thou done? Never can these expostulations be forgotten by his people, and never can they give him the full glory which his grace deserves. Though they spend an eternity in praising him, it will be but to acknowledge that he alone is worthy to be praised; that all honor and glory are his due; and to unite their hearts and combine their efforts in "forming one refulgent, unequalled crown, not to be placed on his head, for it would be unworthy, but to be cast at his feet."

CHAPTER XIII.

The First Promise.

WONDROUS truth, there was no great interval between the first sin and the first promise. Those portentous clouds which hung over the garden, had scarcely begun to cast their shadows, when the halo of an unexpected and bright prediction encircled these first transgressors, and sent its radiance to distant times. Strange prediction! marvellous promise! "I will put enmity between thee and the woman, and between thy seed and her seed; it shall bruise thy head, and thou shalt bruise his heel."

This is the *first promise* recorded in the Scriptures. And that hope might gently and gradually find its way to the despairing bosoms of the transgressors, it is contained in the *sentence pronounced on their betrayer*. He was the first and great transgressor, and on him incensed justice first fell. What was death to *him*, was life to *them*. They could not comprehend its import; bright as it was, it was but a ray of light that illumined their dungeon. Nor did it at first disclose the full, rich truth, that his degradation was man's honor, his defeat man's victory, his overthrow man's redemption. Our first parents probably understood it to imply no more than that it contained a prediction of *life* to the woman, because it spoke of the "woman's seed;" a prediction of conflict between her seed and the serpent, in which the tempter should be vanquished by One in a nature inferior to his own, and in which the woman's seed should be ultimately triumphant. It was the *woman's* seed, and not the offspring of *the man;* and could therefore be applicable only to him who was the Virgin's Son. It is a singular promise, but so emphatic and compendious as to require subsequent revelations to develop its import. It includes the sum and substance of the gospel; it is the germ of that Tree of Life whose leaves are for the healing of the nations. A brief analysis of it is the design of the present chapter.

It contains the FIRST REVELATION OF GOD'S PURPOSES OF MERCY TO OUR WORLD. There is nothing contingent, or accidental in the arrangements of the divine mind. "Order is heaven's first law." Nothing can happen which is not foreseen by an all-knowing God. There never was a period when everything that he does, did not come within the arrangements of an antecedent and eternal purpose. He is wise and immutable, and therefore thought of everything beforehand; everything exists "according to the counsel of his own will." The purposes of creatures discover weakness and imperfection; and therefore are liable to change. On God's part, everything is fixed and permanent. The mind of creatures is too narrow to comprehend many things at once; their heart is too inconstant to remain undivided in their pursuits; their passions are too unstable to flow long in any one direction. God is "of one mind, and none can turn him, and what his soul desireth that he doeth." It is a revealed fact, and not a problem to be solved, that the infinite God, whose thoughts are as far above man's thoughts as the heavens are higher than the earth, has interposed in the concern of man's salvation by a settled purpose and a stated method. If his perfections require definiteness of arrangement in all the minor affairs of the world in which we dwell, so that a sparrow falls not to the ground without his providence; much more is it required in the method of the great redemption. The purpose is not fortuitous and unexpected; it belongs to "the everlasting gospel," and this revelation of it is the first explication of that "mystery hid from the foundation of the world."

Whether a Being who never began to exist, formed some of his purposes before he formed others, is a question which need not embarrass us. It is not necessary that his master-purpose should have priority in the order of time, and only in the order of nature. Nothing is more obvious from his word, or from an extended view of his providence, than that his first purpose in importance—his most comprehensive and all-concentrating purpose—is his purpose of mercy to apostate men. It is the purpose which is most endeared to his benevolent mind, the one for which he has made the greatest sacrifices, and to which he has made all things subservient. Treasures of divine thought were to be developed by it, which otherwise never could have enriched the universe, and changes effected by it which would arrest the attention of angels and men. The divine mind was here to employ itself on a large scale; it was to occupy ages; wondrous were the manifestations it was to make of the unsearchable Godhead. There were "utterances of the Deity" in the few words of that single promise, which will be echoed in the everlasting song of the redeemed; there were excellencies of the Deity of which that promise is the mirror, which will be the more effulgent and the more transforming, as the effects of it are seen and felt with increasing interest by every rational being, when these material heavens and earth shall be no more.

The reasons for the formation of this great

purpose, have been revealed. God himself is his own supreme object. He must be so, from the eternity of his existence, and the perfection of his character. All nations are as a drop of a bucket compared with him. In the eternity past, there was no other in existence except himself; and in the eternity to come, though worlds be created upon worlds, they may not be compared with him. If God himself be not the chief end of all things, creatures must be that end. Yet the heavens are not clean in his sight, and his angels he chargeth with folly. And what is man who is a worm, and the son of man who is a worm? If we ask why, with unwasting resources of joy and blessedness within himself, did he give existence to the race of man; the most natural and obvious answer must be given in the words, "Thou hast created all things, and for *thy pleasure* they do exist and were created." If we ask, *why was it his pleasure;* a field of thought here opens which it is impossible for creatures to travel over, impossible for them to survey, or even to glance at, without adoring views of God, and without veiling their faces before him.

That is an amazing declaration which affirms that *God is love.* How much these few words contain, neither the tongue of men, nor angels can express. It is God's nature, to love. He would not exist alone; he must have something to love.

He created angels that he might love them, and make them holy and happy. But he would stoop lower than angels; his heart was set upon man; he would make them lovely, and give them the happiness of being loved. When his love puts on its most attractive forms, and he would deck himself with it as with a garment, he smiles upon the cheerless and desponding; he hears the groaning of the prisoner and looses them that are appointed unto death. He stoops to this agitated, convulsed, and almost distracted world—this house of mourning, this home of the miserable, these suburbs of hell. His highest delight and joy are that from this once fair, and now fallen creation, those most demonstrative expressions of "the exceeding riches of his grace" should go forth which must otherwise have been suppressed, but which are now destined to receive eternally-accumulating responses of grateful and admiring praise.

Here we may perceive something of the import of this *first promise.* The all-sufficient God was, if I may so speak, urged to it by his irrepressible love. The fountain was full, and must thus transpire though it were by a streamlet in the desert. It is a wonderful promise; and one which illumines the pages of God's entire revelation; lights up many a dark and inexplicable dispensation of his government, and sends its cheering radiance from the dawn of creation to its declining sun.

When oppressed with sin, and writhing under the sting of guilt, it was no easy matter for our first parents to comprehend that there was hope for such sinners as they. Dismal and sullen was the silence of that scene when they were first summoned before their offended judge; and when that deep silence was broken on their part, pitiable must have been those notes of woe. And, delightful thought, guilty as our fallen humanity was, its wretchedness had a voice that entered into his ear; man's helplessness was his most affecting appeal for deliverance from death. The fountain of eternal love was opened, that the thirsty and perishing might drink and live. "Deliver him from going down to the pit; for I have found a ransom." The iron grasp of inexorable justice was broken; that hopeless grief assuaged, and the tears of Paradise exchanged for the "glad tidings, I will put enmity between thee and the woman, and between her seed and thy seed."

There is in this promise, in the next place, A PREDICTION OF HIS ASSUMPTION OF HUMAN NATURE BY THE SECOND PERSON OF THE ADORABLE GODHEAD. "Without controversy, great is the mystery of godliness; God manifest in the flesh." It is one thing to reveal a mystery; it is quite another to explain it; to say that mysteries are revealed is no absurdity, to say that they are explained is to make them no longer mysterious. The Bible has higher aims than to make men acute reasoners and profound metaphysicians. The incomprehensible mystery of the Incarnation appeals to something else in man beside his reason; it appeals to his conscience and addresses his wants and his woes.

The Saviour we need must be *God*, and not a creature. Men have sinned, and deserve the curse pronounced by that law which can no more change than God can change. They need pardon and peace; and though they search through creation, and go up to the heavens, and down into the deep; though they inquire of the past, the present, and the future; though they address the most exalted and the most perfect of all the creatures that ever came from the hand of God; they can find none so good, so powerful, so perfect as to effect their reconciliation with their offended Maker. It would be temerity and crime for the loftiest of creatures, who has no righteousness beyond his own necessities, to entertain the proud and sacrilegious thought that by anything he could do, or suffer, he could satisfy or relax the bonds of immutable justice, and justify the Holy One in justifying the ungodly. Condemned and dying men could not trust a created Saviour; redeemed sinners may not be under this debt of gratitude to a created Saviour.

But while the deliverer they need must be truly and properly *divine;* he must be also the "woman's seed," and clothe himself with flesh. Man is the transgressor; man is the one that needs reconciliation; the great and satisfactory expiation must be made by man, and have a special reference to man. Man is the one who must suffer; and therefore, it is in the nature of man, and for man that the expiation must be made.

The great Mediator must therefore be both God and man, thus supplying the deficiencies of the created by the infinite efficacy and worthiness of the uncreated; and thus applying the infinite merits of the uncreated to the created nature. It is this Incarnate Deliverer which the sinner needs; one that is not hidden from his view by the light that is inaccessible and full of glory; one that he may venture to approach, because, with all his majestic brightness, he is related to humanity; and one to whom he can repair without distrust, without timidity, and with joy.

While, therefore, there is inexplicable mystery in the truth disclosed in this first promise, it is an arrangement full of heavenly love and wisdom. In no way does God so stoop to men, as by becoming one of them; and in no way does he so encourage men to draw near to him, without fear and without reserve. The promised Saviour *was* the "seed of the woman," the Virgin's son. He whom "all the angels of God worship," who "was in the form of God, and thought it not robbery to be equal with God," took upon him the form of a servant, and was made in the likeness of men." Nothing could have induced this disrobing himself of the splendor of the Godhead, and this enrobing himself with the properties of a well-known and degraded humanity, had he not a special fellowship and sympathy with the great brotherhood of man. He linked himself with the race by this fraternal tie. "Forasmuch as the *children* are partakers of flesh and blood, *he likewise* took part of the same." He would be a child with them, and participate in the children's destiny. "Verily he took not on him the nature of angels, but the seed of Abraham; because in all things it behooved him to be made like unto his *brethren*."

The "Seed of the Woman" is a designation that he glories in; he claims to be the "Son of David," and the "Son of Abraham," not less than the "Son of God." He speaks of himself more than sixty times, as the "Son of Man," everywhere and always identifying himself with humanity. We look back to those gloomy scenes in Paradise, where man fell, and was doomed to labor and toil; where woman was condemned to be the daughter of sorrow; where the ground was cursed for man's sake; and where our first parents trembled in apprehension of the coming wrath; and in this sentence upon the serpent, we see them, dark and gloomy as they were, illumined with brighter rays even than those of hope. The predicted Incarnation of the Eternal Word gives an interest and importance to them which belongs to no other part of the universe. This earth we tread upon is immortalized by the fact that it was once his cradle and his grave; and man is immortalized from this wondrous alliance to the Deity. We feel humbled as the descendants of an apostate progenitor; but it is no mean genealogy that we belong to a race of which Mary's Son was the "first born among many brethren." The pride of family has no such lineage to boast of as this common heritage of the race; descent from earthly princes has no such armorial ensigns as the babe of Bethlehem "wrapped in swaddling clothes and lying in a manger."

The "Seed of the Woman," how comprehensive a truth is this!—announced by prophets, shadowed forth by the prefigurations of the ancient law, demonstrated by miracles, confirmed by the cross, reassured by him who rose from the dead, and raiseth them up, because "he quickeneth whom he will!" How momentous this historical fact, that the Son of God left the glories of heaven and descended to the abyss of human woes! What a new face did it put, not only upon the original Paradise, but upon all earthly things, and what transformations has it effected and is yet destined to produce in the history of the world in which we dwell! What an announcement to sinners like ourselves! What amazing interest is thrown around this affecting reality,—interest as intense and as fresh as though it had been just revealed from heaven, although it was announced six thousand years ago! What should interest and electrify us, if not the tidings that the "Seed of the Woman" came to seek and save that which was lost; to satisfy divine justice, and reconcile us to God; to restore the fallen to fellowship with their Maker; to welcome the exile to his Father's house; to make the conquest of the sinner's heart, and carry it with him to those unseen heavens whence he came; to bid the despairing hope, to give the confiding comfort, strength to the weak, and to the struggling victory!

This first promise, also, in the next place, REVEALS THE ONLY WAY OF LIFE. We know not how distinctly the way of salvation was revealed to our first parents; but it was in sufficient fulness to keep them from despair, and encourage them to offer acceptable sacrifices to God. Of this one truth they were persuaded, that salvation *by the works of the law* was to them no longer a practicable thing. What they had done, or what they could perform, might no longer be the ground of hope. They had no reason for self-exultation in their obedience. No repentance and reform could come in the place of the threatened penalty. No morality, no religious duties, no promises of good behavior, much as all these became them, could justify them in the sight of God. As well might a murderer promise repentance and amendment as a satisfaction to violated law, as the sinner look to any works of righteousness of his own as the ground of his pardon and acceptance. "Moses describeth the righteousness which is of the law;" it is a legal obedience, a character and conduct which the law requires and justifies. "The man that *doeth* these things shall live by them." Punitive justice has no claims upon such a man, because he has no sin to be punished, or forgiven. Remunerative justice pronounces him just, and entitled to the life which it awards to unsinning subjects. But the mournful fact is, there is no such man; "*all* have sinned and come short of the glory of God." "There is none righteous, no, *not one*." So that the man who now stands upon his own righteousness, is condemned and lost. He may not be so bad as other men; but in the article of his justification on the ground of what he himself has done, he stands upon the same level with the vilest of the race. "Every mouth is stopped, and the whole world is guilty before God." For man the sinner, there is no hope from the law. "Yea, though I wash myself in snow water, and make myself never so clean, yet shalt thou plunge me in the ditch, and mine own clothes shall abhor me." It is no longer in himself that he can find a justifying righteousness; it is too late; be it ever so agonizing, the effort is desperate, it is a forlorn hope. "If thou, Lord, shouldest mark iniquity, O Lord, *who* could stand?" The thing is impossible. Sooner may men scale the heavens, or dive to the bottom of the ocean. It is more than God can do *thus* to justify the *ungodly*.

Yet shall the seed of the woman bruise the serpent's head. There is salvation by Jesus Christ, and that salvation is altogether a practicable attainment. What cannot be affirmed of a legal justification by the deeds of law, can be affirmed of a gratuitous justification by the seed of the woman. There is such a reality as "the righteousness of faith." This was the way of life revealed to our first parents, and which is so clearly and abundantly revealed to their apostate descendants. What men cannot do, Jesus Christ has performed. The work is finished by him; nothing can be added to it, and nothing can be taken from it; and God hath done it, that men may fear before him.

There is perfect simplicity in this way of life, and perfect reasonableness in its revealed conditions. There is nothing in it which an intelligent child cannot understand; it has no duplicity, no subtlety, no abstruseness. It has not one set of doctrines for the initiated, and another for the vulgar; its teachings are open to the world and accessible to all. It is not locked up in mysterious hieroglyphics, and confined to the cloisters of learned and privileged orders of men. "The word is nigh thee, in thy mouth and in thy heart." It is simply that the righteousness, on the ground of which the sinner is justified, is not in himself, but in another; not wrought by himself, but by God manifest in the flesh. And it is perfectly reasonable in its revealed condition. It is the "word of *faith* which we preach, that if thou shalt confess with thy mouth the Lord Jesus, and believe in thine heart that God hath raised him from the dead, thou shalt be saved." It is no longer "This *do* and thou shalt live," but "he that *believeth* shall be saved." It is an honest and true faith.

It is not enough, that the ground of acceptance is laid in the perfected work of Christ; that finished redemption must be *received* by a trusting confidence. The testimony which God has given concerning it must be practically honored. Men must be so persuaded of the truth and importance of it, as to rest upon it the whole weight of their immortality. If they demand, Is there nothing for me *to do* to be saved; I answer, this is the work of God, "that ye *believe* on him whom he hath sent." They have nothing to do as a work of righteousness, or as adding to, or giving strength to the foundation which

God has laid in Zion. They have *this* to do, to *believe* the promise in which there is so much reason to conclude, our first parents believed—to believe on the Son of God as the only and all-sufficient Saviour. "Him hath God set forth to be a propitiation, *through faith* in his blood." This is a very different thing from "going about to establish a righteousness of our own by the deeds of the law." The one is the "righteousness of the law," the other is the "righteousness of faith;" the one is of works, the other is of grace—a received and imputed righteousness. The former is impossible, there is no impossibility in the latter. Millions have thus believed; and millions upon millions more will rejoice in this way of life, thus early disclosed, and to the "glory of his grace who hath made them accepted in the Beloved." Men may not work for it, but they must believe for it. They have nothing to give for it; but they may have it without money and without price. They are not worthy of it; and it is because they are so unworthy that the gift and grace are so rich and free. They have nothing to cover their poverty and shame but rags of filthiness; yet may they take these heaven-provided robes and be clothed in fine linen, clean and white. The word on which God caused our first parents to hope was not a stipulation, but a promise; and it is worthy of remark, that so far from their worthiness having anything to do with it, it was not uttered to *them*, but embodied in the sentence upon their greatest foe.

Another fact comprised in this promise is, that IT IS THE GREAT SOURCE AND MEANS OF HOLINESS. This is a fair inference from what was said in the chapter on the subject of spiritual death constituting a part of the penalty threatened to our first parents for their disobedience. Personal holiness flows through Christ as well as pardon. The redemption he bestows is as truly redemption from sin as redemption from hell. Personal holiness is too great a blessing to be bestowed except for the sake of Christ; nor could it, in the nature of the case, be bestowed where the penalty of the law is executed. And if it could be, who does not see and feel the unfitness of sanctifying a sinner without making him the object of pardoning mercy? Those who hold to the doctrine, that forgiveness is the only blessing which is bestowed for Christ's sake, must be driven to the conclusion, that, so far as this theory is concerned, God may, in the mere sovereignty of his grace, sanctify a sinner, and yet send him to hell. Would not this be an anomaly in the divine government? How much more in keeping with the beauty and symmetry of all the arrangements of heavenly wisdom, that pardon and holiness should never be separated in their objects, should flow in the same channel; and from the same source? It is a beautiful view of this first promise, that it not only binds together the divine attributes of truth, justice, and mercy, but is the golden string that binds the unwithering flowers of holiness, in all their beauty and freshness, to the parent stock on which they grew. There is nothing in the gospel that transforms man's physical and intellectual nature; it is impossible for him to be holy while in despair. The great design of Christianity is to make him holy, by encouraging him to hope. "Perfect love casteth out fear." The love of God is essential to the existence and progress of holiness in the heart. Wickedness could not indeed be *justified* in a state of absolute despair, any more than our first parents could have been justified in persevering alienation from God before the utterance of this first promise. Yet, no more than they would have returned to him without this promise, would their descendants, without hope, ever become holy.

It is the method of God's grace to rouse men from their thoughtlessness by the terrors of wrath, and to persuade them to repentance by the attractions of love. The promise which so early taught the first transgressors the only true method of justification, contained those great truths by which alone they and their descendants could become holy. The apostle Peter instructs us, that "exceeding great and precious promises" are given to God's people, "that by *these*, they might become partakers of the divine nature." They have comforted the hearts and revived the hopes of millions, and thereby promoted their holiness. The influence of this first promise has extended to untold millions; nor has it been uncertain, or feeble, nor its tendency questioned to promote every grace and virtue. This was its great object, and these the most important things it promised. It supplies the means and inducements to holiness, and that power of the Spirit of God by which alone men ever become holy. Just as it supported and propped up the drooping heart of our first parents, who, in that dark hour, needed something to lean upon, does the system of grace and truth it reveals support the drooping hearts of that great multitude which no man can number who are washed, and sanctified, and justified in the name of the Lord Jesus, and by the Spirit of our God. There never was, and there never will be a holy creature among all Adam's posterity, whose personal character is not influenced by this promise. Take this promise and the great truths and realities which it involves from the word of God, and you leave the world under the influence of error, dreams, and fable; you leave it without any such knowledge of right and wrong as would exert a practical effect on their character; you leave it under the dominion of wickedness, and with no hope that its wickedness will ever end, or that a brighter day will ever dawn on this lost and undone world. There is heavenly light from this promise on the wayward character of man. There is no provision made for this, but in the religion of which this promise is the germ. Here the heart is relieved from its sense of guilt, and cleansed from sin. It is no longer shut out from all communication with God. There is a renewal of the lost fellowship. There is a closer and still more close communion; until, at last, it becomes unbroken; and beholding, as in a mirror, the "glory of the Lord, the believer in it is changed into the same image, from glory to glory, even as by the Spirit of the Lord."

There is one more remark we may not suppress, in our amplification of this promise: it contains A PREDICTION OF THE SAVIOUR'S TRIUMPH. After his fatally practised wiles upon our first parents, the Great Adversary enjoyed a malignant and momentary victory. Man was ensnared, and this great foe vainly imagined the race was lost. The thought not improbably entered his mind, that what he sought by his own revolt was now secured; that the object of the benevolent Creator in calling into existence this lower world was defeated, and that the gloom and sadness of his own prison must now be transferred to those bright heavens from which he had been so lately exiled. But how short the triumph, and what a death-blow to his malignant hopes were those words, "I will put enmity between thee and the woman, and between thy seed and her seed: it shall bruise thy head and thou shalt bruise his heel!" How degrading the sentence, and what a poor, degraded being must he have felt himself to be, to learn that, after all his subtlety and malice, and all that teeming hostility which then brooded within his fiendish bosom; the most that he could ever hope to accomplish was to crawl upon his belly through a redeemed world, be trodden upon and crushed by the woman's seed, and that the only retaliation he could now inflict was to "bruise its *heel!*" And how degraded must they be who condescend to enlist themselves in the service of such a poor, degraded devil as this!

Glad visions cheer the Son of God as he now looks down on the world where we dwell. Ten thousand blessings drop from his hands, and fountains of joy spring up in his path all over this redeemed creation. In the progress of time, not a nation, not a tribe, and not an island of the sea but will lay their honors at his feet. His triumphs will be complete, and everywhere confessed. His conquests are conquests of truth over error, holiness over sin, joy over sorrow, heaven over hell. He is as emphatically the King of truth as the

Great Adversary is the prince of darkness. He himself is the way, the truth, and the life; truth in its thousand forms constitutes the weapons of his warfare. When his arrows are sharp and reach the hearts of his enemies, he "rides victoriously, because of truth, meekness and righteousness." When he girds his sword upon his thigh, and his right hand teaches him terrible things, "grace is poured into his lips," and his "sceptre is a righteous sceptre." He gains his victories by making the people *willing* in the day of his power, and by those moral transformations which are multiplied like the dew of the morning, and resplendent with the beauties of holiness.

When this "rod of his strength goes forth out of Zion," the love of self is supplanted by the love of God; the love of heaven predominates over the love of earth: the law of the spirit of life in Christ Jesus over the law of sin and death; and the new creation, the temple of God is erected upon the ruins of the fall. This is all his work, the consequence of his incarnation and sacrifice, and the result of "the exceeding greatness of his power." Not more certainly did this beautiful world come forth from the depths of chaos at his command, and shine forth in all its brilliancy, than his command calls into being a new and regenerated intellectual and moral creation, and bids it shine in progressive and everlasting splendor.

This was the object he had in view when he stooped to the cradle, and expired on the cross; and this is his joyous reward. The balances of earth cannot weigh the burden of his degradation and sorrows; nor can the arithmetic of earth measure the exaltation and extent of his victories. The "heathen are given to him as his inheritance, and the uttermost parts of the earth for his possession." He shall "have dominion from sea to sea;" they that "dwell in the wilderness shall bow before him," and his throne shall be as the days of heaven." "His name shall be called Wonderful, Counsellor, the mighty God, the everlasting Father, the *Prince of Peace;*" and "he must reign until all enemies are put under his feet." The victory shall be complete, and the shouts of it be heard in every land. The devil, that old serpent, in a little while shall be bound a thousand years, and go forth to deceive the nations no more. And when the predestined time shall come that his chain shall be loosed for a little season, it shall be only that he may be more inexorably bound at last. "He shall bruise thy *head*, and thou shalt bruise his *heel;*" this is the comment upon all his struggles. He shall have no ultimate triumph. Whatever may be the relative number of the saved and the lost, of this one thing we are assured, the proportion will be such, that heaven and hell shall see that the seed of the woman is victorious. He has made a show of the powers of darkness openly, triumphing over them in his cross. In commemorating his death, we commemorate his triumphs. The destroyer shall still destroy; but the Saviour shall be mighty to save. It shall yet be as it ever has been, that while the devil's path shall be traced only by the serpent's slime, the path of the conqueror shall be marked by the footsteps of light, and impress of love, by the honors awarded to him by redeemed men, and by wreaths which earth and heaven have prepared for the head that is to wear "many crowns."

Such is this first promise. And it is like the rainbow which the exiled apostle saw round about the throne. It encircles the earth where we dwell. This is the promise under which we were born. We are the descendants of a fallen ancestry; nor are there wanting humbling reflections which force themselves upon us, and thoughts that cover us with shame in contemplating such an origin. But these form the deep and lowering background, from which stand out the strongest lights in the moral firmament.

The brightest gems that adorn our Immanuel's head are gathered from this low earth; the sweetest song is the song of those who "are redeemed from among *men*." And let not the remark be forgotten, that notwithstanding all their sins, men cannot come short of this character and blessedness, except through their persevering unbelief and impenitent rebellion. Yonder infant in its cradle, if it employs its opportunities of religious instruction as it may and ought to employ them, will know more of its redeeming God, and enjoy him more; will be brought into nearer relations to him; will adore him more humbly, and more gratefully praise him, than the favored angel who now leads the chorus of the skies. To have been thus an embryo fiend, and to have thus become an embryo seraph, is the privilege of every believer in Jesus. Wondrous truth! and one which we may well press to our bosoms, —to pass through this wondrous transformation—to learn thus to "esteem all things but loss, that he may win Christ"—to find his highest good in him, and good in everything because it flows from his love—to be the workmanship of this Great Restorer, and occupy his assigned place in the "Temple not made with hands"—is the privilege of the meanest believer in Jesus. This is a privilege which belongs not to angels; they have no such interest in Christ; they bear no relation to him as their Redeemer. In heaven they cannot sing his praise as their Redeemer; and should they come down to earth and worship with us in these earthly sanctuaries, they could never have access to the communion-table of his saints, and there show forth his love.

I thank my Maker that I was not created an angel; for if I had been, right sure am I, that, left to myself, I should have been among the fallen. I give him praise that I am a native of this favored earth; that I occupy a place on the soil consecrated by the mission of patriarchs and prophets, and the greater mission of his Son; and that I belong to this habitable earth, where "his delights are with the sons of men;" that I live in a world where that Incarnate One first drew his infant breath, and where one of Adam's daughters called him *Son!* Here lies man's dignity, that his nature has been thus associated with Deity. He belongs to the earth the Saviour trode upon, and which was vocal with his prayers, and wet with his tears and blood. And, if a believer in Jesus, he is one with that redeemed humanity, in which, from the eternity past to the coming eternity, this Redeemer takes such a joyous interest, and of which he is the accredited, honored, adored Representative in the court of Heaven.

This promise is appreciated only by appreciating its corresponding *obligations.* And how vast and extended are they! Who makes a just estimate of them? What a world is this we live in; what a world to labor for, and what mighty objects are here to be secured by a faithful devotement to the will and glory of its great Redeemer! The smallest church, the meanest family, the most unworthy minister, the most unnoticed individual, is here exerting an influence for good or for evil. It is an influence that acts always and everywhere. It is felt far off and near; and not only while men live, but after they are dead; it laps over, and fastens itself upon succeeding generations.

And how amazing is the responsibility which rests upon every man for his own soul! He inhabits a world which belongs to him who "came to seek and to save that which was lost." With the exception of the short period between the first apostasy and the first promise, this earth has never been without a revealed Saviour. Not a generation has passed over it for whom there was no gospel; never was so miserable, so touching a sight presented to the eyes of angels or men. Amid all the changes in human affairs, God's revelation of grace has never been withdrawn from the abodes of time. Almost from its very birth, this earth has been wrapt in the mantle of heavenly mercy. Here "God commands all men everywhere to repent," and makes them the offer of the great salvation. They have a reprieve from the condemning sentence; and this is their day of grace. But it is a short day. Nothing shuts out *death* from the abodes of men. It is found in the purest and most salubrious sky; it reigns in every zone; its elements are combined with every clod, every stream, and every breeze. This world is the only place of education for eternity. Within this little span are comprehended decisions which determine an unalterable retribution. O does not this stamp a value on earth and time, which time and earth cannot calculate! This single fact throws around this habitable globe, and the least considerable of its inhabitants, an interest and a responsibility, that are overwhelming.

"Just as a tree cut down, that fell
To north or southward, *there it lies;*
So man departs to heaven or hell,
Fix'd in the state wherein *he dies.*"

Think of this, Christian, when you inspect the work you have to do, and the place which it is given you to occupy. Be thankful for the high vocation to which the grace of God has called you, and be solicitous and in earnest to honor the law of your being and your destiny. Let this earth have the same place in your hearts which it has in the heart of your eternal Saviour, and for the same reasons; take heed that you put a due estimate upon it, by putting a due estimate upon his claims, and the advancement of his kingdom where he lived and died.

Think of these things, ye also who forget God. There is no world like that in which you dwell, so fitted to draw out your character, and fit you for your eternal state. Hear ye this, both high and low, rich and poor together. "O earth, earth, earth, hear the word of the Lord!" There is given to *you* this short space for repentance. Around you are men forgetful of God like yourselves. A little farther back in the career of human life, you see the young who have fallen, and made shipwreck of their immortality in the days of their youth. Onward, and at a little distance, is many a veteran neglecter of God's salvation, cast up as a withered hulk on the shores of time, a beacon to warn *you* of the danger of delay. Just beyond the ground on which you are treading is the *grave.* It is a dark valley; a darker night than ever yet encircled the earth, will soon enwrap its folds about you. And now, from "the top of high places, by the way in the places of the paths," the voice of wisdom cries, "*Flee to the stronghold*, *ye* PRISONERS OF HOPE."

We solicit for this promise a glad and thankful and confident reception. There is no imposition in this first promise. It is but for this Saviour to fill the circle of our moral vision, and we may say with Paul, "I *know* whom I have believed, and am persuaded that he is able to keep that which I have committed to him against that day!" There are realities in his divine character and perfected work, so sure as to remove doubt. There is nothing obscure, or fluctuating in them. They will never alter. God's covenant with the day and the night shall come to an end; but the covenant of which his blood is the seal, is "ordered in all things and sure." I am "persuaded that neither death, nor life, nor angels, nor principalities, nor powers, nor things present, nor things to come, nor height, nor depth, nor any other creature, shall be able to separate us from the love of God which is in Christ Jesus our Lord." It is no marvel that when our back is turned upon this Sun of Righteousness, our way should be dark; nor need we wonder that the winter of our comforts comes on when his beams fall scantily and obliquely on our path. If you seek not shadows and gloom, study to know more of this first promise. Be familiar with the pages that develop its import, with the mercy-seat on which it is inscribed, with the sanctuaries which it illumines, with the ordinances and emblems of which it is the substance. And learn to dread not too deeply those dark passages in the wilderness where the light of it shines with unwonted loveliness; nor those hard and tempestuous waves where the wind is contrary, and in the appointed watch of the night, Jesus himself comes walking on the sea. "Stagger not at the promise through unbelief;" and if he bids you come to him on the waters, take heed lest you extort from his lips the deserved, though kind rebuke, "O thou of little faith! wherefore didst thou doubt?"

Human life is not worth its toil, its perplexity, its

weariness, its disappointments, its trials, its solitude, its ten thousand ills, if there be no hereafter. Man would be the sport of delusion, his hopes mocked, and his best affections cheated, were not life and immortality brought to light by the gospel. O ye, who make light of this gospel! approach and see what a wreck of human hopes this fallen world would be, if this ark of God did not float upon its waters, or if its doors were shut. Cast your eyes over this broad earth; mark the woes that rest upon it, and then turn to this one hope of man.

END OF VOL. I.

www.ingramcontent.com/pod-product-compliance
Lightning Source LLC
LaVergne TN
LVHW020115110826
845151LV00001B/167

* 9 7 8 1 4 2 5 5 4 2 8 6 3 *